Gracie's Tail: Conversations with DoG

Copyright © 2014 by Julie Bloomer

All rights reserved, including the reproduction in whole or in part in any form without the written consent of the author.

ISBN 978-0-692-32407-3

Photographs Copyright © 2014 Julie Bloomer

Book Design by Blue Jay Ink, Ojai, California

bluejayink.com

Published in the United States by

DoG Books Ojai, Ojai, California 93023

juliebloomerdogbooks.com

All profits from the sale of this book will be donated to better the lives of animals.

Gracie's Tail:
Conversations with DoG

JULIE BLOOMER AND GRACIE

PREFACE

I am grateful for all that I have, all that I have been given, and all that I am. I have always believed that the Universe is abundant, that lack is in our heads, but I acted as if that concept only applied to money and my ability to have the house, the car, the job, even the guy, I wanted in this life. But in reality, all of the divine aspects of the Universe are abundant: love, peace, compassion, kindness, joy, creativity, happiness, gratitude, generosity, grace, and a host of others. They are all there for the asking—to be given and to be received by all.

I've always been a spiritual seeker. The problem with being a seeker is that you're always looking for something else out there, always doing, and mostly forgetting to just be. Then I remembered that there are no problems, only opportunities to learn and grow. So, to rephrase that, I have recently recognized that, for most of my life, I've looked for something outside of myself to complete me, to give me purpose, to make me happy. Only lately have I begun to understand that all I need or seek is within—that all of those divine, abundant traits of the Universe exist inside of me, too, just waiting to be expressed fully.

I never believed I was good enough, or did enough, no matter how kind, thoughtful, or generous I tried to be. Now I'm trying to accept who I am and embrace my soul's journey . . . the good, the bad, and the ugly parts of it. It's taken me a lifetime to understand that I'm not the stories I constantly replay in my head, that I'm not my mother's words or thoughts about me, and that I'm good enough just the way I am. I'm now aware that

I add something to this world just by being a peaceful, kind, compassionate being who likes to laugh.

Meditation has been a key to this growing awareness. While I've meditated off and on for forty years, I have to admit that it has been mostly off. I was too busy with work, studies, and life's events to meditate. As Deepak Chopra once said in a global meditation for peace, "If you have the time, it's good to meditate at least once a day. If you don't have the time, meditate twice a day." Only in the last few years has meditation become a daily practice for me. With steady meditation, my consciousness has started to change, and my life has naturally become calmer and more joyous without me having to work at it so hard. Quitting the practice of law also helped.

I do believe that all of the events in our lives, which on their face appear negative, provide avenues for growth. Some days, though, I think I've grown enough. Other days, when faced with obstacles, I remember that it's all perfect in the cosmos, even if *I* don't like it. I still slip and fall back into old patterns and thoughts, but sometimes now I consciously notice when I do that, forgive myself, and then move forward, remembering that every moment gives me the chance to restore balance and begin again. I get the occasion to express myself in a new way, with new insight and understanding, every second of every day, and I get to choose how I will act in the next moment. And I give thanks to the divine energy of the Universe for creating another opportunity for me to become aware of a behavior or a reaction that I'm not so enthralled with. Not in a critical way, but because I have a choice to let my divine spark shine. It is all perfect in the moment, including my desire to change how I show up in this world.

I am grateful for all of the teachers in my life, in particular, my dog Gracie, who helped me discover who I am, or at least who I am becoming, and has guided me along the road of personal discovery and transformation. In many respects, I've traveled along that road unconsciously: working hard, worrying, getting caught up in the human struggle, being critical of myself and others, repeating the same lessons over and over, trying to control things that clearly I had no control over, and often missing the beauty and joy of the present moment. I am trying to stop such behaviors. But, as Yoda said, "Do. Or do not. There is no try."

Through the years, I've had many incredible teachers besides Gracie: Walter and all of my other animals, Crystal, my spiritual teacher, Buddha, Jesus, The Little Prince, Siddhartha, Don Juan, Yoda, the Dalai Lama, the monks from Bhutan, the Air, Water, Fire, and Earth, the trees, the oceans, Barbara Janelle, St. Francis, don Alverto Taxo, a shaman from Ecuador, Howard Wills, a peacemaker in Hawaii, Joy, my guardian angel, all of nature, Deepak Chopra, and many other human and nonhuman beings who have entered my life. I'm grateful to them all for helping me along my journey, including the difficult human ones, who have perhaps been my greatest gurus.

My life has changed dramatically since my days as a lawyer. These days I'm studying animal communication so that I can serve as a bridge between people and animals. I hope to help people open their hearts, even just a little, to feel compassion and understand how we are all connected. Once we feel that connection at a heart level, and show kindness to all, healing can and will occur, and the world will become a peaceful place.

Thank you for taking a step with me across that bridge.

> A human being is a part of the whole, called by us the "Universe," a part limited in time and space. He experiences himself, his thoughts and feelings, as something separate from the rest—a kind of optical delusion of his consciousness. This delusion is a kind of prison for us, restricting us to our personal desires and to affection for a few persons nearest to us. Our task must be to free ourselves from this prison by widening our circle of compassion to embrace all living creatures and the whole of nature in its beauty. Nobody is able to achieve this completely, but the striving for such achievement is in itself a part of the liberation and a foundation for inner security.
>
> -Albert Einstein (1879-1955)

INTRODUCTION

What can you say about a fourteen-year-old Labrador retriever who died? That she was beautiful. And brilliant. That she was the best writing partner a person could have. That she loved to smile and dance and swim in the ocean. That she loved to sing along with the harmonica, as loud as she could. And that she loved me. That she wanted to be with me always. I was good enough for her just the way I was. No judgment, no changes necessary.

You often hear that dogs make our lives better because they love unconditionally, but I think it is also in how they allow us to love them back: pure, uncomplicated love without expectation or explanation, just heart to heart, no questions asked. I am grateful for every minute Gracie was in my life.

The depth of my sadness at Gracie's passing was profound. I never knew I could feel such grief, a grief that some days wanted to keep me in bed. But I had promised her I would finish this book, a book I started years ago with her but was too wrapped up with my internal critic to complete. I was too concerned about what people would think about me if I told them that my dog was communicating with me, giving me a glimpse into how the Universe works, and imparting knowledge and spiritual advice that she felt was important for people to hear. Gracie reminded me on a daily basis that we are all connected on a very deep level. It has taken me a long time to get it.

Gracie lived her life, and communicated, with a grace and beauty that is often found in nature if we will only stop to listen. My hope is that people will suspend their disbelief just a tiny bit in order to hear what Gracie had to say through the years. Gracie's dictations, while not in chronological order, are just as I heard them, whether I understood them at the time or not. The actual dates of the dictations, when I remembered to date my notes, are listed in the parentheses following Gracie's insights.

I'm still working on forgiving myself for my self-doubt, and for believing, all those years, that I wasn't good enough just the way I was. Gracie knew that I was. Gracie knew that we are all divine creations—perfect, whole, and complete just as we are.

So this is *Gracie's Tail: Conversations with DoG*, which really began before she was born, back in late 1997 when I was getting divorced for the second time, dealing with the sad part of finding myself alone again, and yet feeling eager to move on with my life.

> Yesterday I was clever, so I wanted to change the world.
> Today I am wise, so I am changing myself.
> -Rumi

CHAPTER 1

CHANGE

I dragged myself outside, coffee cup in hand, climbed onto the giant rock in my front yard, and cried. I kept my tattered pink robe wrapped tightly around me to keep out the early morning chill. The threads in that robe had absorbed the very essence of survival and security from many hospital stints and still offered a cocoon of comfort to me in times of stress. I was somewhat shocked to find myself sad and living alone in the middle of nowhere. Well, Ojai isn't exactly nowhere, but it is quite a bit different from Brentwood in Los Angeles. I knew I needed to make some changes so that I could move on, but I didn't know where to begin. So, instead, I cried about how I had really messed up another marriage.

Finally I looked up and tried to breathe in the peaceful energy of the mountains that surrounded me, and was startled to see my favorite go-to guy on the ranch, Tino, staring at me with concern from across the driveway.

"Qué pasa?" he said in his kind and gentle manner. "Usted está triste."

I wiped away the remnants of tears and looked at him, wondering how long he'd been standing there witnessing my distress. Yes, I was sad. I mustered up my best Spanish, which was not that good, and said haltingly,

"Mi esposo is no más aquí." I brushed my fingers away from me through the air and added eloquently in Spanglish, "He vamanosed."

Based on my delivery, I wasn't surprised that Tino continued to stare at me as if he didn't understand what I was saying. Then he shook his head bewildered and said, "¿Por qué? Usted una bery, bery nice lady. Esposo está loco to leave you." And he walked away to turn on the water in my avocado orchard.

I thought about what he'd said, started to smile, and then couldn't help but burst into laughter. The whole scene came into perspective as the sun peeked over the mountains to greet me head on, and I let it sink in how grateful and blessed I was to be alive on this beautiful morning, on this beautiful sprawling avocado and citrus ranch, surrounded by mountains, streams, and the national forest.

I followed the same predawn ritual, coffee and crying on that rock, for a few mornings, and suddenly I was over the sad part of getting divorced. Tino was right. Harry, my second ex-husband, was loco. I was a nice person, and I deserved more. Actually, I was shocked at how quickly I felt better, as if a gigantic weight had been lifted from my shoulders. It dawned on me that I'd spent almost every waking hour since graduating from law school in 1980 either working twelve hours a day or trying to make someone else happy.

As I thought about it, my life with Harry had required tiptoeing on eggshells, not just walking on them. No matter what I did or said, I couldn't make him feel better. He often seemed depressed or just cranky unless he was drinking fine wine. He taught me to enjoy great wines, too, but our relationship didn't improve with age. Finally, after seventeen years, I was free. I had a good job and plenty of money, but I didn't know who I was or what I liked. I realized that I had taken on Harry's life and lost mine.

Even my studies with my longtime friend and spiritual teacher, Patricia Chuse (affectionately known as Crystal to those who worked with her), had been at Harry's initiation. Although I recognized my tendency to throw myself into the interests of whatever man was in my life, I'd embraced my spiritual studies with Crystal wholeheartedly, and it was one of the good things that came out of my marriage to Harry. So, I was grateful for that.

Crystal constantly stressed the importance of following one's inner voice and feeling the connection between everything. I believed, at least on an intellectual level, in the concept of oneness with everything around me, but I didn't know if I really felt it or understood it on a deeper level. Even though I'd been studying with her for more than ten years, I still doubted myself and questioned my ability to connect with that small, still, intuitive voice within. I never knew if I was getting it right or just making it up.

I knew that things went smoothly and easily when I gave up my judgments and expectations. But that was extremely hard for me. Mostly I was fighting every moment and thinking I could control everything around me, even those things that clearly weren't in my control, like someone else's feelings. I knew I should relinquish that tortuous trait, but I didn't know how. I felt responsible for it all. And why couldn't I just let it go and stop thinking about it? He was gone, and that was that.

As I sat on that rock in my front yard, under internal pressure to figure out my next step, I suddenly heard my mother's voice, "Pick yourself up by the bootstraps. Get over yourself. You are one tough cookie." Where the heck did that phrase come from, anyway? I thought. And what did it really mean? I liked cookies. I certainly had eaten my share of hard, soft, chewy, crunchy, and lots of other kinds of cookies, but I couldn't remember ever experiencing a tough cookie. Maybe that was my mother's way of acknowledging I was unique and a survivor; even though what I'd usually heard from her was, "No one will ever love you" and "What makes you think you're so special?" Maybe she was right, I thought. Maybe no one would ever love me. I shook my head in an attempt to turn off the internal negative monologue and come back to the natural beauty that surrounded me. Despite my mother's words, I realized I'd survived a lot worse than just another divorce.

My butt was getting sore, and I could feel the pins and needles starting in my feet, so I got up, walked back inside the house, and went to the kitchen to make some more coffee. I moved to the overstuffed chair in the living room, which was a lot more comfortable than that rock, sipped my coffee, and looked through the glass walls toward the trees and the mountains beyond. Outside it was very green, very peaceful, and yet seemed effortlessly alive. When I looked around inside, though, it was immaculate and monochromatic white, and it felt very lonely. A light bulb went off. I realized that I had been feeling empty, unhappy, and lonely for quite some time, even during the marriage, but I had kept myself busy and numb by immersing myself in work. Oh well, I thought, at least I wasn't so sad about getting divorced anymore. Now what?

I briefly thought about getting a dog as a companion but immediately dismissed the idea as impractical and illogical given my current work and living circumstances. I still considered myself a practical and logical person even though I dabbled in metaphysical pursuits. Harry hadn't allowed any pets, and I had gone along with that mandate during our marriage since pets didn't seem compatible with my busy career and travel schedule. He'd convinced me that managing young lawyers and multimillion-dollar cases required all of my time. So, even though he was gone, I'd convinced myself that adding the responsibility of a dog to my newfound single life was simply out of the question.

But I made a decision, right then, to get rid of Harry's vibe in the house to make room for a new relationship. I was done with mornings on that rock. I was done with that husband and everything that went with him, and I was tired of being alone. Out with the old, in with the new—a clean slate so to speak.

The logical place to start redecorating seemed to be my bedroom, so I marched downstairs, looked around and noticed a dead plant in the corner. "That looks like a good place to begin," I said out loud as I picked up the plant to toss it out. Then I decided I would get rid of everything in the room, the bed, the bedding, and all the memories and energy that went with them. And I wanted to get it done right then.

I took a final look around, got dressed, hopped in my brand-new Mercedes SUV, which I had purchased as a divorce present for myself, and drove to Los Angeles to the most expensive bedding boutique that I knew. I plunked down an extravagant amount for a white silk duvet cover with white embroidered bees on it, bought the matching sheets and European pillowcases, and drove back to Ojai. I thought that I shouldn't really keep spending money now that I was single and solely responsible for my expenses, but what the heck, easy come, easy go and, anyway, I was helping the economy. Besides, I thought, I deserved something new for the house, and the car didn't count toward that.

When I got back to Ojai, I still wanted to tackle the bed situation. Since it was already 7 p.m. and stores were closed, I called a mattress place from the yellow pages to discuss options. I talked to a nice salesperson on the phone about the environmental, comfort, and health aspects of each type of bed, and he convinced me the solid latex mattress was the best choice. Of course it was the most expensive one he had, and I could feel the hard sell through the phone, but I was in the mood to get it done.

"I'll take it," I said, knowing it was nuts to buy an outrageously priced bed, sight-unseen. "But only if you can have it delivered to Ojai before 10 a.m. tomorrow morning."

"No problem," he said. "I'll deliver it myself."

When I got the bed all set up the next day, it was nice to have a new bed and beautiful bedding, and all, but it hadn't made the change I was hoping for. So now what was I supposed to do? Rearrange furniture? Call an interior designer? Get some color going against the all-white backdrop? I wanted more change.

I knew it was important to get some "new energy" flowing, and just randomly, I'd been reading about Feng Shui. I'd always been interested in how alternative realities work in our lives, and the ancient Chinese method for placement of objects to create good energy and alter negative influences intrigued me. So, even though I didn't know too much about it, I decided to find someone to do a Feng Shui analysis of my house. I called Ms. Anna Lu, a Feng Shui practitioner in Santa Barbara whom Crystal had heard about. I explained to Ms. Lu that I was just getting divorced and wanted to change the energy in my house so I could move on. She said she'd just had a cancelation so I could have an appointment for the very next day. I was surprised because Crystal had said it could take months to get time with Ms. Lu. At 10 a.m. sharp the following morning, an attractive Chinese woman, dressed in what looked like hand-painted red silk, walked purposefully into my living room and started to look around. I had no idea what to expect.

"The chi is not correct in here," Ms. Lu said matter-of-factly.

"I'm sorry," I said, while wondering what the heck that meant.

"You have nothing to stop money from flowing out of this house. It comes in here, in this door," she said, pointing to the west-facing front door, "and goes directly out the opposite glass door over there—just as quickly as it came in."

Without acknowledging the accuracy of her statement, I nodded pleasantly, thinking to myself that I didn't need an additional $300 to flow out to Ms. Lu to gain that insight. I was well aware that money had been flowing away from me ever since Harry left. He'd been the one with the stable, predictable monthly income. After leaving my corporate-oriented New York law firm, I'd started representing plaintiffs on a contingency basis, so it was more of a feast or famine mentality for me.

"Let's take a look at your bedroom," Ms. Lu said. I led her downstairs and thought I heard a slight gasp as she perused the entire room. She looked toward the empty southeast corner of the room and said, "What was in that corner before?"

"A dead plant," I admitted sheepishly. "I just threw the darn thing out a few days ago." Hoping for some approval, though, I added, "But the bed is new."

Ms. Lu stared at me for a moment, taking it all in, and then she said, "I'm not surprised you got a divorce." Coming from her, it didn't sound judgmental, but I really didn't know what she was talking about.

"That's your relationship corner," she said. "Look at it."

I looked and realized I had allowed a lifeless plant to linger there. Just like my relationship with Harry. Lifeless. Joyless. Dead.

"Let's find something alive for that corner immediately," she said. "Something romantic."

So we drove to the nursery, and I bought a beautiful plant with heart-shaped leaves and a colorful pot. Ms. Lu selected two iron frogs from my frog collection and placed them in the dirt under the plant, facing each other, as if they were kissing. And we put the plant and the frogs in that empty corner of my bedroom.

"Now you must hang a painting in that corner, which represents your idea of love," Ms. Lu said. "Think about this carefully. I gave this advice to a client a few months ago. She called me recently and said she was meeting lots of men, going out all of the time, but she couldn't understand why all the men she was meeting were alcoholics. I asked her what was in her picture. She said she had chosen a beautiful, romantic Paris café scene with a small bistro table and a bottle of wine with two wine glasses."

I understood immediately what Ms. Lu was implying but felt slightly incredulous about the potential effect of a picture on my wall.

"Do you understand?" she said very quietly and softly. "We must live in harmony with the elements of nature and reside in surroundings that properly balance these elements and tap into the energy lines of the earth. There is an intelligent spirit in every thing and everyone, which has an effect on us. Our environment can have a profound effect on how we feel. And we can manifest things in our lives through our intention. It's that old adage come to life—be careful what you wish for. Your intention must be clear."

I didn't totally believe that a painting could have that much effect, but with that admonition, I was petrified that I might pick the wrong picture for my relationship corner. I really wanted to meet my forever partner so I didn't want to take any chances. The picture had to be exactly right. It had been a rough few months on my own, and meeting men in bars or elevators, like my previous two husbands, clearly hadn't worked, so I decided to have faith in this process.

I looked and looked in every gallery and art store for miles around for the perfect symbol of love. During my rare free days, I went to art walks, art fairs, and art auctions, but the correct painting never materialized. Finally after months of not finding my precise representation of love, I decided to commission a painting. I'd seen some stunning paintings of flowers by an artist named David Scott. Flowers always made me happy, so I thought they'd be just right for my relationship corner, and David's paintings were spectacular. So I tracked him down and called him to explain my dilemma. He said he'd love to come over and talk about the project.

When David arrived at my house, I told him about the Feng Shui analysis and showed him my relationship corner. He seemed to understand, without question, my need for a painting representing my idea of love. I was still wondering what the heck I was doing. Then we wandered around up by my pond, and he took pictures of Matilija poppies and the many other flowers which grew wild on my 45-acre parcel of the ranch. We decided on a painting with a green vase to match my new green bell-curved lamps, but otherwise I left the choice of flowers up to him.

Several weeks later, David phoned. "Hey, your paintings are done," he said.

"Great, I can't wait to see them," I replied. Oh no, I thought. Did I ask for paintings? Plural?

"I'm really pleased with how they came out," he said. "Can I come by to show you?"

"Sure. I'm around today if you have time."

David arrived in a rusted old pick-up truck filled with canvases of different colors and shapes. He pulled out the painting he had crafted to go in my relationship corner and carefully carried it into the house. It was circular, painted on dark wood, with a gigantic bouquet of calla lilies overwhelming a gorgeous green vase. Lying on the table, in front of the vase, out of water, was a solitary coral rose, which looked alive but exhausted, as if it just couldn't take any more and had jumped out of the vase to rest.

At first glance, the painting was striking and beautiful—it seemed like the perfect representation of love to me. The coral in the picture was my favorite pink. But as I studied it in more depth, it sunk in. I was well aware of the phallic use of calla lilies in paintings by such artists as Georgia O'Keefe. Here, the small banana-like centers of the flowers in the vase thrust themselves out of the painting in all directions. And the wilting flower in front? Well, of course, that represented me. The sexual symbolism and connotations were obvious to me and not exactly what I'd had in mind—on many levels—for my future as a single person. I wanted a boyfriend but not lots of them, coming at me, exhausting me. I'd been there and was done with that.

"It's a gorgeous painting," I said truthfully. I really didn't want to get into my issue with the phallic images and the dying rose for my relationship corner, but I did worry what such a painting might bring into my life, just in case Feng Shui really did work.

"Did you say you did two?" I asked.

"Yeah, I was inspired," he said. "I'll go get the other one from my truck if you want."

"I really can't afford two paintings, but I'd love to see it." Fortunately for me, the other painting was smaller, simpler, and more straightforward. It was a painting of blissful-looking Matilija poppies sitting calmly and comfortably on a table in a celadon green vase. Those gorgeous Matilija poppies with their lacey leaves and vivid, cheerful yellow centers brought a smile to my face instantly. I knew I had been right. Flowers were the perfect choice for my relationship corner, and this painting was it.

"How much are they?" I asked. I couldn't believe it, but I'd forgotten to ask. I was a little shocked when David said the big phallic one was $3,500 and the smaller one with Matilija poppies was $2,000.

"They look great in your house," David said hopefully. "You can have both for five."

I didn't want to explain my predicament, but I also didn't think I should spend that much money to buy two paintings. I really didn't have an extra $5,000 lying around to spend on a sketchy theory about how to bring a new man into my life. I mean, the Chinese have been practicing Feng Shui for 5,000 years, but it was new to me—not to mention a little bit "out there" as a way to meet men.

But, bottom line, I couldn't stand the thought of disappointing anyone, so I simply said, "I'll take both. They're beautiful."

When David left, I switched the paintings. I put the Matilija poppies in my relationship corner in my bedroom and hung the coral rose in the living room.

∞∞∞

The weird thing was, just one week after hanging that painting, I met Bill at the 49ers Party, an impromptu gathering a group of us had orchestrated at my pond where the Matilija poppies were in full bloom. My neighbors and best friends on the ranch, Maggie and her husband,

Fred, had invited Bill and his three kids to the party so we could meet. The excuse for that party was to celebrate everyone who was born in 1949 and was turning 49 that year. Both Fred and I were 49ers. Bill was a few years younger, recently divorced, and Maggie thought he'd be a good match for me. She told me that his oldest daughter, Anne, wasn't able to come, but that Bill would be at the party with his two youngest children, Roy, 12, and Jane, who was about 9.

    Once everyone arrived and the party got rolling, I got up the courage and walked over to Bill to introduce myself. He was very good looking, and I got nervous and tongue-tied around him, so I wandered away to mingle with some friends. Instead, though, I wound up playing with Roy and Jane for most of the party. We laughed a lot while we played horseshoes, and I caught Bill watching us. Somehow the painting had worked to bring an intriguing man into my life, and now I hoped a relationship would miraculously materialize.

> Amazing Grace, how sweet the sound
> To save a wretch like me
> I once was lost, but now I'm found
> T'was blind, but now I see.
> -John Newton, 1779

CHAPTER 2

MEMORIAL DAY

I woke up, stretched, looked around my bedroom and, for some unknown reason, felt hopeful about the day. I looked out the big picture window opposite my bed and felt the peace and power of the mountains that surrounded me in this magnificent and isolated spot I now called home. A certain happiness emanated from the corner of my bedroom where the newly acquired painting of the Matilija poppies hung, and I was warmed by the thought of seeing Bill again at the Memorial Day barbeque that afternoon.

Five weeks had gone by since I'd first met him, and I sort of wondered why he hadn't gotten in touch since then, but I remembered he was tall and handsome, with a great half-smile, kind, sparkly green-brown eyes, and an infectious laugh. I thought he would be easy on the eyes around the house and hopefully even easier on the heart. I knew I was getting ahead of myself, but I was the eternal optimist. My two priors didn't scare me, although it did cross my mind that perhaps Bill was too good looking for me. But my friends said he was really nice, and he had seemed like a happy person based on our first, brief encounter. And having three kids was a definite plus in my book. I loved kids, but I was never able to have children of my own.

I got out of bed, walked to the kitchen, brewed my morning ritual, and sat in the living room, thinking. I wondered what was in store for me. A few days before, my ranch manager had called out of the blue and asked if I wanted a dog igloo. He said his dog had outgrown it and he didn't need a doghouse any longer. The logical part of me said I didn't need one either, since I obviously didn't have a dog, but for some unexplained reason, I said, "Yeah, sure, bring it over. That'd be great."

Then, as I sat in my chair and looked at the wondrous scene outside my living room, this incredible need welled up inside of me. It was like an outside force was urging me on, and I couldn't stop myself. Rather than analyze everything to death, like I usually did, I just went with the flow of it. I followed the feeling, got up from my comfy chair, and drove to Pet Smart in Ventura where I bought all of the things I thought I might need for a puppy. I bought dog bowls, puppy food, treats, training books, the cutest stuffed hedgehog that squeaked, pink and yellow tennis balls, toys, and a beautiful comfy dog bed that matched my white and pale grey sofas and rug. This is nuts, I thought. What am I doing? I am not getting a dog.

I brought the dog paraphernalia home and laid it out in strategic locations around the house. I put the dog bed right next to mine, and I felt a deep sense of peace. Now what? I guess I would just wait and see what the Universe had in mind.

The last six months of my life, living alone and trying to hold it all together, hadn't been the best, but I had a sense that things were about to change. As I wandered from room to room, delaying getting ready for the Memorial Day party, I looked at all of the dog stuff lying around my house. Even though it had only been there a few hours, it seemed like it belonged. It seemed like it had been there forever.

I often heard the phrase, "Relax, just go with the flow." To me that meant to go along with what everyone else was doing at the time and not try to control the situation. But deep down I knew there was much more to the meaning of that statement, and I was trying to allow that flow to work in my life.

Just get yourself together and go to the party and have a good time. You think too much, I thought to myself. "Besides," I said out loud, "Bill will be at the party, so maybe things really are looking up."

ooooo

I finally made it to the small Memorial Day gathering at Ken and Fay's house in town. I thought I looked cute in a recently divorced, just lost 15 pounds, kind of a way, with my pressed white jeans and new navy top. When I walked in, I saw Bill, dressed casually in an old, sloppy Hawaiian shirt, shorts, and flip-flops, standing with his kids by the pool, talking to Maggie and Fred. I felt way over-dressed in comparison to Bill.

"Hi, Julie. Nice to see you," Bill said as I joined the group. I noticed him looking me over with an appreciative grin, and I got uncharacteristically nervous around him for the second time. "Do you remember my kids, Roy and Jane?" he asked.

"Of course. Good to see you again."

"And this is my oldest daughter, Anne," Bill said introducing me. "She couldn't make it to the 49ers party."

"Nice to meet you," I said and then smiled at each of his kids gently, trying to ignore the pounding in my chest.

I chatted with Anne for a minute about her junior year at Nordhoff High School and the advanced placement classes she was taking. Maggie and Fred soon wandered away to talk to our hosts in the kitchen and Bill's kids jumped in the pool to join a game of water basketball with Ken and Fay's kids.

"Do you want a beer?" Bill asked.

"Sure," I nodded. Bill walked over to the cooler and brought back two beers, and we sat on the lounge chairs and started talking. It was easy to talk to him, and my nervousness disappeared. I felt an immediate connection and, by the way he looked at me, I thought he did, too.

"Have you ever been sailing?" Bill asked. "A friend of mine called this morning and asked me to go soon."

"Sure, I love sailing," I replied. "I actually started racing small boats when I was a kid. My parents didn't have any idea how to sail, but my dad plopped me and my two brothers into boats, and told us to figure it out."

Bill laughed.

"I even taught sailing for a few summers at our summer place on Long Island," I said.

"Good to know. Maybe you can teach me something," he said mischievously. "We should go sometime."

And so it went, we discovered that we both loved opera, that we were the only two people on the planet, or at least at that party, who proudly had not seen the movie *Titanic*, and that we both had just purchased cars to treat ourselves to something new after our recent divorces.

The kids got out of the pool, and we gathered at the table to eat. This group of mutual friends all had dogs, except for me, so it was not surprising that the conversation turned in that direction. We often joked about how most of our conversations wound up being about crops and pets. I told everyone how I had gone out earlier that day and gotten all set up for a puppy. "I have the training books, the bed, the toys," I said.

"What kind of a puppy do you have?" Bill asked with interest.

"No puppy, just the stuff," I responded.

"What kind of a dog are you getting then?"

"I don't know. I don't have any real plans."

"Isn't it a little weird to have all the stuff for a dog and not even know what kind of a dog you're getting?" Bill asked kindly. "They do come in different sizes, you know."

"Not weird to me," I replied with a smile. Even as I said it, I secretly thought maybe it was a little weird. The idea of a Labrador, just like I'd had as a kid, popped into my head. "I was thinking maybe a yellow Labrador because the hair would blend in with my carpets."

Bill raised his eyebrows slightly and gave me one of those "really, that's your criteria for a dog?" looks.

"What? I'm just ready," I said. I hesitated before giving any more information as I looked at Bill. I saw a kindness in his eyes in spite of his comments, so I continued, "And I know her name."

"Interesting. What's her name?" he asked.

"Amazing Grace of Ojai. Well, that's her full, official name," I replied as I looked around the table and saw amused expressions appear on my friends' faces.

"Don't you think Amazing Grace of Ojai is an awfully long name for a little dog you haven't even met yet?" Bill added, chuckling.

"I'll call her Gracie, for short. And don't laugh," I said good-naturedly. "I know the right dog will come." Did I know that? I wondered. But Amazing Grace, how sweet the sound, I thought.

Bill just smiled at me without further comment.

"I'm going to change the topic now, so everyone will leave me alone about my non-existent, maybe-someday-I'll-get-a-dog, dog," I announced. "I'm having a charity event for the Land Conservancy at my pond next week. Does anyone want to come?" I asked, looking directly at Bill, who was sitting across the table from me.

"Maybe I could come over and help you get ready for it," he said.

"That'd be great. The event is Saturday. Can you come over Friday night to help me cook? You can cook, can't you?"

"I can take direction pretty well," he said with a glint of enthusiasm in his eyes.

∞∞∞

The following day, the phone rang. It was Gail, a law school friend from Los Angeles who I hadn't talked to in a long time. I had stayed with her in Santa Monica for several nights when Harry first moved out, and she was checking up on me. I told her about being hopeful about a great new guy I'd clicked with at the Memorial Day party. Then I reported on my conversation with Bill and the group's amusement about my invisible dog.

"You should get a dog," Gail said. "We got our Labrador, Molly, from a breeder fairly close to you, in Saugas. His name is George. He's a unique old guy, but his dogs are incredible. I did a lot of research before we got Molly, and she's the best. Let me give you his number."

"What about my job? What would I do with her when I go to work?"

"Oh, just bring her here. She can stay with Molly."

"Thanks, that's a sweet offer, but I'm not really sure driving a dog back and forth between Ojai and Santa Monica is such a great long-term plan," I said.

"You'll love having a puppy, Julie. You need something to take care of now."

"Yeah, well, I don't know," I said.

As I hung up the phone, I thought it couldn't really hurt to just call this breeder guy, and see what the deal was. I wondered whether this was another sign from the Universe since Gail had called out of the blue, after months of not being in touch, and offered me the number of a Labrador breeder, one day after I'd bought all of the stuff for a dog and had contemplated getting a Labrador. Of course it was—even I wasn't that dense. Before I thought about it too much, or changed my mind, I dialed the number.

"Hello, George?" I inquired.

"Yeah, this is George. Whad da you want?" the gravelly old voice on the other end of the line asked abruptly.

"Hi. Uhhhhh...." What did I want? I was really struggling to let go of analyzing everything so much. In my heart I knew that magic occurred in the spaces in between thoughts, in the quiet spaces where we connect with something much larger than ourselves. But it was really difficult for me to go there. "You were recommended to me by a friend. She got a Labrador puppy from you a few months ago." I paused. "Do you have any puppies available now?"

"Yep. As a matter of fact, a litter was just born."

"Are there any females?" I asked, feeling like I was getting on a moving train.

"Yep, two, but one's spoken for," he replied.

Then I got nervous. My logical brain wrestled control away from my heart. How could I care for a puppy? My life was in an uproar. I'd just bought my ex-husband out of the Ojai ranch property. I was transitioning from living in Brentwood to small-town life in Ojai, even though I still had an active law practice almost two hours away in Beverly Hills. I traveled frequently to conduct discovery in my cases, which were located all over the United States. There were no pets allowed at the tiny apartment I had just rented over a garage in Santa Monica for when I had to stay overnight in Los Angeles to go to Court or attend an early meeting. And I had finally met a guy I really wanted to get to know better. There was no time for a puppy. And who would care for the dog when I had to travel or spend long hours at work? A dog just seemed impractical at this stage of my life.

"Don't worry," a little voice said. "It will all work out. It always does. The things you need come at the right time."

"I'll take the other one," I blurted out, listening to that quiet, intuitive voice within and ignoring the loud, negative, practical one.

"OK. Just give me a $150 deposit and she's yours," George said, without even asking me any questions.

"Don't you want to know anything about me? Don't I get to see her or anything?" I asked. I was becoming a little bewildered by the process of getting a dog.

"Not now," he said. "They're too little. Come out to the kennel in about four weeks and take a look. If you don't want her, you'll get your money back."

There's a leap of faith, I thought. An old fogey on the phone wanting a $150 deposit on a $550 dog, sight unseen. But I just said, "OK. Will you take a credit card over the phone?"

"Yep," George replied. "Hate them darn things, but got to these days."

"Her official name is going to be Amazing Grace of Ojai. Gracie for short," I said enthusiastically.

"Yeah, well, call her what you want, but you have to do that registration stuff yourself. I don't do that no more," George said gruffly. "I'll give you the paperwork, though."

"Sorry, I didn't mean.... When did you say she was born?" I interrupted myself to ask.

"Yesterday, May 25th."

Ahhh, that explains it, I thought smiling inwardly at the phone. Memorial Day—the day I'd gotten ready for Gracie, without knowing why I'd done the things that I did. There it was, magic: Gracie had been born that day. Gracie was the motivating force behind all the events the Universe had orchestrated so perfectly. I had followed every step that had presented itself without thinking about it too much. I had gone with the flow and gotten out of my own way. And now I understood why.

"Hey, lady, I'm ready for the credit card number," George said, his husky voice interrupting my epiphany.

"Oh, sorry, here you go," I said as I rattled off the number to George. "I'll see you in four weeks to meet Gracie in person."

"Call before you come out, so we can be ready for you," he said and hung up the phone.

ooooo

My relationship progressed quickly with Bill over the next four weeks. He helped me prepare for the event at my pond to raise money for the Land Conservancy, as he said he would, and we had a blast hosting the event. Our first alone date was watching a Lakers game on TV at my house a few nights later. After that, we just skipped the dating part of a relationship and became an instant couple. Maggie said she was surprised when she saw Bill driving out of the ranch one morning not long after the Land Conservancy event, coffee cup in hand, looking very happy.

Anne, Roy, and Jane were with their mom every other week, so Bill and I took advantage of the in-between weeks, when we didn't have to worry about the kids, to spend time together. Bill would stay over at my house in Ojai or meet me in Los Angeles for a night at my apartment. We were consumed by the easy, early days of falling in love. We talked about my plan to get Gracie, and he promised to help me take care of the dog.

Bill and his kids quickly became permanent fixtures in my life. I didn't think too much about the relationship or ask myself too many questions. I just moved forward to make it happen. I felt so lucky to have gotten together with him. We got along really well. It was easy. I adored his kids, and we had a lot of fun together.

One of the first things we all did was attend a charity benefit for wild animals at which Crystal and her dog, Delphi, were invited to speak. Among other things, Crystal frequently taught about animal communication at events or workshops, and I was fascinated by that topic. We drove to the event in the canyon behind Malibu, attended their talk about the importance of love, and got to see and interact with many different animals who had been in movies or were rescued from injuries or abusive situations. The kids even got to help wash an elephant who had appeared on screen many times. On the way home from the event, Roy, Jane, and I sang Bob Marley's "Don't Worry 'Bout a Thing, Cause Every little Thing's Gonna Be Alright," at the top of our lungs, with the car windows open, and the CD player blasting the music in the background.

> The trick is in what one emphasizes. We either make ourselves miserable, or we make ourselves happy. The amount of work is the same.
> –Carlos Castaneda

CHAPTER 3

MEETING GRACIE

The four weeks went by in a flash, and it was already exceptionally hot and dusty as Bill and I drove out to George's kennel in Saugas to actually meet Gracie for the first time. George came out to the car as we pulled into the driveway. We got more of a grunt than a greeting as he motioned us to follow him into the house. His jeans were caked with dirt, especially at the knees, and his shirt was so threadbare that I had to stare intently to notice that it had started out as a blue plaid cowboy shirt with fake pearl buttons.

As we followed George, barely able to hear each other over the barking which seemed to be coming from behind the house, George yelled over his shoulder, "Oh yeah, forgot to tell ya. The other people backed out, so you have two little yellow girls to choose from."

"Why'd they back out?" I countered, as Bill and I trailed behind George through the house trying to step lightly on the exhausted avocado shag carpet while navigating a path through the canine odds and ends that littered the floor. The TV trays and tables were overwhelmed with plates of half-eaten food, stacks of papers, magazines, pictures of dogs, hypodermic needles, dog supplements, and ashtrays overflowing with cigarette butts, all intermingled with bowls of dog food. I wondered whether the total chaos had anything to do with the other people's decision to pass on the puppy.

Clearly the distinction between man and dog had been lost in this house.

"I don't have any idea," George said as he walked ahead of us. "Nothin' wrong here."

We continued on through the house and out the back door. Then he led us down a gentle hill to the kennel area below the house where dogs were dashing about every which way in a large enclosed yard. There were at least thirty of them barking enthusiastically at the fence as we passed by. The sound was deafening.

George took us into a large darkened room with pens lined up on both sides of a cement hall, each pen having doggy-door access to the outside yard and a chain-link gate to the inside hall. "Wait here," he said, pointing to the two steps going down to the kennel area. It was slightly quieter inside the kennel, and Bill and I sat down on the cement steps to wait as instructed.

"Well," I said. "This is a little weird, don't you think?"

"I'll say," Bill replied. "I couldn't even hear myself think out there."

"I know. How do these dogs cope with all of that noise?"

"I guess they must get used to it. Dogs are adaptable, you know."

"Do you think we should be getting a dog from a place like this?" I asked, as ten tiny whirlwinds of varying colors came blowing into a pen just to my right. A smallish lactating black dog and George simultaneously entered through the door just behind the steps we were sitting on, so Bill and I jumped up to let them pass.

"This black one," George said, pointing to the dog who entered with him, "is Sadie, their mom. She's a great dog and a good mother. It's a mixed litter—some black, some white, but all purebred. The sire of this litter was my champion dog."

"You can get in there with them if you want or let them out," he continued. I didn't hesitate and opened the door into the pen and was immediately covered with puppies. I was overwhelmed with how cute and sweet they were.

"See this little gal with the red nail polish?" he said, pointing. "She's the one reserved for you. But you can have the bigger one over there if you want. She's the other one I told you was available. Those are the only two yellow girls I got now."

"Oh," I said. "They're both adorable."

"Hold 'em," George said. "See which one's yours."

When I picked up both puppies and took them out of the pen, the little one with the red nail polish turned her face toward me and kissed me all over without any hesitation. I kissed her back. I knew that she was the one for me as I breathed in the sweet smell of puppy breath. How delightful. Bill cuddled both puppies as we handed them back and forth.

When we finally had to leave, I placed Gracie on the floor. Gracie's mother was close, and the other puppies were scattered. Gracie saw an opportunity and raced toward her mother to steal a little sip of milk while her siblings weren't looking. That independence sealed the deal as far as I was concerned.

"I think that one's Gracie," I said pointing to the little puppy who had quickly turned her attention away from the milk and was running back toward me, her little tail held proudly, making slight propeller circles as she ran. "What do you think?" I asked Bill. Even though I knew which one I was taking, I thought I should ask.

"I agree," Bill said.

"George, we'll take the one with the red nail polish," I said as I kneeled to give her one last kiss on the head. "The one reserved for us."

"OK. You can come back in four weeks to pick her up. She'll have her first shots and be ready to go."

"You won't mix her up with any of the other pups, will you?"

George just looked at me, like, "Where did such a stupid idea come from?" Of course he wouldn't mix them up.

ooooo

Bill and I had fallen into a comfortable silence as we drove along, but I couldn't stop thinking about Gracie or the extraordinary feeling I got from her. It had been a long time since I'd had a dog, but I remembered that feeling of love and connection with an animal from my childhood. I'd lie on the floor with my black lab, Sheik, and talk to him endlessly or just hold on to him for comfort when my mother was acting weird. I also remembered that as I grew up, my mother tried to thwart the relationship I had with Sheik, or any other animal in my life. I could still hear her yelling at me to stop acting crazy when I talked with the dog. Then other random thoughts about growing up in my family started to rattle around in my brain. I hadn't had time to share too much of my past with Bill, so I thought this might be a good opportunity to tell him about some of it. Besides, he was a captive audience in the car.

"Hey," I said glancing over at Bill who was driving calmly. "I think the idea of getting a dog has stirred things up from my childhood. You want to hear some of the stories of growing up with my mother?"

"Sure," Bill said. "We have time to kill before we're home."

"It's not pretty. Almost four funerals over the years—all mine."

"What!" Bill said startled. "Go for it."

"Well, let's see, might as well start with the commencement of this lifetime, since I don't really remember any of the other ones," I said with a grin, as I paused to think about what to say. "To begin with, my mother constantly reminded me that I should have died when I was born. I don't know if that was a wish or the reality of the times. She's long gone, and I never asked. Apparently, I was a 'blue' baby."

"What's that?" Bill asked with a twinkle in his eye. "You don't seem blue to me."

"Supposedly it's a blood thing, and you turn weird colors when you're born. It happens when you're the accidental third child of RH-positive and RH-negative parents. My mother was 42 when I was born, which was really old to be having a kid back in those days. My father said I was a 'wonderful surprise.' I think he was thrilled with having a little girl after two boys. I was always a daddy's girl, but I didn't have the same warm, fuzzy relationship with my mother, that's for sure. I heard my mother refer to me once as a 'mistake.'"

"Ouch," Bill said.

"Yeah, that stung, but I guess it was a miracle I even survived in 1949. I was told they had a tough time finding compatible blood for a transfusion back in those days."

Bill didn't say anything, but he appeared to be listening, so I continued.

"When I was six, I came down with scarlet fever. Rather than post the required quarantine sign on the front of their new house, my parents got the brilliant idea to hide me and my illness away in a friend's mortuary in the next town over."

"That sounds scary," Bill interjected.

"It was, but they were ashamed of me being sick. I only remember my parents coming to see me once during my month-long stay in that place where death seemed to ooze out of every pore. I heard the doctor tell them he'd done all he could, and he didn't know if I'd live or die. I always wondered why he said that in front of me. I was sick but not deaf," I said, trying to interject a little levity into a story that I thought perhaps was starting to sound too serious.

"That's pretty harsh," Bill said.

"Yeah, well, apparently my father thought my illness might hurt his business and my mother was afraid that it might have a negative impact on her status with her new, upper-middle-class neighbors, and she really wanted to fit in. You know, a quarantine sign would have been like the Scarlett Letter, but on her house, and obviously a bad reflection of her.

She wanted all of the family secrets kept hidden. Besides, it was the '50s. Everyone wanted to fit in and keep up with their neighbors."

Bill gave me a half-smile that seemed to show an understanding of the mores of the '50s.

"Then, the next year, my appendix almost burst. I stayed home from school for six days and complained to my mother about my stomach pain that just kept getting worse and worse. Eventually she got it together, got all dressed up in her red silk suit, matching red pillbox hat, and white gloves, and took me to the doctor. Before we went she fed me pizza and strawberries, which still are two of my favorite foods, in case you're interested. So... that was a nice thing she did. Totally wrong, but nice," I said reflecting back. "As they wheeled me into emergency surgery, I remember hearing the doctor say, 'I hope she hasn't eaten anything spicy or acidic today.'"

Bill laughed, acknowledging the irony.

"I survived that one easily. It doesn't even count toward the four funerals."

"You really almost 'kicked the bucket' four times?"

"Yup."

"That's incredible. What's the next one?"

"When I was sixteen, I almost died in a car crash," I continued. "A drunk driver crossed the dividing line and hit my oldest brother Vince and me head on as we were coming back from a ski trip in Vermont. I don't want to bore you with all the gory details of that accident, but, suffice it to say, my head went through the windshield, and I wound up with 108 stitches across my forehead and over my eyelids and nose. I had a bunch of broken bones and needed several facial reconstructive surgeries. That's what all these scars are on my face. See, right here," I said, pointing to the obvious scars on my forehead. "Just in case you wondered."

"I never really noticed," Bill said, looking at me adoringly. "You look great to me."

"Yeah, well, I'm telling you some of my story so you still have time to back out of our relationship if you want to."

"Continue," Bill said, ignoring my comment.

"So, then, when I was twenty-six, living in Aspen, married to my first husband, this ugly black tumor engulfed my ovary. I was managing a popular Aspen restaurant and bar back in those days. I remember writhing on the floor in my office in pain, with this huge extended belly that almost looked like I was pregnant. Typical of the '70s, the doctors in Aspen told me to go home and take pain pills. Vince, who was a psychiatrist by that time, told me that was crazy advice and made me fly immediately to California. They rushed me into emergency surgery to remove the tumor. I spent thirty days in the hospital after that one. I got really sick with some weird infection and the doctors didn't know what to do. Antibiotics weren't working and everyone thought I was a goner."

"That sounds terrible," Bill said with real concern in his voice. "I've never had anything major happen to me. I can't even imagine what it must have been like being in a hospital for thirty days."

"It's not fun, that's for sure," I said, thinking about the pain of those thirty days, mostly alone in that hospital, not knowing if I was going to live or die. I wanted to share some of my experience with Bill, but I didn't want to reveal all of my vulnerable parts quite yet. It just seemed too much to tell Bill that my parents never bothered to come see me during either the car accident or the tumor hospitalizations, so I made light of it. "But I fought back because I knew I had things to do in this life. Unfortunately, I still haven't figured out what those things are yet," I said, laughing at my ongoing internal struggle. "Anyway, finally they did more surgeries and gave me multiple transfusions to save my life."

"Wow," Bill said.

"Enough about me," I said abruptly as the full story washed over me. "What was it like growing up in your family?"

"Let's see," Bill sighed. "There was always a lot of commotion in the house. Six kids, pretty close apart, and we had lots of friends over all the time. It seems like my mother just wanted us out from underfoot so she constantly told us to go outside and play. Since I was the oldest, after about 4th grade, my mother had too much to do taking care of the younger ones, so I was allowed to ride my bike pretty much anywhere I wanted to go. They left me to my own devices to figure it out..."

"...You're lucky," I interrupted. "Sorry, I interrupted you. Go on."

"That's Ok. I actually think it was the Boy's Club that saved me as a kid. I was into sports, and I always found something sports related at the Club to occupy my time after school or on the weekends. My father was never around. He was always working or off doing something. He had a small manufacturing company, which took a lot of his time. It was OK, but none of us kids ever got much individual attention or guidance." His voice trailed off as he stopped talking and he seemed far away. I wondered whether I'd opened an old wound. I wasn't sure why, but it didn't seem appropriate to ask him about it and he didn't elaborate.

"I got attention all right," I offered more quickly than I intended to since I didn't know if he wanted to add more. "Not necessarily the kind you want as a kid, though."

"What do you mean?" he asked, coming back to our conversation.

"A typical night in my family went like this," I said looking over at Bill to watch his reaction. "I'd come to the dinner table. My mother would say or do something that would make me cry. I don't remember what I was crying about, but it seemed like I cried every night of my childhood. My father would say in a kind and loving voice, 'Go wash your face, honey. You can't eat while you're crying,' but my mother would say, 'Don't be such a baby. You want something to cry about? I'll give you something to cry about, young lady,' and she'd raise her hand toward my face, and my father would interfere to stop her from hitting me. Then I'd go to the bathroom and wash my face. I can still see the yellow and grey tile in that bathroom, and I can still hear my mother's voice sometimes as she calls out to me from the heavens, or wherever she is."

"But you seem so happy... and upbeat," Bill said.

"I've always been a glass half-full kind of a girl, I guess. I don't know why, but I am. That's just fundamentally me. Every day when I wake up, I realize I have a choice to be happy or not. Most days I choose the happy, positive route. Not always, but I try."

"Me, too," he said.

"I noticed," I said, continuing to look at him. "It's one of the things I really like about you. You wake up in the morning and look at me with a smile on your face."

"What's not to smile at?" Bill asked.

"You'll see. I haven't even scratched the surface of the details of life with my mother. I don't want to tell you too much right at the beginning, though. You might get scared that I could turn into an axe murderer or something."

He shook his head. "I'm not worried."

"At forty-six, I had multiple abdominal surgeries to remove recurrent tumors and ultimately a hysterectomy. Uterus gone, tubes gone, ovaries gone, cervix gone, all of it—gone. The doctors keep taking out body parts, but I keep on going." I laughed. "Sometimes it seems like we have a lot of unnecessary parts, doesn't it? You hear about it all the time. Doctors taking out one thing or another. Maybe our bodies really don't have much to do with who we are."

"What?" Bill asked confused.

"It's our spirit, our soul, that makes us who we are. Not our physical bodies. You know, like Yoda says: 'Luminous beings are we... not this crude matter.'"

Bill looked at me like I was at least one bubble off of level and I was sorry I'd even mentioned it, so I quickly changed the topic. "So, here we are. I'll be forty-nine in July. I've had two weddings and almost four funerals—my personal variation on that Hugh Grant movie, and mine also has a good ending. I never let any of those events keep me down for long. In spite of it all, I've always felt happy and healthy. And, as far as I'm concerned, I'm done with illness."

Bill smiled in solidarity.

"I'm also hopeful about our relationship, and I love your kids, but..." I paused to think. "I am a worrier. A happy worrier, but still a worrier."

"It doesn't really help, you know."

"I know, but that doesn't stop me from worrying about things."

We both got quiet as we continued toward home, and my mind wandered again. I started wondering what *was* my purpose in life. I'd been trying to figure that out for a long time without any real answer. I always believed I'd survived my upbringing and all of those illnesses for a reason, and I didn't believe it was to be a lawyer. That was my mother's idea. According to her, I needed to be able to take care of myself since no one else would ever want that job.

Vince told me Mother used to rant at him about having a career, too. One time he asked her, "What about being happy?" He said our mother slapped him really hard and said being happy was not important, and he better not talk like that ever again. The only thing that was important was not being poor, getting an education, having a career, and making money.

Now I realized I needed to figure out what was right for me. Perhaps a puppy and the great new guy was the answer. Maybe I'd finally found my soul mate. I looked at Bill and realized this was the first time I hadn't felt tense with someone else driving in a very long time.

"Thanks for being such a good listener and a good driver," I said looking at him with a deep tenderness. "I appreciate it. I feel safe with you."

∞∞∞∞∞

After meeting Gracie, Bill and I had a day alone to relax together before I jumped back into work and resumed my business trips. I had decided to take time off work after Gracie came home, so I had to run constantly on the legal treadmill for the next four weeks to get ahead, or at least catch up.

As had been Bill's custom every summer for years, he made a beeline with his kids to Montana, his birthplace, to visit relatives. We discovered we didn't like being apart and talked five or six times a day on the phone. Bill said it was the first time in all the years he had been going to Montana, that he was anxious to leave Montana so he could get home to me. Bill made it home a few days before we were scheduled to bring Gracie home.

> Whatever relationships you have attracted in your life at this moment, are precisely the ones you need in your life at this moment. There is a hidden meaning behind all events, and this hidden meaning is serving your own evolution.
>
> -Deepak Chopra

CHAPTER 4

GRACIE COMES HOME

I was anxious to get Gracie out of that strange, uninviting kennel and home with me, but I had been delayed in New Jersey for an extra week on a business trip. And here it was, almost five weeks after first meeting Amazing Grace of Ojai, that I was on my way home with Gracie in my lap.

I sat in the passenger seat, looked over at Bill and then looked down at this adorable white fluff ball, with remnants of red nail polish on her toes, curled up asleep in my lap, breathing peacefully in and out, in and out, in rhythm with my own breath. I looked again at the tall, handsome guy driving my new car and questioned my sanity for just a second. Rushing into another relationship and simultaneously getting a dog was nuts. What was I doing?

Bill smiled at me lovingly. "Don't worry, sweetie, it's gonna be fine. I told you I'd help with the dog, and I will. They're not any trouble."

I continued to stare at him, trying to see what was underneath this calm, kind exterior. I was sure this time it was going to be different. Bill was a nice guy. And as an added bonus he was a happy person and his offbeat sense of humor made me laugh. I couldn't ask for anything more. Perhaps the third time really was the charm.

"I guess I'm just a little nervous about the dog," I said, looking down at this sweet bundle of responsibility sitting in my lap. I love animals, and I had pets as a kid, but I haven't had any for a long time. Harry, my second husband, was afraid of dogs so he wouldn't let me have one."

"Really? There's nothing to be afraid of. Dogs are easy."

"I know that, but apparently Harry didn't. Anyway, it's been almost forty years since I've had a puppy, and I don't remember what to expect." As I continued to stare at Gracie and feel her presence, I knew deep down, no matter what, getting her was the right decision. I was already in love.

I realized we needed to stop when Gracie started to squirm in my lap. "I think we need to pull over and let Gracie out to pee. She's getting anxious," I said.

"OK, no problem," Bill said kindly as he maneuvered the car to a deserted area by the side of the road and opened the door.

"Do you think I should put her on a leash?"

"I think it'll be OK. There aren't any cars around here."

"What if she runs away?" I said.

"She won't run away."

"Are you sure?"

"She's already attached to you, don't you see?"

Even though I'd asked his opinion, I wanted to make sure nothing bad would happen. I thought it was probably a better idea to have control of her, so I ignored his advice as I reached for her collar.

"Or, just do what you want and put her on a leash, if you're worried," he said wryly.

I snapped on her new pink leash and set her on the ground. Gracie immediately squatted, peed, and raised her cute little tail, then walked over and pressed herself against my leg as if to say, "Thanks, let's go home now."

As we continued on Route 126 towards Ojai, Gracie once again settled on my lap, I noted how quickly my life had become filled with kids one week and career the next. I was happy and busy, and I started thinking about my two marriages in comparison.

The first one was a good starter marriage that occurred in Aspen, Colorado, back in the '70s and, through the haze of the times, I couldn't really remember much of those years. Sex, drugs, rock and roll, and the 2 a.m. shuffle at the bars *are* what I remembered. I even married one of those really nice handsome guys I went home with after a late night of carousing and hustling for beers at pool. A skier, house painter, high school drop out, and hippie—he was perfect for the times. My mother hated him because he didn't have an education or a real job, and that, of course, made him even more appealing to me.

My parents actually showed up in Colorado for that first wedding, conducted by a Catholic priest out in a field filled with wild flowers, nestled up against the Rockies, followed by a raucous reception at the ski lodge at the base of Aspen Highlands. It was one of the few times I remember my mother looking happy. There was a picture of her looking up at one of the local drug dealers, enthralled, with a big smile on her face, and her eyes sparkling. I later learned that someone had spiked the punch with a mild LSD. I was a little sad that it was a drug-induced happiness, not a real one. But one thing my mother was really good at throughout her life was being nice to strangers and acquaintances, or at least pretending to be. The outside picture was always perfect; the inside story quite different.

In Aspen, I went to one of the first EST (Erhard Seminar Training) courses, which were very popular back in those days for encouraging transformation, personal responsibility, and accountability, and it caused me to start taking some responsibility for my life.

But my near-death experience with the black tumor was the actual catalyst that caused me to grow up and grow out of that first marriage; and it allowed me to transition out of the Aspen fantasy life to law school and all that followed. What that first marriage did was prepare me. But prepare me for what? To make the same mistakes a second time? That's what it had felt like when I was going through the second divorce. I never really believed that anyone would love me. That's what I'd heard from my mother when I was growing up, and so I tested that theory non-stop, without even knowing it.

As to the second marriage, I remembered that the wedding itself was also a blast. But the marriage seemed to fall apart quickly from there, and I was having trouble remembering my part in it all.

Maybe I'd been so desperate to have a relationship after law school, to try to obliterate the random affairs and one-night stands with men whom I now couldn't pick out of a crowd of two, that I'd settled for Harry, the first reasonable, professional person with a real job who asked me to marry him. It did make my mother happy to know I'd married a lawyer before she died. Maybe it should have been a clue of things to come when, shortly after Harry and I got married, I agreed to move to Switzerland for six months because the high-powered law firm I worked for at the time asked me to go and take care of a client there. Even early in our marriage, the grass was always greener for me somewhere else.

Maybe it'd always been thorny between us, but I was so busy raising Harry's son and trying to do things that I thought would make everyone happy, that I didn't even notice that things weren't right. There'd never been much passion between us. And I didn't really get much out of sex. Sometimes I'd attributed it to work or wanting to pursue a more spiritual life, and somehow sex didn't seem to fit in. At the same time, a part of me secretly wondered whether anyone could love me for anything other than sex, a thought deeply embedded in my psyche by my mother. So I tested that theory, too. I even questioned Harry once whether, hypothetically, he would continue in our marriage if sex were not a part of the relationship. He said he would.

Without even realizing it, I'd struggled my whole life between listening to my mother, believing her, not believing her, rebelling against her, not wanting to be like her, and yet constantly trying to please her, all to no avail.

As I thought about the end of my second marriage, one of the most perplexing memories popped into my head. I replayed the days before Harry announced he was leaving me. We had just returned from a wonderful trip to Poland and Lithuania with Harry's parents. In Poland, we unearthed some old relatives of Harry's dad on a small farm in the Polish countryside. They were happy, simple people. They still used horse-drawn carts for farm work and slept against a common wall with the pigs for heat. And yet they opened their home and their hearts to us and pulled out every jar of food they had canned for the winter just to be gracious to the long-lost relatives from America.

They didn't speak English so it was a bit difficult to communicate, but the old grandpa broke into his stash of Vodka and offered us shots—the universal language. Harry and his parents declined. When in Rome, I thought, as I smiled and accepted his invitation to drink even though it was only 10 a.m. Vodka and farm fresh eggs—perfect, I thought. He and I tossed back a few shots, and he laughed at my grimace as the vodka burned its way down. Drinking together seemed like the only polite thing to do under the circumstances. Later, the old man held my hand and proudly showed me around his town. I could tell I was his favorite relative from America when he gave me a present to bring home—a precious string of dried wild mushrooms that he had painstakingly collected in the forest.

We had a wonderful time those two weeks with Harry's parents, as we had had on many other trips just the two of us. The day after we got home, though, Harry announced out of the blue that he wanted a divorce. He was leaving me to get back together with the same woman he'd cheated on with his first wife. And I had been clueless. And how long had it been going on? I never believed that third parties break up relationships, so I knew that his infidelity wasn't the only reason we were splitting up, but what was? What had I done? And why had he waited until after this incredible trip, where we had dug into his Polish and my Lithuanian roots, to tell me? And why couldn't I just let it go and stop thinking about it?

I thought about what Crystal, who also worked with Harry, had said about us splitting up. She simply acknowledged that things change. Crystal said I had other things to do in this world, which, of course, put a lot of pressure on me to get it right. She said that I should stay connected to the present moment, use my intuition, connect with my inner voice, and feel the oneness and perfection of it all. When the divorce was happening, it didn't really feel that perfect to me. I remembered feeling betrayed and exhausted by it all, but now I was glad to be out of that relationship, out of that struggle, and on to a relationship with the nice guy sitting beside me.

I glanced at Bill driving calmly and quietly, country western music playing softly on the radio in the background. Then I looked down at Gracie and realized that this new puppy and this new man had all happened so easily and effortlessly. So I guess I just needed to let go, trust in the Universe, and see where this road was going to lead. I bent my head down, kissed the puppy on the top of her head, and whispered, "Welcome to my world, Gracie."

CHAPTER 5

GRACIE EXPLAINS IT

Julie thinks she picked me, but that's not quite how it worked. I had the entire thing orchestrated. I knew I needed to rescue her from the beginning, even before the beginning. You see, I am part angel. She needed me, and I knew it, but I needed her, too. I have wanted to write this book for a long time, but it has taken many lifetimes to find someone who would listen with her heart and then be willing to suspend judgment and write it down. It takes a certain leap of faith, you know. So I was born, part yellow lab, part angel, when she was ready. I needed to be in a dog body, so that it would be easier for her to learn to connect through her heart. Dogs have many gifts for their human companions to help them open their hearts. At first, she was pretty resistant to the idea of writing a book with her dog, but I kept working on her, little by little.

I remember the whole thing like it was yesterday. She had strayed pretty far from the natural path and her true essence. She had always loved animals, and yet she didn't have one living thing in her house; even the plants were mostly dead. Her natural connection with animals was strong, just buried very deep, and she didn't believe in herself. She had no idea how her life was about to change. And she certainly didn't know I was behind it all.

Just so you know, she can tell her part of the story anyway she wants, but remember, what I say is the truth because it comes from my heart and the heart of every being. She was studying and reading about oneness, but she didn't really feel it. She never experienced it directly. Intellectually, she was on a spiritual path, whatever that means. We are all on a spiritual path; it is just a matter of how open or receptive we are to different levels of consciousness at any point in time. But for her it was work. It's not supposed to be work to feel oneness with the universe, to feel a conscious union with spirit, to feel the interconnection of everything. That is our natural state. The human stuff is what is work.

Every being—whether human, non-human, animal, plant, the earth, air, water, trees, rocks, whatever—has an essential spiritual nature. The physical presentation may be different, but the spiritual essence, the life force in each being, is the same. It's all energy. This is the connection between all of us and the basis for us to understand and respect each other, regardless of our differences. How can that be so hard? People have made it that way.

She has drifted away from her connection with nature and now is struggling back. That is my job. To snap her out of it or maybe snap her back into it, depending on how you look at it. It really is all about love, gratitude, and respect for all beings: no matter what, no matter who, no matter where. Be kind. There is no hierarchy. No better or worse. Just different presentations of form. I am love. We all are. Love is all there is.

CHAPTER 6

THE EFFECT

Once Gracie arrived home, it took her only one night to figure out how to escape the gated enclosure beside the bed and leap up, so that she could sleep between Bill and me. In the heat of the summer she also loved to sleep by the air-conditioning vent with the stuffed hedgehog I had bought her before we had even met.

One morning a few days after Gracie had taken up residence in my heart, I woke up early and looked out my picture window as the sun just peaked over the mountaintops. I glanced to the right of the window and once again absorbed the effect of the beautiful painting of the Matilija poppies hanging in the corner. I rolled over and stared at Gracie and Bill, who were both still asleep beside me. A deep sense of peace filled me as I watched them sleep. Bill opened his eyes slowly and then instantaneously smiled at me.

"Good morning," I said looking at him lovingly. "Want some coffee? I'll get up and make some if you want."

"Sure. That'd be great."

"Do you know that it was the magic in that painting that brought you into my life?" I said slowly as I looked at him tenderly and nodded toward the painting of the Matilija poppies in the corner.

"What are you talking about?" Bill said, barely awake.

"When I got divorced from Harry, I hired this wonderful Chinese woman to Feng Shui this house. She told me to hang a painting in that corner that depicted my idea of love. Apparently, that's my relationship corner. That's the painting I chose."

"Yeah, so?" Bill said, as he seemed to try to focus on what I was saying.

"So, one week after hanging that painting I met you at the 49ers party up at my pond, where the Matilija poppies grow."

Bill stared at the painting and then at me with disbelief. "It's a nice painting, and I love flowers, but I don't know about its effect in that corner of your bedroom," he said after a minute. "It sounds a little nutty."

"It's true, just one week later I met you."

"Yeah, but it didn't have anything to do with the painting."

"How do you know?" I asked.

"Well, I don't, but you hardly paid any attention to me at that party anyway."

"I know, you made me nervous."

"Why'd I make you nervous?"

"I don't know, maybe you were too good looking or something."

"I don't see myself that way," Bill said.

I stared at him in surprise. How could he not see himself as gorgeous? "Well, maybe you were too nice then," I said.

Bill just stared at me as if he didn't have any idea what I was talking about.

"Maggie was trying to finagle a way for me to meet you," I continued. "She told me she was going to invite you and your kids to the party so it would be casual, not like a date or anything."

"What'd she say about me?"

"She said you were really nice, recently divorced, had three kids, and that I should meet you."

"All true," Bill said, with a pleased look on his face. "I'll have to thank her."

"Since dating options in Ojai for our age group are slim, I agreed to the party concept. Besides, I love parties. I remember hearing you laughing and seeing a bunch of kids struggling to get in a boat by my dock. I got up my courage, walked over, introduced myself, and asked if you needed help. Remember?"

"No," Bill said. "Not really."

"Well, I do. You introduced me to Roy and Jane. Anne was away at a leadership conference in Northern California and wasn't there. I remember smiling at your kids and looking away from you. Then I said, 'It might be breast … best to climb in the boat this way…' I'll never forget it. I was so embarrassed. I could feel the red start to rise up my face. I was totally tongue-tied and couldn't put two thoughts together, let alone words. I felt like an idiot and hoped you or the kids hadn't heard. Finally, I couldn't take the knots in my stomach any longer, so I walked away in mid-sentence. I didn't want to say anything else embarrassing on that first encounter."

Bill laughed at my memory.

"I mingled, played horseshoes with Jane and Roy, and kept contact with you to a minimum for the rest of the party. You were a lot more youthful than any of my recent dates in Los Angeles, and I didn't want to blow it. In spite of two divorces, I still believed in the triumph of hope over experience."

"I watched you play with my kids," Bill said remembering. "It seemed so natural for you to be with them, and it looked like you were really having fun."

"I was. I love kids. I've done a lot of stuff in my life that I'm not necessarily proud of, but I don't regret any of it. I learned from all of it. But if I did have one regret, it would be that I never had any children of my own."

"You want mine?" he joked. "No, seriously, I appreciate how good you are with my kids. Always coming up with things to do and including them," Bill said. "It's really important to me. I can tell they like you, too. I always thought they deserved better from me and their mother than a divorce."

"Divorce is hard on kids. No question. I think it's really hard to have a good divorce as far as kids are concerned."

"I guess," Bill said, as the first look of sadness I had seen from him flitted across his face.

"You can try and minimize the pain, but it's still tough on everyone. I'll try to step in the best I can to help you," I said as I reached over to touch his hand. "Just talking to your kids is a good start. But no matter how you feel about things with their mom, remember kids love both of their parents no matter what."

Bill didn't say anything.

"It'll be OK," I said softly, looking from Bill to Gracie and back.

"By the way," I said after a minute of silence, "you didn't call me or anything after the 49ers party. What was up with that?" I laughed.

"I know. I wanted to, but I got crazy with students and classes at the end of the school year and trying to figure out how to be a single parent. I was overwhelmed with work and finances. Besides I thought you weren't interested since you didn't pay any attention to me at the party. I didn't think anyone was loony enough to want to date a poor college teacher with three kids."

"I guess I am." I smiled. "It took another party to actually cement the relationship, though. Memorial Day. The day Gracie was born. Maybe that painting actually brought both you and Gracie into my life," I said tenderly, as I adjusted my pillows and looked at the little puppy lying sound asleep between us.

"Well, I don't care what did it, I'm just glad I'm here."

"Me too," I said.

"By the way, Ojai is full of woo-woo," Bill said affectionately. "You'll fit right in. There are all kinds of nuts in this town."

I laughed.

"Hey, what about that coffee you promised?" he said.

CHAPTER 7

CRYSTAL

When I told my friends about the Feng Shui experience and meeting Bill just one week after hanging the painting, they were happy for me but amused by my forays into alternative means for meeting men. I, on the other hand, was convinced there was something to all of this woo-woo stuff. No matter what anyone said.

I'd been fascinated with the idea of alternative realities since my college days and the Carlos Castaneda books, which I read over and over. I had been going to psychics, palm readers, astrologers, and tarot card readers since the late '60s, but I'd been seriously studying mysticism, the inner voice, indigenous wisdom, the idea of animal communication, and the connection between everything for the last ten years with Crystal. I believed that there were unseen forces at work in our lives, and as I'd traveled and studied with Crystal, some amazing things had happened that continued to alter my view about how things work. But parts of my very left lawyer brain were still extremely active in putting on the brakes.

Crystal had three golden retrievers. She often told me about her communication with them, in particular with her dog Delphi, who was constantly working with her to help people understand the importance of intuition and love. I loved animals and was curious about Crystal's gift of communication and attended all of her workshops on animal communication.

On one of our early trips together, Crystal and I went to Costa Rica to talk to Dr. Robert Muller, a visionary and author of many books, who had recently retired as Assistant Secretary-General at the United Nations, to continue his life's work to promote world peace. We sat on his farm overlooking the University for Peace, which he had co-founded, and discussed his world core curriculum and its potential use at an online university Crystal wanted to start in the United States. It was one of those encounters I will never forget. We discussed at length how we could make a conscious choice to be happy and peaceful and thus create a peaceful world. Dr. Mueller said he prayed every day that all human beings would become instruments of peace.

"Always remember that the peace of the world is the sum-total of the peace of all individuals. It starts within," he said. "Always affirm to others the vision of the world you want."

I saw that Dr. Muller did this tirelessly in every letter, poem, or book he wrote, every speech he gave and every word he spoke, and he encouraged me to do the same. I was inspired to do more to promote peace even though I didn't really know how I would accomplish such a task.

After spending a few days with Dr. Muller, Crystal and I decided to tour Costa Rica a little, and I decided to do a touristy thing and go for a horseback ride on the beach one afternoon.

"I don't want to ride," Crystal said, "but I'll come talk to the horses and tell them to take it easy on you, if you want. I know you haven't ridden in a long time."

"Sure, that would be great," I said, still a little skeptical about talking to animals but open and interested in the idea. I got on this big chocolate-colored horse and sat there, waiting for the other people to get settled on their horses before we set off. Crystal walked right up to my horse, looked him square in the eye, and tried to get some information from him.

"I'm sorry, Julie, but the only thing this one will say is 'I am the King.' I'm trying to argue with him about God/spirit being king, but that's all he'll say, 'I am the King.' I don't know, maybe he doesn't speak English." She laughed.

"OK, thanks. You tried," I said, happy about her effort. And we left it at that, and she went back to her room at the hotel.

A few minutes later the local guide came up to us, explained where we were going to ride, and said he would like to introduce our horses to us. He turned to me and said, "Your horse's name is King."

I remember being blown away. There was no way Crystal could have known the horse's name. I thought of every angle because, in spite of my belief that Crystal had a special connection with the Universe, I had a real hard time believing that she, or anyone else, could talk to animals. That was the first time of many that I had independent confirmation that she wasn't just making it up.

Over the years Crystal and I went to Egypt, Ghana, Brazil, and Lourdes in France to put on workshops or participate in conferences. Crystal said she had assignments from other realms in these places and asked me to travel with her to help hold the energy for her. I didn't always understand what she was doing, or what I was doing, but she was a very powerful and inspirational speaker, and we always met interesting people on our travels.

In Ghana, we met with several spiritual leaders and the Vice-President of Ghana to discuss holding a children's peace conference in that country. At the United Nation's Earth's Summit in Brazil, I spent a lot of time with indigenous elders and chiefs whom we had sponsored to be part of a panel discussion at the conference. Our hope was that indigenous wisdom, including assessing the impact of any decision on seven generations down the line, would be considered in any future environmental plans made by the various governments.

Crystal and I also encountered animals along the way who had interesting things to say. She told me to tune in to my inner voice and listen to the animals. I would try, but I didn't really know if I could hear them or not.

So, wherever we would go, I'd ask Crystal to tell me what the animals were saying. I trusted her intuition. When I went to the World Women's Conference in Beijing to support Crystal as a keynote speaker, I asked Crystal to talk to a donkey that I found tied up by the Great Wall in China. According to Crystal, the donkey reported that animals were getting tired of carrying the burdens of man. Apparently the donkey was also clear that he was happy that someone was finally listening to him, and he really wanted to come home with us to the United States. I agreed with Crystal that he seemed sad when she told him that she didn't think she could arrange such a trip.

Another time she talked to a polar bear in a zoo who anyone could see was stressed by the way he paced back and forth in his enclosure. He said it was too late for him, but that I should help the others. Without exactly hearing those words, I certainly got the sense from that encounter that I should do something to help polar bears, so I immediately donated money to the World Wildlife Fund, the only thing I knew how to do to help them. Since money was abundant in my life at the time, I was constantly giving money to organizations that helped animals, children, the environment, or indigenous people.

Whenever I was with Crystal, we meditated and connected with our inner voices. When left to my own devices, however, I couldn't seem to make meditation a permanent part of my daily practice. No matter how much I enjoyed the peace and clarity and no matter how much I knew about the benefits to reduce stress, life took over. I was just too busy with my law career to make time for meditating. I felt I was too busy for even five minutes a day. Maybe I just wasn't that disciplined.

Yet I was struggling to find meaning in my life and to figure out what I was supposed to do to be of service on this planet. No matter how much

I did for others, no matter how many charity events I hosted, no matter how much money I gave to good causes, it never seemed enough. I was always seeking to do more, give more, and be more. I was rarely content with where I was or what I was doing.

CHAPTER 8

CHILDREN AND ANIMALS

I started working with Julie early on. She really didn't know what she was doing, but I coached her about love for all animals from the sidelines. I really wanted her to trust and believe in herself more. I wanted her to tune in to things going on around her. She tried, but the critical part of her brain often spoke up louder than the intuitive part in her heart, and she had learned to listen to the critical and skeptical parts inside her. Those parts had taken over and she doubted herself. I needed to be patient for the right time to work with her directly, but I encouraged her along the way. She didn't know it was me, though.

-Gracie

For the first few months, Gracie went with me everywhere—to weddings, tucked in a shopping bag at the supermarket, and occasionally to my office in Beverly Hills. I could tell she preferred the peace and quiet of Ojai, so I started staying in Ojai more and going to Los Angeles less. Gracie loved to swim at the pond on my property. From the very beginning, she was enthralled with kids and water. She loved to ride in the boats or play with Bill's son, Roy, on the surfboard. She slept in Jane's lap and played with the kids on the slip and slide. Her smile said it all. Life was good.

Within weeks, Bill and I started talking about blending our lives to simplify raising his children when they were with us. Since we were together all of the time, it seemed silly to keep up the expenses of two houses. Although we hadn't made a final decision, we talked some about the details of living together.

"I only make a set amount from the college every month to contribute," Bill said.

"Not to worry. We can contribute equally, to a joint account or something, for our day-to-day expenses, and if we spend more, I'll just cover it. Besides, I believe in abundance. Ever since I can remember, contrary to what most people say, I've always thought money does grow on trees and is just out there for the picking. Now that I own an avocado and orange orchard, that metaphorical-metaphysical concept has turned into a literal one," I said with a laugh.

"I don't know about abundance," Bill said. "It's hard with three kids. Sometimes when I'm struggling to pay bills, it doesn't feel so abundant."

"I think we've been conditioned to feel that way. Some people believe what they see—others see what they believe. I guess I've been pretty lucky to mostly be in the latter category. I mean, I've always worked really hard and everything. And I've had constant jobs since I was about twelve, but I've always been grateful for everything I had, and I always had everything I needed. Money has never been a problem, even when I didn't have any."

"That's great," Bill said. "You're one of the lucky ones."

"I guess I am." I paused to think. Was it luck or belief? I wondered.

ooooo

One day Jane and Roy were at my house playing on the back deck when Jane turned to me, looked me straight in the eye, and said, "I'd really like to live here. It's so great."

Roy looked at me shyly and very quietly said, "Me, too."

Bill and I just looked at each other in surprise, but we took it as a sign.

Right before the new school year began, less than three months after we got together, we sold Bill's house, paid off his debts, and Bill and his children moved in with Gracie and me. I never explained to Bill that some of my motivation for acting so precipitously came out of worry that our relationship and my life with his kids might disappear if we didn't create an immediate family. I was afraid that if I wasn't indispensable to his life, that it all might fall apart and I'd be left alone again.

When they moved in, Bill and the kids came with Carl and Bert, two shelter rescue dogs. Carl was about three years old at the time. I suspected he might've had some bad experiences during his early years because he was incredibly protective of his food. He would growl and bite if anyone tried to take anything away from him, or if he just didn't like someone. Everyone was afraid of him when he was in those moods, except Gracie. Gracie loved Carl.

I could see how kind and attentive Gracie was to Carl. I often found them cuddled together, arms around each other, on the same dog bed. I worked hard with Carl on what I called 'love training,' thinking I'd come up with that term all on my own. It wasn't until much later that I learned Gracie was supporting me from the sidelines in working with Carl and all of the other animals. Carl blossomed under the extra attention. He loved being able to run off leash and eventually became the love bug of the group. Everyone wanted to try and cuddle up with Carl. If he didn't growl and allowed someone to pet him, it was like they had passed some animal test. I was the only one who would take something directly out of his mouth. I knew he'd never bite me, and he never did.

ooooo

The next few years were filled with happiness, love, travel, work, laughter, tears, and the challenge of integrating Bill, Anne, Roy, Jane, Gracie, Carl, and Bert into my life, or maybe me into theirs. We laughed a lot, and Bill and I started redecorating to make my house seem more like us. We made room for the kids. In the process, we moved furniture around and started painting each wall in the house a different color—rust red, butter yellow, sage green. Only the trim remained white. I was constantly humming happily to show tunes or tunes I made up in my head as I worked around the house. Gracie grew quickly and was my constant companion.

Roy loved birds and had moved in with his pet Cockatiel named Grey. We decided Grey needed a friend. Roy and I went to our local pet and feed store, Wachters, and bought a very pretty little yellow and grey Cockatiel, whom we named Francine, as a friend for Grey. Of course, we needed a bigger cage and all sorts of bird accoutrements, so I bought those, too.

When the kids were asleep and I waited up for Bill to come home from his work as a professor at the Community College, Francine would sit on the stainless kitchen table and eat seeds off of my tongue. Bill taught Grey how to do a great wolf whistle, which always made me smile. Then friends started giving us orphan birds, or birds they could no longer care for, so I had an aviary built for them. Grey and Francine moved outdoors and started having babies, and more orphan birds kept arriving. We built a second aviary for the sweet Finches and Rosy Bourkes that arrived. Those little birds lit up the ranch with their song each morning, and Grey continued his wolf whistle every time I walked past the aviary.

ooooo

One day I looked out and saw Roy running down the driveway with a cup bouncing in his hand and a concentrated look on his face.

"Look, look, Julie. Look what I've got. Please come out. Come out quickly," I heard him yell through the open screen door.

I rushed outside. "What's wrong?"

"Nothing's wrong," he said. "Look what I found. I went back to our old house in town. No one lives there now, and I snuck in the back to see if I'd left anything behind. There was an old bucket full of icky-looking brown water. I started to play in it, and I was swirling a stick as fast as I could in the mud at the bottom and out popped Bob. Do you believe it? Look," he said, shoving an undulating cup of brown liquid in my face. "This goldfish has been living in that bucket for months with no one taking care of him, and he survived. Just think of it. Look, Julie, in the cup," Roy said urgently.

As I peered into the old cracked ceramic mug, I saw a fish that was the shape of a large goldfish but the color of dirt. It certainly didn't look like any goldfish I'd ever seen. So there it was, a large brown fish whose name apparently was Bob, trying to swim in about two inches of murky water in the bottom of a cup.

"Well, well," I said. "I think we need to find Bob a bigger home than that cup." And so another of the many strays and rescues came to live with us.

Roy and I immediately went to Wachters and bought a large goldfish bowl. We were becoming one of Wachters' best customers. While we were there, we decided that Bob needed a friend, so we picked out a beautiful fish with a long white feathery tail, whose golden scales sparkled in the water. We plunked the two of them together in their new home.

"What should we name the other one?" Roy asked.

"Umm," I said, thinking, "Obviously not Bob."

"That's perfect." Roy sighed in relief. "Now we have Bob and Not Bob."

I smiled but didn't say that wasn't exactly what I had meant, and so the fish got their names.

The most amazing thing happened over the next few weeks. Bob's color slowly changed from a dirty ugly brown to the most vibrant shade of crimson orange. Bob simply shimmered as he swam proudly around his new bowl. Bob and Not Bob grew quickly, eventually getting so big that I insisted we build a giant fishpond with a waterfall, pumps, and a filtration system in the front yard, so the goldfish would have a nice big home. When I got an idea in my head, I made it happen. Bob and Not Bob moved outside, and each one grew to be about a foot long, with hundreds of offspring swimming around them. Apparently either Bob or Not Bob was a girl.

○○○○○

Jane came home from school one rare drizzly day with a sad look on her face. "Julie, there are the two most adorable baby goats at the store right down the street. They're a few days old and soooooo cute. You'd just love 'em. They're sisters."

"What? At Wachters?"

"No, not Wachters," Jane said. "We need to rescue them from that mean guy at the store down the street. You know the one."

It didn't take much pleading. I had real difficulty saying no to anything Bill's kids wanted. They were good kids, and I just couldn't stand disappointing them. Besides, having animals around made everyone happy.

Jane looked at me again with those imploring, sad eyes and said, "Please, please, Julie. They need us. Let's just go look at them."

I suspected I was being manipulated, but I immediately drove Jane down the hill to "just look." We came home with two baby goats who were seven days old. On the ride home, Jane named them Natalie and Claire. We had no corral, no barn, and no place for goats, so these little babies moved into my newly remodeled kitchen, with its stainless appliances and hand-crafted cherry cabinets. We bottle fed them, and they were supposed to sleep in a giant black bucket which we had placed smack in the middle of everything, constantly causing a traffic jam around the refrigerator.

Somehow the goats learned to jump in the bucket to pee and poop but then would jump out to sleep with Gracie or Carl in the corner of the kitchen.

Every morning for almost two months, I went to Vons and bought all the pasteurized goat milk they had, usually about 12 quarts at a time at $3.49 a quart. No one in town could understand why Vons never had goat milk, and I wondered how people with less income than I had could afford to raise goats. It wasn't until the goats were almost weaned and ready to be put outside that I mentioned this predicament to Katy, one of the owners of Wachters.

"Katy, don't you guys have anything to feed baby goats?" I asked. "There's got to be a better way than going to Vons for goat milk everyday."

Katy laughed. "You do realize, Julie, that we have powdered milk for baby goats?" she asked. "You just mix it with water."

"Really?"

"Yeah. For about $20, you can make at least 100 quarts of milk."

"Why didn't I know about that?" I asked rhetorically.

We were at Wachters almost daily for some kind of animal food or supplies, and I'd never thought to ask them about the goats. I realized I had a lot to learn.

"You know what they say—no use crying over spilt milk," I said with a laugh as I paid for the bag of powered milk, which lasted until the goats were weaned and out of the house. At least I would know what to do if we ever had baby goats again.

∞∞∞

At the beginning of my relationship with Bill, Crystal was living in Ojai, and she was integral in our lives. She continued to give workshops, teach, and write about oneness, intuition, and connecting with the inner voice. She loved children and animals, and she worked tirelessly to give a voice to those who could not speak for themselves. Crystal, Jane, and

I worked on a project where Jane collected messages from kids around the world about world peace and helping the environment, and then Jane delivered those messages, along with a speech, at a panel discussion at the United Nations in New York. Jane did an incredible job of promoting peace and representing children all over the world.

Bill and I took the kids with us everywhere. I didn't want the kids to feel that I was taking their father away, so I bent over backwards to make sure they were included in everything. Sometimes I wondered whether I thought more about the kids' and the dogs' needs than Bill's or mine. We had a baby-sitter for the dogs so they could stay at home while we were gone, but I never liked being gone more than a week or ten days because I really missed the animals, Gracie in particular. But I loved doing things with the kids. They were enthusiastic, and we always had a blast.

I encouraged Bill to do things alone with his children, or talk to them about what was going on in their lives, but he rarely did. We were a new family unit, and I was in charge of planning family activities. I arranged a trip to Italy and a cruise to Alaska. We went skiing in the winter and to Montana in the summers. Bill seemed to love being outside, tending to the plants, so when we weren't working or traveling we stayed home, and he worked in the garden and I played with the dogs. Gracie loved to swim in the pond.

The every-other-week arrangement with the kids' mom was stressful on everyone. It seemed like they would just get used to one place and then have to move again, or they'd forget stuff at the other house. It always took Jane a few days to settle back in with us when she returned home, but it was the best we could do under the circumstances. During the weeks when the kids were with their mom, I desperately tried to cram in all of the law work I needed to do to maintain my job, so I would be able to give the kids more love and attention when they were with us. Eventually Roy got tired of going back and forth between two houses, so he just stayed full time with Bill and me. It became difficult for me to juggle being a lawyer in Los Angeles with the demands of the kids' schedules, soccer games, school activities, picking them up and dropping them off at various places in Ojai, and taking care of the dogs.

I tried to work from home for a while, and I went to Los Angeles less and less. I declined work travel whenever I could and took more and more conference calls from the house. The house was always filled with kids, laughter, and barking dogs, so the mute button became my friend during work time. I loved the fact that I could be sitting at home in my pajamas, talking on a conference call with fifty lawyers around the country, or arguing a motion with some Judge somewhere, and no one knew I was home. Gracie was with me always. She sat at my feet while I worked. If I took two steps forward, so did Gracie. Two steps backwards, Gracie was there.

CHAPTER 9

GRACIE AND STORMY

Roy, Jane, and I talked about mating Gracie so we could have a litter of puppies. I didn't know whether Gracie wanted puppies, or if I was just projecting the joys of motherhood onto her. I thought maybe I'd missed out in not having any children of my own and wondered whether Gracie would feel the same if we had her fixed before she had a family. We hadn't made any firm decision, though. Bill thought puppies would be great, but he didn't really weigh in one way or the other.

As things worked out, the answer came easily and unexpectedly. Gracie and I were at Wachters, waiting at the check-out counter with a bag of gourmet dog biscuits, when we ran into B.B, the sister-in-law of a well-known local character and an acquaintance of mine from the many charity events we had both attended.

B.B was admiring Gracie when she said, "You know, Julie, Larry really wants a Lab puppy and wants to breed Stormy. Do you know anyone who might have a female?"

"Well, I've been thinking about breeding Gracie," the words just popped out of my mouth. "She's just over two, so that's a good age. She's a purebred Lab and a wonderful dog—sweet, kind, all the traits you could want. She does have a little independent streak, though, and likes to do things her own way."

"That would be great. Gracie is beautiful," B.B said. "I'll talk to Larry to arrange details. They probably should meet first but call us if she goes into heat soon. Here's our number."

And just like that, I was Gracie's pimp, even though I wasn't one-hundred percent certain I wanted her to have a litter of puppies. I thought it might be a lot of work, but I didn't know how much.

Larry, with a ten-gallon cowboy hat perched on his head, his wife Maj, dressed beautifully in clothes I later learned she'd made herself, and Stormy all arrived for a pre-conjugal visit a few days later. Jammed into their new Prius, they all had big smiles on their faces. The giant yellow Lab, with a kind and gentle face, was crammed in the back, his head hitting the ceiling as he bounced around, trying to get a look at Gracie.

Just like Larry, I thought, to be the first in the Hollywood crowd to trade in the Ferrari for a hybrid and do what was right for the environment.

"How do you like this car?" I asked, as Stormy jumped out of the back and immediately ran up to Gracie to check her out. "I've been thinking about getting rid of my Porsche and getting one. I really like the idea of a hybrid."

"It's fantastic," Maj said. "We just love it."

And so a friendship began. Gracie was enthralled with her new big, handsome boyfriend. It was love at first sight, so I made marital arrangements with the new in-laws.

A few weeks later, Gracie went into heat. She was just over two years old. Perfect timing, according to what I had read in one of my "breeding for dummies" books. I called Maj, and she dropped Stormy off to stay with us to see how things worked out. For a few days, Stormy tried, but he just couldn't get it right. Gracie would approach Stormy and then turn around so her butt was right in his face, but it seemed as if Stormy just couldn't figure out what he was supposed to do. Everyone was worried and fretted over the dogs because they weren't getting together.

I finally called our vet, Dr. Matt Bailey, to ask for advice. "I told you we are trying to breed Stormy and Gracie. Well, time's running out on Gracie's heat, and they haven't gotten together yet. Any suggestions?"

"There's nothing you can do," he said. "Leave them together. Just see what happens today. If they don't hook up, bring Stormy to the office in the morning. We'll see what we can do here as a last resort."

"What does that mean? You'll see what you can do there?"

"We'll give him a hand job, Julie, and then artificially inseminate Gracie," Matt replied in his calm voice.

"Ooohhh," I replied, a little embarrassed that I hadn't even imagined that as an option, while visions of that process simultaneously went through my head. "I see."

So the next morning, after talking to Larry and Maj about the slight wrinkle in our plans, I piled Stormy in my car and dropped him off at Matt's office.

I waited for the call to bring Gracie in. But when Matt finally called toward the end of the day, he said, "Sorry, Julie. We didn't have any luck."

"What do you mean you didn't have any luck? How could you not have any luck?"

"We tried and tried, but we weren't able to get any sperm. It was like he just wasn't interested in the whole process. Highly unusual."

"So what should we do now?" I asked, at a loss, since supposedly that had been the last-ditch effort.

"Let them be together and see what happens. Keep the other dogs away and give them some space and quiet," Matt said. "That's all you can do. Let nature take its course. But don't be too hopeful. Maybe Stormy is just too old to be a daddy."

The next morning I got everyone out of the house. Let's leave them alone, I thought. No visitors.

I locked the other dogs in the backyard and took Gracie and Stormy out on the front lawn. Then I sat down on the bench quietly to see what would happen. Gracie went over to Stormy and moved her butt in position, and Stormy tried, but he just couldn't get it right. It was awkward, and Stormy seemed frustrated and ready to give up. Stormy walked over to me as if to ask for reassurance.

I said quietly and tenderly, while holding his dejected looking face in my hands, "It's OK. Don't be nervous. You're a good boy. You just need to get up a little higher on her back. You can do it. I know you can. Go try again. It's OK," I whispered in Stormy's ear.

As I turned to go back into the house, resigned to giving up on the breeding process, I saw Stormy do exactly what I'd instructed. He walked over to Gracie and got up a little higher on her back than in all of his other attempts. And they joined together as nature intended.

I had read every book I could get my hands on about the process, but none of them suggested just talking to the dogs to explain what to do. I walked into the kitchen to leave them alone, but I checked on them through the window and saw that they were locked together. About fifteen minutes later, Gracie appeared at the front door and scratched to be let in; she had a big smile on her face, and Stormy was right behind her. I called Larry and Maj and told them what happened. They found humor in Stormy's ordeal, but were delighted. They decided to leave Stormy another night just in case the first joining didn't take.

The next day I was walking all of the dogs on the little street that wound through the orchards on the ranch, when all of a sudden, right opposite the mailboxes in front of the ranch office, Stormy mounted Gracie again, knowing exactly what to do this time without being told. So I had to wait until they were done, looking around nonchalantly as if nothing were going on, not wanting to be a voyeur, and hoping the neighbors wouldn't drive by. Maggie came out of her driveway, saw the copulating dogs by the side of the road and laughed. I was embarrassed, and it seemed like a long twenty minutes, but out of those unions came the best puppies ever.

○○○○○

In the hot days of July in Ojai, just before the puppies were born, Gracie started to get frantic. I could tell she wanted to create a nest for her pups. She ran around everywhere, looking for the best place. She tried to dig a hole and get under the patio deck; I boarded up that spot so she couldn't get in. She tried to create a spot outside under the bushes; I fenced that area off. None of the places Gracie chose were acceptable to me. I wanted the puppies to be born inside, so I could protect them. I didn't want to worry about coyotes or bears or rattlesnakes getting to the puppies, let alone the problems associated with the birthing process if I had to squeeze under the deck to be close to Gracie. Bill thought I was nuts.

"Just let her be," he said. "Stop worrying so much. She's a dog. She'll be fine."

I thought I knew what was best for all concerned, and I encouraged Gracie toward a corner in my bathroom where it was cool and quiet. There was an alcove under the counter where I kept the laundry basket; when I removed it, the space was almost like a little dark cave with only one opening. Finally Gracie agreed and settled in, spending hours in that room before the birth. It was hot out, and the cool sandstone floor made it a good place to retreat. I bought a blue plastic kids' wading pool and placed it on the floor in the bathroom close to the alcove. I lined it with paper, blankets, and soft towels to make it comfortable for Gracie. I waited, checking on Gracie frequently as the gestation period came near its end.

One night just Roy and I were home. Jane was with her mom in Maine for part of the summer, and Bill was teaching a computer drawing class in summer school. Assuming that the puppies were not going to be born that day, I poured myself a large glass of chardonnay and was just settling in to start dinner. Although I'd been a vegetarian for more than ten years, I was too busy to make two or three meals a night nowadays, so I'd compromised and started eating meat again. It was just easier that way. I was planning to grill hamburgers that night, one of Roy's favorite meals. I often kidded that Bill and Roy had turned me to the dark side.

I went down to check on Gracie before I began cooking, and there she was, lying stretched out in the alcove, towels all wadded up, and a pool of blood on the floor. I panicked. Oh, my God, I thought. Something's gone wrong.

"Roy, Roy, come down here," I yelled. "Something's wrong with Gracie. We need to get her to the vet. She's bleeding."

I didn't know what to think, and I couldn't make sense of the scene. I yelled again for Roy who came running down the steps. I saw more blood under Gracie's tail.

Oh, no, I thought as my anxiety about Gracie's welfare rose. What have I done? Gracie was my baby, and something had gone terribly wrong. Why had I bred Gracie? What was I thinking? What would I do if anything happened to her?

I peered in through the dim light in the alcove and noticed Gracie was licking intently at something hidden from view. Suddenly she looked up at me with a proud smile on her face, and … a tiny blob appeared. Roy and I simultaneously realized that Gracie was licking a little puppy. I tried to clean up the area a little while I recovered from my embarrassment that I hadn't realized what was going on. I said as calmly as I could, "Good girl, Gracie. I'm so proud of you. I love you."

When Gracie started to strain like she was going to give birth again, I went over and picked up the first puppy, weighed it on a kitchen scale, realized it was a boy, and named it Lyon after our other vet Dr. John Lyon. Roy and I wrote the name, weight, sex, and time of birth down on a piece of paper. I called Bill, who said he couldn't come home for hours because he was in the middle of teaching his class. I called B.B, who said she would be right down to help because Larry and Maj were out of town. Then Roy and I waited. I was concerned that another puppy wasn't coming. Based on what I'd read, the puppies should have been arriving every fifteen minutes or so. Gracie seemed to be straining, but nothing was happening. I sipped my wine as I watched and worried. I didn't know what to do, but I was trying not to panic again. Wine seemed like the best idea.

More than an hour later, a giant male puppy, whom we named Jackson, arrived, but he didn't move in spite of Gracie's licking efforts. I tried to clear his tiny nasal passages with a syringe and breath life into him, as one book had suggested, but he never moved. I tried everything I could, but Jackson was dead. I cried and showed the puppy to Gracie who looked at it tenderly and sadly. I tried to explain to Gracie that he hadn't been born alive.

"I'm so sorry, Gracie," I said tenderly. I gently wrapped him in a cloth, and Roy helped me place the lifeless little body in a shoebox for burial later.

After that, another puppy was born quite quickly, a little girl, Angel, who had gorgeous long ears that looked like wings. Then another and another, fast and furious, so that Roy and I barely had time to put them on the scale, weigh them, name them, record their birth statistics, and get them safely into the wading pool, which was about three feet away from Gracie, before another one arrived. My bathroom was a very busy place that night.

Gracie was incredible through it all. She was calm, licked each baby dry, and then relinquished it to Roy or me. By the time Bill got home, all of the puppies had been born and Gracie was nursing them calmly in the wading pool.

One of the remaining puppies was tiny and couldn't latch on to drink from Gracie's nipples even though he tried. We named him George. Matt, the vet, said to just keep trying to feed him, so Bill or I sat on the floor in the bathroom, holding George and tried to bottle-feed him every few hours, but George just didn't gain weight. Matt said that happens sometimes, that perhaps George had something wrong with him, and that nature would take its course. George passed away within a few days. Everyone was sad. I showed George to Gracie, so she could mourn his loss and see that he had passed away. Gracie moped around and didn't want to eat unless I fed her from my hand. I observed her count the puppies in the pool, seven distinct nods around the perimeter, and then she would embark on a frantic mission to scour inside and outside the house for her two missing puppies.

"Gracie, Jackson and George are gone, sweetheart. They didn't make it. I'm so sorry," I said to Gracie.

Gracie soon accepted that they were gone and settled in as mom to the seven remaining puppies. I assumed the search had been her way of making sure they had actually passed on, and were not just lost, so she could move forward and cope with the loss.

The other puppies all thrived. Larry and Maj had pick of the litter. After visiting and studying their behavior, Larry chose Lyon for himself, and one of the little girls for his grandchildren. At the insistence of Jane and Roy, Bill and I kept the female named Lily and the male named Pug Bailey, after our other vet, Dr. Matt Bailey, but affectionately referred to as Puggers. The two new puppies added significantly to the dog energy in our house. I had really only wanted to keep one, but Roy and Jane said they each wanted a dog, and since the puppies were Gracie's children, I acquiesced. I just wanted everyone to be happy.

Maggie and Fred took a little girl they named Katie. Fred's brother took Angel, who kept her name and the sweet personality that went with it. Another law school friend took the remaining male puppy. I was just happy that Gracie's puppies all stayed close and remained in our extended family.

CHAPTER 10

A NANNY AND A PET PSYCHIC

Tino, my ranch guy, approached me one day and said his niece, Maria, needed a job and a place to live with her three-year-old son, Sebastian. I thought it might be a good idea to meet them because I realized I really needed reliable help and the current baby-sitting arrangement wasn't working out. I worried every time I had to go to Los Angeles for work and leave the puppies at home. I had pretty much arranged to be home when the kids were with us, but I still had to be in LA a few nights every other week, and Bill worked late, so there was no one to watch the dogs.

"Stop worrying," Bill said. "They'll be fine. They're just dogs."

"Sorry, but they're not just dogs to me. I totally stress if they're alone for too long." I didn't want them to be sad and lonely. I wanted them to be cared for and loved just as they would have been if I were home. And so after I met Maria, I asked her to be the dogs' nanny.

Besides, although the kids said they didn't need it, I thought it would be nice to have someone else around for them in case Bill and I weren't home. Jane was twelve and Roy fifteen, but I still worried about them since we lived in such an isolated place. Anne was off to college and not around to help.

Maria and Sebastian moved into the guesthouse, and Maria took over taking care of the house, the animals, and the kids when Bill and I were away. Maria loved the dogs, and they loved her. Sebastian was afraid of the dogs at first but soon settled in as part of their pack. I became the mother figure for Maria and Sebastian; Sebastian became Roy and Jane's little brother, as our blended and extended family grew.

It seemed like just a blink of an eye before Puggers and Lily had grown into wonderful dogs. Puggers was athletic, and Lily was sweet. They were very attached to each other.

Sebastian and Puggers became best friends; anything to do with balls, especially footballs or baseballs, was their passion. Maria and Sebastian created all sorts of games of chase to give the dogs some nighttime exercise. Maria would toss a ball up the stairs from the living room, and Puggers or Gracie would try to get it before Sebastian did. I often came home from work to find everyone in a mad frenzy, chasing each other around the living room and dining room area.

ooooo

Several people I knew used Laura Stinchfield, the local pet psychic in town, to communicate with their animals. Gracie was three years old now, and I thought it would be fun to see what she and the puppies had to say. We had lost Bert to seizures, so it was just Gracie, Carl, Lily, and Puggers. Crystal wasn't around, so I called Laura to have her come talk to everyone.

Laura said the dogs were very happy living with us at the ranch. That comment didn't prove much to me in the way of psychic abilities since all my friends said they wanted to be reincarnated as one of my dogs, so they could be so well treated and loved. The pet psychic also said Gracie and Puggers were concerned about me being sick, and they wanted me to sit on a certain rock up by the pond every day. How did the dogs know about me being sick? I'd just found out a week earlier that I had Hepatitis C. I hadn't told anyone except Bill, and I knew he hadn't talked to Laura or the dogs. He thought the idea of the pet psychic was absurd.

The doctors thought the Hepatitis C was probably from the transfusions I'd received in the '70s when I had surgery to remove the black tumor from around my ovary. They suspected that the Hepatitis C had lain dormant, quietly sapping me of strength all those years, and was just now showing itself. But no one really knew. I didn't feel that bad, but I instantly became hyper-vigilant about anyone coming in contact with my blood. I didn't want anyone to touch me or come close, especially if I cut myself or was bleeding. Also, no more sharing food or complicated kisses, just to be sure. Only the dogs were allowed to be near. Gracie was my comfort. Other than that, for the time being, I'd decided to just ignore the Hepatitis C. I thought perhaps I would try sitting on the rock as suggested by the dogs, though.

> *I really wanted her to meditate or sit quietly on that gigantic rock every day. She only did it a few times. It would have given her more strength to get through the illness, but she was not prepared to do that yet. Things unfold as they should. The natural world has great healing powers. The divine healing energy is available to all. People have gotten out of balance and have forgotten their training in these arts. It's time to remember.*
>
> -Gracie

CHAPTER 11

NEVADA BELLE

There can never be too many animals around. I knew Julie had the ability to communicate with animals, she just didn't trust it yet. But I encouraged her at every opportunity. Just putting the intention to communicate with other species out there, into the universe, is useful. Nature is available to communicate anytime with anyone who is ready to listen. I was biding my time, waiting for her to be ready. We had something to do together, but she didn't know it yet.

— Gracie

Crystal called me one day to tell me that I really had to rescue a horse named Nevada Belle who was living in less-than-ideal conditions close to her. Crystal said she talked to the horse each time she drove by, and Belle was very unhappy. The people who owned her needed to find her a new home, or she was going to become dog food. Although Crystal always told me to check with my own inner voice before doing anything, I rarely questioned requests like this from her because the mandates seemed to come from some other realm.

We didn't have a proper corral for a horse, and Bill was a little reluctant to take on another animal. Tino had left me two chickens on the front porch for my birthday, and we'd built a spur-of-the-moment home for them up by the garage. When the goats moved out of the kitchen, they had joined the chickens in the temporary pen. We all recognized that the goats and the chickens needed a better place to live. In the meantime, Jane got a rabbit, named Halo, and Roy and I got more beautiful chickens: some speckled black and white ones with tufted headdresses, some shimmering gold and red, some with feathery feet. Roy and I named them all.

Apparently anyone who knows anything about chickens knows naming them is a no-no. Roy and I learned this the hard way. Bill was away in Montana, so we were in charge of the farm chores. As we approached the coop to feed the chickens one morning, it was unusually quiet. When I looked in the pen, my heart started to beat out of control as I absorbed the scene. Something had decapitated all of our beautiful chickens and scattered their body parts around the yard. Roy and I just stared at the mayhem, and then each other, confused and scared. It was horrible—not a single chicken was alive.

Then I noticed that the goats were huddled in a corner of the pen, with big raw claw marks running down their sides, as if two giant hands had grabbed them from behind as they struggled to get free of the grasp. Roy discovered a broken fence and bear scat close by and we realized that only a bear was large enough to have done so much damage. The rabbit was still in its sturdy enclosed cage, untouched. The incident shook us up.

I called the forest service and told them that a bear had eaten our chickens.

"I'm sorry," the ranger said. "But there's nothing we can do."

"What do you mean? Can't you move the bear somewhere or something?"

"No, not once a bear has killed a domestic animal. If we relocate it, and it kills someone else's livestock, they can sue us and try to hold us responsible. So we don't do it anymore."

"So what do I do?" I asked, feeling dismayed at the state of our litigious society.

"We'll give you a permit to shoot the bear."

"I don't want to shoot it," I said calmly. "I just want you to take it away."

"The permit is the only option we've got. Sorry."

"OK. Give me the permit," I said, finally exasperated, and not knowing what else to do.

Without any fuss, the ranger arrived that afternoon with permit in hand. He gave me the name of some hunters to call. The hunters arrived, decked out in camouflage and carrying gigantic high-powered rifles, and took up residence on the roof of our garage to wait for the bear. It felt wrong to have two men with rifles perched on my roof, like a scene out of one of those violent movies I wouldn't watch. The rifles didn't even give the bear a chance. The whole situation seemed out of balance, unfair, and it stressed me out.

I didn't even know why I was allowing hunters to be on my property. To put it mildly, I had never been a fan of hunting, but I felt bad about the chickens and thought it was my responsibility to protect the goats from further harm. Hunting animals seemed wrong to me even though I was acutely aware of how hypocritical that was since I was eating meat again. But I still had trouble going to restaurants that had animal heads hanging on the walls. There were a lot of competing thoughts in my head. Whenever I thought about the bear attacking the goats, though, my heart started to pound and the hunters seemed like my only option.

I periodically went outside to check in with the hunters to see what was going on and to find out if the bear had been around. Gracie was always at my side.

When I was out of earshot from the hunters, I said out loud, but quietly, to make sure they wouldn't hear, "Please, bear. Please stay away. There are hunters here who want to kill you. I'm sorry I called them. Please stay away. I don't want you to get hurt. I just didn't know what else to do. Stay away. Please don't hurt the goats." I knew I was rambling at the bear, but I hoped some part of the message would get through.

After two days and nights of camping on the roof with no bear sighting, the hunters got bored and left without saying anything. I was grateful and ripped up the permit.

That night the bear came back. Bill had returned from Montana and heard a commotion up by the goat pen. He jumped out of bed, got in his truck, started to yell, and drove up to the pen to shine his headlights on what was happening. He said he saw a medium-sized black bear, probably a teenager, climb over the fence and run away, frightened. The goats were scared but unhurt.

Neither Bill nor I knew what to do to keep the bear from coming back. I came up with the idea to blast human voices on the radio all night long up by the goat pen to scare the bear away. It seemed silly, but in the middle of the night, that's all I could think of to try. The only station I could find on the radio that had constant talking was a religious station.

So our poor goats had to listen to, "You weeilllll be saved! Bel--lieeve and you weeeilllll be saved!" at full volume all night, every night, for a week. I never knew the effect on the goats, but apparently the bear didn't want to be converted because it stayed away.

After that incident, Bill agreed that we needed to build a proper corral and a secure pen for the goats. The potential arrival of Nevada Belle accelerated this process. Bill also knew the presence of a horse would help to protect the goats from predators. So without much further thought or discussion, I went to the lumberyard, purchased the necessary materials, and hired someone to help Bill build a corral and a more secure goat pen. As Bill said, when I got a construction project in my head, just stay out of my way. The job was done quickly.

I went to visit Nevada Belle and asked whether she wanted to come to live with us. I was pretty sure her answer was yes. And so a week later I paid $200 to Belle's owners for the privilege of rescuing an old horse who they didn't want to take care of any longer. This was a little less than they would have received if they'd sold her for meat, but the owners were happy that she was going to a new place, and so was I.

"Welcome to your new home, Belle," I said when I brought her home. "Meet Natalie and Clair, your roommates." The goats seemed happy to have someone much larger than them around as security and often parked themselves right underneath the horse.

CHAPTER 12

COURT

I had been working late into the night at home for several nights to complete my opposition brief to a motion filed by the defendant pharmaceutical company in a big multi-district litigation plaintiff personal injury case I was handling. If the pharmaceutical company could win this pre-trial summary judgment motion, the case was over. There would be no jury trial and no money for my client. So it was important that I do a good job, not that I ever tried to do anything less.

I stayed up most nights to work, so that my days were free for the kids and the animals because I wanted to do it all. It wasn't ideal, but it was a solution. As the sun came up on the last day for filing my brief, I did one final proofread and realized I was proud of the finished product. It wasn't perfect; I knew I could make it a little better, tinker with it just a bit more, but I was out of time. I faxed the final changes to my secretary in Los Angeles, so he could put the finishing touches on the brief, attach the exhibits needed as evidence, and get the document filed with the Federal Court and served on the defendant by that afternoon. Then I went downstairs to make coffee and breakfast for everyone. The defendant had a few days to reply, and the hearing was scheduled for two weeks later.

The defendant pharmaceutical company argued that there were no questions of fact for a jury and that the defendant was entitled to judgment as a matter of law because the FDA had approved the drug in question. This drug caused aplastic anemia and other serious injuries, requiring a bone marrow transplant for one of my clients and hundreds of other individuals. The defendant was trying to do whatever it could to avoid paying damages, including playing lawyer games. I was disgusted by the deceit and dishonesty in the defendant's papers, but thought I'd done a good job refuting their factual and legal arguments.

To be on time for the 10 a.m. court appearance, I decided to spend the night at my apartment in Santa Monica. Because I was rarely in LA anymore, I now shared the apartment with my friend Laura, a lawyer from San Francisco, who came to Los Angeles to work on cases with me. Laura, who was twenty years younger, had become one of my best friends. Since we rarely saw each other anymore due to our complex work and lifestyles, we had a lot to talk and laugh about over a bottle of wine that night.

I felt good that Maria and Sebastian were at home to take care of the dogs, and I'd arranged for Bill to drive Roy to school in the morning. With any luck, I could get back home after the hearing in time to pick up Roy from school since Bill would still be at work. There was always a lot of scheduling, but I made it work. Maria was always there for backup if needed.

The wine from the night before and Ojai's slow pace had sort of lulled me into complacency, so I wasn't thinking about how much traffic there was in Los Angeles, or how long it took to get downtown from Santa Monica. I woke up late, dashed out, and had to sprint up the steps to get to the courtroom on time. I made it out of breath with only minutes to spare.

"Hey, Bob," I said as I took a deep breath and nodded politely to the string of overly eager young men sitting at the defense table next to Robert R. Jones, the defendant's lead counsel from Dewey, Cheatem, and Howe. Obviously that was not the firm's name, but that old "Car-Talk" joke summed up how I looked at them that morning. I took my place at the plaintiff's table, on the opposite side of the courtroom, and had plenty of space to spread out since I didn't travel with an entourage like the defense lawyers did. After all, they were being paid by the hour while I didn't get paid unless we won the case.

The bailiff said, "All rise. The Honorable Tallac Washim presiding."

"Good morning, Your Honor. Robert Jones for the defendant and movant."

"Good morning, Your Honor," I said. "Julianne Bloomer for the plaintiff and respondent."

"Good morning, counsel. I have read your papers," the Judge said. "Mr. Jones, do you have anything to add?"

"Yes, Your Honor. I would like to point out the case from Georgia that we cited in our reply papers. It is right on point …"

"I've read your reply papers too, Mr. Jones. Anything else?" asked the Judge with a palpable edge of annoyance in his tone.

"As a matter of public policy, Your Honor," defense counsel continued, "drug companies need to develop new drugs for our society to move forward. We need advances in medicine. If the FDA approves a drug, the pharmaceutical industry should be protected from claims of injury caused by those drugs, or companies will stop spending the vast sums of the money it takes to develop new drugs. Society and medicine will not advance. Someone is always going to have an adverse reaction. This is one of those unfortunate cases, but my client should not be responsible as a matter of law."

"Ms. Bloomer, do you have anything to add?" Judge Washim asked politely. I hoped he was being polite because I was smart and a nice person, not because he was going to rule against me, but I couldn't be sure.

"Yes, Your Honor, I do," I said as I stood and walked to the lectern. "There are many questions of fact for a jury here that mandate denial of the summary judgment motion. Those facts are laid out in our papers, and I will not repeat myself here. What most people in our society don't realize is that the FDA does not have laboratories, and it does not do any independent testing of drugs that are submitted for approval. The FDA relies strictly on the information the drug manufacturers submit to them, as to both efficacy and side effects. So when a drug company makes misrepresentations in its submissions to the FDA, the FDA has no independent means to verify the facts." I paused for emphasis. "Besides the serious, life threatening injuries my client sustained from this drug, we will present evidence to the jury that this defendant made serious misrepresentations to the FDA; and therefore the FDA's approval to put this drug on the market, with minimal warnings, was not warranted."

"Anything else, Ms. Bloomer?"

"Yes, Your Honor. I think this motion was merely another attempt to delay by this defendant. The drug company knows it will be cheaper for them if people ultimately die, and they do not have to pay for a lifetime of suffering, so they want to drag it out as long as they can. This motion was a waste of time and money, both yours and mine. This case should be set for trial."

"I tend to agree, Ms. Bloomer."

"Especially if the best the defendant can come up with to support its ridiculous position is a public policy argument and a state court opinion from Georgia, which has no binding effect on this Federal court, besides not being relevant or on point," I continued.

"Ms. Bloomer?"

"Yes, Your Honor?"

"I'd quit while I was ahead, if I were you."

"Yes, Your Honor. Thank you. I just wanted to make sure I was ahead. Nothing further, Your Honor."

"Defendant's motion is denied," the Judge said. "Let's set a trial date for three months. So get it resolved, counsel, or be ready for trial in three months."

"Thank you, Your Honor," I said as I continued standing, and the Judge turned to leave the courtroom.

"Thank you, Your Honor," Bob said as he rose, and the Judge disappeared into his chambers. "Hey, Julie. Can I talk to you outside the courtroom?"

"Sure. What's up?"

"How are you?" Bob asked. "Haven't seen you for awhile."

"I'm fine. You?" I asked semi-politely.

"I'm great."

"Really? You used to be such a nice, ethical guy when we started out in law school. What happened to you?" I asked with a smile, trying to muster up some compassion in my heart for this man who now looked old and tired.

"Don't take things so seriously, Julie. It's just a money game. You know that. And you know I like playing games," Bob said, winking at me. "Besides, my client would rather pay me than shell out earlier than they have to for these alleged injuries."

"Oh, quit the crap," I said cringing, just thinking about his wink. "This is a bad drug and you know it, and your client knew it before it even went on the market. Your client needs to pay. Big time."

"You always were the feisty one."

"What do you want, Bob?" I asked curtly, thinking that I was glad he wasn't aware of the kinder, gentler me struggling against the painful parts of being a lawyer. "I'm sure it's not just to chit-chat."

"We don't want to go to trial on this one," Bob said. "Your client is too sympathetic, a squeaky clean mother of two kids. No way. We'll pick one with a more messy background and pre-existing medical conditions for our first trial, so I'll have a settlement offer to you next week."

"OK, call me, but please don't even bother if the offer is less than mid-seven figures."

"Are we talking three?"

"No, double that," I said firmly, "and I'll see if I can get my client to accept."

"I'll see what I can do," Bob said as he maintained a forced smile and walked away.

It was a game, and I realized I didn't like playing it anymore, even though I was really good at it. I had gotten to a point where I couldn't stand the deceit, negativity, stress, and egos involved in a high-powered law job anymore—especially the men who seemed to just love to hear themselves talk; it drove me nuts. It was affecting me on a deep level, and I knew it was time to move on, no matter how successful I'd been. I'd never lost a case, and the judge's words "Quit while you're ahead" rang in my head. And so I did.

By the time I drove home to Ojai, I'd made the decision to quit being a lawyer and to settle down and focus my efforts on raising animals and children. I realized I was miserable when I was away from Gracie, and I worried about everyone's welfare without me—almost as if I didn't believe anyone could survive if I wasn't around. Only I could take care of it all. Only I could do it right. I wanted to be home and available for Bill, the kids, and the dogs. I constantly thought about the Hep C, too. I started to feel bad just thinking about it.

I settled my case with Bob, cleaned up loose ends at work, and submitted a termination letter to the senior attorney I worked with. He still owed me substantial amounts of money from past and pending cases, and we worked out a deal on those. But other than protecting my financial interests, that was it for the practice of law. I knew I would miss Laura and the fun we had in that tiny apartment in LA, but that wasn't enough to continue. Besides, I knew she would always be a part of my life. Bill didn't have too much to say about my decision, but he was supportive. Now—just like that—I was a farmer and a full-time caregiver for Bill's kids and all the animals we had accumulated.

CHAPTER 13

SPICE

Julie didn't even recognize that she was receiving communications. Inner and outer transformation sometimes occurs slowly as our awareness expands, so she needed to do whatever she felt was right at the time. It's a process, but everything unfolds as it should.
-Gracie

It wasn't too long before Bill came home one night and said that a friend of his had told him about a thoroughbred racehorse who needed to be rescued. Eastern Spice had been a money-winner and then a brood mare for 15 years. After she went through menopause and was no longer useful, she was on her way to the glue factory, when she was rescued from that fate by a racehorse organization. They were temporarily housing her, but she was at the bottom of the pecking order and competing with 80 other rescue horses for food. Since she was losing weight, the organization really wanted to find her a new home.

I thought perhaps we had enough to take care of and enough mouths to feed, but I didn't say anything because Bill wanted the horse. Besides, I couldn't stand the idea of terminating a horse's life just because it had gone through menopause. I certainly wouldn't want anyone to do that to me. My hot flashes were punishment enough; although, on some days they were so bad that I wished someone would put me out of my misery. Putting practicality aside, I encouraged Bill to bring Spice to join Belle.

"But, Bill, this is it. No more animals," I told him. "We have enough to take care of."

"OK," he said.

Since we hadn't seen this horse before agreeing to take her, we had no idea what to expect. A few days later, a gorgeous black thoroughbred, with a shooting star-shaped white marking on her nose, arrived in perfect health, to become part of our family.

"Well, well. Aren't you the beautiful, spirited one," I said to Spice as I stroked her nose and felt her nuzzle up to me. "Meet Belle. I hope you two will be happy here."

Bill really seemed to love Spice. Many a morning, I'd find him just hanging out with the horses in the corral. Bill often said he thought he'd been a cowboy in another life, and he did seem the happiest when he was in Montana.

Our friends often said, "Those horses think they died and went to heaven when they came to live with you guys." Although the horses had a corral for nighttime, they were pretty much allowed to roam free on the ranch during the day. We had no fences to keep them in, but they never went far. When Nevada Belle had to be put down due to old age and an inability to walk, Spice became despondent and wouldn't leave the corral on her own even though we left the gate wide open.

When this behavior continued for weeks, I got worried. Even though Spice had been going in and out of the corral for years, she now was extremely fearful to pass through the gate. I tried to talk to Spice to calm her down, but it didn't seem to help. It seemed as if she was anxious about what might happen to her if she went out of her corral.

I called Laura, the pet psychic again, and she said Spice was afraid she would disappear, just like Belle did, if she left the corral. Spice didn't know where Belle had gone and she wondered. I realized that was the same thought I'd had when I was talking to Spice a few days before. I went and spoke to Spice again and tried to explain to her what had happened. I apologized for not explaining ahead of time. I told her that Belle had been very old and in a lot of pain, that she couldn't stand any longer, and we hadn't been able to lift her when she fell. I told Spice that Belle had left us to be in a better place, a place of peace, where she would not be in pain. I may have even used the words 'horse heaven,' but I'm not sure.

It took a bit of continual reassurance, but Spice calmed down and formed a stronger bond with the goats, and she eventually ventured out of the corral again on her own. I often would find Spice playing on the front lawn with Gracie or the goats. Spice took herself back into the corral when she'd had enough, and the goats would follow.

CHAPTER 14

MARRIED AGAIN

Bill and I were driving up the hill toward home in his beat-up 1988 Ford pick-up truck. He was adjusting the side vents to allow air in to dissipate the nasty smell that had developed from all the years of creatures living in the truck, and I was trying to push the mouse droppings into a pile on the floor with my sneakers. Groceries were sitting between us as we headed home.

As we drove up the hill, Bill turned to me and said, "Do you want to get married?" I looked at him, surprised, and thought for a minute. Something didn't feel right about the proposal, no ring, no romance, but it did seem like the practical thing to do. At that point, we'd been together six years, and we loved each other. Maybe romance is highly overrated, I thought.

"OK, but you have to surprise me with a diamond ring," I said.

Bill got me a beautiful ring, and I got caught up in planning the party. Since we had blended our finances and I paid the bills, the ring wasn't much of a surprise and there wasn't any romantic ceremony attached to it, but I appreciated the effort. In the interim, I took a stand-up comedy class and prepared what I thought was a very funny routine about getting married again at age 55. I heard Bill's unbridled laughs above the others from the audience on the night of the show.

We went to Kauai with the kids and forty of our friends and got married on the beach in Princeville. It was really a fun wedding, but I was nervous about walking all the way from the hotel to the beach with everyone looking at me. My friend Rachel told me to think of a song and just sing it to myself the whole way while walking. The only song I knew all the words to was Linda Ronstadt's "You and I Travel to the Beat of a Different Drum." So that's what I sang. Getting married didn't change too much in our lives, except now I had good health insurance.

CHAPTER 15

CRYSTAL TALKS TO GRACIE

Although Crystal and I had remained friends, after I met Bill, I stopped my formal studies with her, except for an occasional trip or workshop. She moved frequently, wherever she was guided by her inner voice, to help with opening or transforming the energy of a place. I never really understood it, but I generally helped her move, either financially or physically. During Crystal's time in Ojai, I'd become way too busy with my newfound life as a step-mom to continue attending workshops about animal communication or how we are all connected. But we stayed in touch.

Bill rarely made any comment about my spiritual meanderings, although sometimes I thought he looked at me like I was a nutcase when I told him about one pursuit or another. I sensed that Bill thought Crystal was a little weird, although he never said anything, and he always came through in a crisis when Crystal needed him. I had generally stopped talking with Bill about spiritual matters that were important to me because he always gave me that look like, "Oh, no, not some other wacky idea that has no basis in science or reality." We settled into a comfortable existence and talked about more mundane, day-to-day things. My meaningful discussions were with my girlfriends.

One day Crystal came for a visit to the ranch. I went outside with all of the dogs to meet her as she drove up.

"Hi," I said enthusiastically as we hugged heart to heart. "It's so good to see you. It's been way too long."

Gracie was particularly animated to see Crystal that day. Her eyes lit up, and a smile spread across her whole face. Gracie loved her, and I could plainly see it.

"Crystal, Gracie just loves you," I continued. "Look at those crinkle eyes and that grin. She's so happy to see you."

"Hi, Gracie girl. How are you?" Crystal asked, beaming at Gracie.

"I think she has something to say. Can you talk to her for me?"

"You should try," Crystal said.

"No, please, you do it," I said, not trusting myself. "I don't usually get anything."

Crystal bowed her head slightly toward Gracie and half closed her eyes to listen. "She's really happy. She wants to write a book with you. She says it's important. That you have to start it now."

"What?" I asked. "Write a book with Gracie? That's crazy. I can't do that!"

"Sure you can. You're very connected to her."

"Yeah, but how would I even begin?"

"Just sit quietly with Gracie and ask her a question from your heart," Crystal said as we stood in the middle of the driveway and all of the dogs, except Gracie, started to spread out into the garden to find something to eat. "Pretend like your heart has ears and listen. Then just write down whatever you hear. Don't question it. Just write it down."

"Really, that's it?"

"The secret to animal communication is not to try," Crystal said, "but just be open in the heart. That's where your animal partners are and where they can telegraph their communications to you."

"In spite of all you have taught me, you're making it sound easier than it probably is."

"Have faith," she assured me. "Listen to your heart. That's your transmitter."

"My transmitter?"

"By the way," Crystal added, "I'm in a bit of a hurry today. Sorry. I just came up here to tell you that I'm moving to Santa Fe. I feel called to go. I must help open a record there."

I didn't exactly understand what that meant. I knew it had something to do with bringing energy to a place and opening energy that existed in a place for the benefit of all. But based on our history, I trusted her and didn't really question things like this too much anymore. I'd been through a lot of moves with her, and I was still mulling over the idea of writing a book with Gracie.

"Really, another move? Are you sure?" I asked. "It seems like you're just getting settled and starting to build students in your classes here."

"You know I always listen to my inner voice. I've checked in several times, and I have to go," she said kindly. "I'm having a garage sale tomorrow. You should come."

I knew Crystal was full of love, but she was never attached to people, places, or things. She always followed her inner guidance to move, or do anything else, even if it didn't make sense to anyone else. This move didn't make sense to me, but I'd always liked Santa Fe. Besides, Roy was there, so now I would have two people to visit.

CHAPTER 16

GRACIE TALKS TO ME

I kept thinking about writing a book with Gracie, but it took awhile for me to decide to try what Crystal had suggested. I was a little skeptical, but I took Gracie into the bedroom and sat on a comfortable chair with her at my feet. I pushed the skepticism aside as best I could.

"OK, Gracie, we're going to try it. What do you want to say to me? What do you want me to know? I'll really try to listen and write it down." I tried to get out of my head. I sat quietly, took a deep breath, got centered, and went to my heart to listen, pen in hand.

I love you. You mean a lot to me. Can you see how we become one when we talk? Our thoughts meld. You don't know if it is you or me because we have come together—we are the same thought. It would be great if you could get in tune with all animals, all of nature, in the same way. Become one with it; understand it as if it were you, because it is. Go inside everything. Become everything and everyone, human and non-human beings, feel their experience, understand their experience, and gain knowledge from them. Transform yourself into a new being of light, where you are perfect in harmony, free from pain, free from the attachments around you. Feel life, feel love, feel light. Become love, become light, become life. Be love, be light, be life. You are. (Dictated 12/07/05)

I was stunned. I'd actually received a message from Gracie, and the message was quite clear. I didn't entirely understand it, and I didn't know if I got it down right, but it was clear.

Was it really Gracie speaking or was it just me? I mused. Was this just stuff coming out of my head? Was it stuff I'd heard before? I didn't know and maybe it didn't matter. But it sure felt like Gracie was speaking to me.

CHAPTER 17

DISTRACTION

And then a loveable, gigantic distraction entered my life. Unbeknownst to Bill and me, Larry and Maj had mated Gracie's son, Lyon, who was about four at the time, with a chocolate lab who belonged to one of their celebrity friends. Gracie's litter, including Lyon, Puggers, and Lily, had all been white or off-white dogs. The next generation, which Lyon sired, was all black. Larry picked Walter out from this litter for Bill and me and kept two of Walter's brothers, Thunder and Lightening, for himself.

I remember getting the call from Larry inviting us up to Heaven, the name Larry had given to his magnificent home way up high in the hills above Ojai.

"I've got your puppy for you," he said. "Come on up to Heaven and get him."

"What do you mean? What puppy? I don't need another puppy."

"Sure you do," was Larry's reply. "Come on up to see him. It's Gracie's grandson. I picked him just for you."

"I've got four, sometimes five, dogs, and I think that's enough," I said.

"Oh, come on up and just see him. You don't have to take him. I'll keep him if you don't want him," Larry said. I should have known better than to go.

"Bill, we don't really need another dog," I said as we drove up to Larry and Maj's house. "I have enough to take care of. And remember, we said no more animals."

"Don't worry," Bill said. "He'll be my dog. I'll take care of him."

"Famous last words," I muttered under my breath.

Bill took care of the horses and the birds in the morning, but I was the primary caregiver for the dogs and the other assorted animals who lived with us. Already it was hard for me to leave the animals for any length of time because I worried about their welfare. I loved Gracie and wanted to be home for her and the others so they wouldn't be lonely without me. It was a big responsibility, and I wanted to do it right. I loved the dogs and being around them. They made me happy. I think I made them happy too.

Puggers and Lily were four now, not puppies any more, and they weren't as much to handle as they used to be. But a new puppy would up the ante once again.

"A new puppy is a lot of work, you know," I reminded Bill as we continued our drive. "They need training. They're constantly peeing and pooping in the house. You have to follow them around everywhere. Get up at all hours of the night. Don't you remember all of that? How much work all of Gracie's puppies were?"

"Oh, don't worry so much," Bill said. "I'll train it." I didn't really believe him, but I tried to let it go and not say anything else.

Once we met the new arrivals, it was clear Bill really wanted the puppy Larry had picked for us. Bill had already named him Walter, after the black lab he had when his kids were young. I tried again to convince Bill that we didn't need another dog, but when I really thought about it, I realized one more wouldn't make that much difference. Walter was adorable, and it's a rare person who can resist a puppy, and I was not that rare. So an hour later Walter rode home in my lap to join his grandmother Gracie, his Aunt Lily, his Uncle Puggers, and Carl.

A few days later Maggie and Fred went and picked out Walter's brother, Duke, to add to their family. It was always interesting at our dinner parties when there could be as many as thirteen dogs and six or eight people over. As far as I was concerned, dogs and children were always welcome in my house. The more the merrier.

Larry and Maj called one afternoon. "So, how's Walter working out?" Larry asked.

"What did I ever do to you?" I asked.

"What?" Larry replied.

"Is he revenge for something I don't know I did?" I asked, laughing. "He's a handful. I affectionately refer to him as the devil dog."

Larry and Maj laughed into the speakerphone.

"He's always into something," I said. "How are Thunder and Lightening?"

"They are the sweetest, most lovable dogs," Maj said. "No trouble at all."

Although sweet, Walter clearly was trouble. He was the life in the group, the energy, the animation, the comedy, the tears, and the joy all rolled into one.

"Thank Gracie for such wonderful grandchildren," Maj said.

During Walter's early years, I would often come home to find him with a toilet paper roll in his mouth, one end still attached in the bathroom, trailing toilet paper all over the house. You could tell exactly where Walter had been—up on the couch, under the table, on top of the table, on the counter. I guess Gracie just sat by and watched her grandson make a mess without judgment, criticism, or discipline.

Walter would eat anything and everything; food was his obsession. In particular, he loved bread, especially bread left on a counter top, whether in or out of a plastic bag; it didn't matter. Walter would discreetly steal bread, cookies, or bags of biscuits from the counter when no one was looking and nonchalantly walk into another room, hiding whatever it was as best he could, and then chow down the contents and most of the plastic bag, too. It was the remnants of the plastic bags in various places throughout the house, or hidden on the back lawn, that finally provided me with the clues to the missing bread. Rarely would anyone catch Walter in the act.

He could also consume 20 or more avocados a day, which he'd learned to pick himself from the trees. Walter's daily volume was evidenced by the number of avocado pits scattered on the front lawn. Light bulbs, socks, and underwear were all fair game to Walter. He could go through a dog toy advertised as indestructible in less than a minute. His best time was 30 seconds from delivery to his mouth to unrecognizable as a toy. I timed it once as I watched a purple latex hippopotamus turn into a pile of tiny pieces of purple rubber in 29 seconds flat. Walter quickly grew into the biggest lab anyone had ever seen, tipping the scales at 145 pounds.

Despite Bill's promise, there never was any real training for Walter except from Gracie, Puggers, and Lily. Walter took his cues from them and learned the basics fairly easily. I did teach Walter to sit and give his paw. Maria and Sebastian worked with him a little. Bill rarely. Walter would sit quietly to a 'stay' and allow me to put a biscuit on his nose for a second before tossing it into the air to catch and devour.

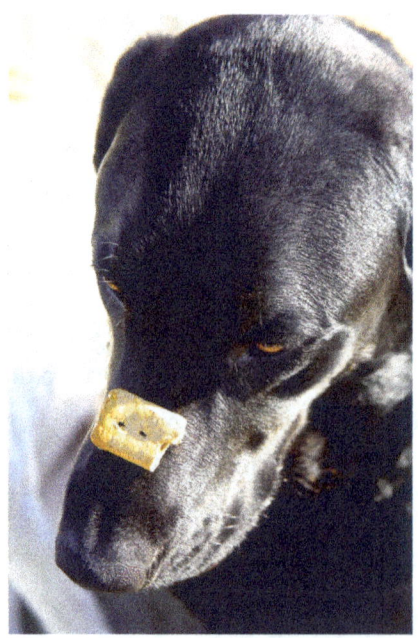

I was playing with Gracie one day and she sauntered over to the toy basket to bring me a present. Just as she approached to give me her favorite stuffed caterpillar, Walter came darting in and snatched it from her mouth and brought it to me himself, wanting to be part of the game and demanding some love. I laughed at Walter's antics but it was almost as if I could hear Gracie's response as I saw her look at Walter tenderly, but slightly annoyed.

Walter is a big baby. He's always butting in to get attention. He steals toys right from my mouth and then delivers them himself, as if it was his idea. But really, he doesn't have an original thought in his head. It can be annoying, but I recognize that he is being who he is, with all that he is, and I accept that. He's my grandson, but for some unknown reason, very insecure. Not at all like me. Besides he makes everyone laugh. And I do like to play with him.

One day I arrived home after going to the market to find Walter in the house. I could swear I'd left him outside. "Maybe not," I said out loud. A little later I went downstairs and noticed that the sliding door to our bedroom was open. Now, who left that open? I thought. I was going to have to remind everyone to shut the doors when they went out, so the snakes and mice didn't come in.

It turned out that Walter had slowly taught himself how to open every door in the house, going in or out, so that he wasn't restricted by what he apparently viewed as artificial barriers. When he was on the deck, I watched him execute his entry maneuvers through the glass kitchen door. Walter pushed up the lever on the kitchen door handle with his nose to release the locking mechanism, then artfully and quickly wedged his nose between the door and the doorframe, nudging and holding the door open with his nose. Since the door swung outwards, towards him, it required him to simultaneously jump out of the way, as he pushed the door open far enough so he could let himself in the house any time he wanted. Then he entered and gazed at me, so proud of himself. I realized that his movements were extraordinary and complicated in that they required forethought, anticipation, knowledge, and dexterity. Going out was somewhat easier, requiring only the nose to lever action, and a push outwards. I gave up trying to stop him, but I did wish he would learn to close the door behind him.

As to sliding glass doors, these were also no problem for Walter. I'd seen him take his big nose and, with a mighty swipe sideways, slide the slider back on its track.

"NO, Walter," I yelled at him when I saw him begin this alternative ritual to breaking and entering the house. Usually he would stop and look at me with his mournful eyes, and I would let him in the proper way. I'd never actually seen the next step of the process, but I knew exactly what he had done based on the evidence.

Once Walter opened a sliding glass door, he was confronted with a sliding screen door that had a special locking mechanism that he couldn't open. When no one was home, this obstacle didn't stop Walter. He'd put his head down and charge the screen door so hard that it came off the track at the bottom but stayed attached at the top. This allowed plenty of space at the bottom for Walter to squeeze past and sneak into the house.

Many a night I came home to find dangling screen doors with Walter in the house, a big smile on this face, tail wagging, so happy with himself. I could usually find a warm spot on the couch or on our bed where he'd been lying comfortably after he broke into the house. The interesting thing to me was that all of the other dogs respected the doors and barriers erected for them. I would find them lying outside, right next to a broken door, with plenty of space to come in, but they rarely followed Walter's lead.

It became a constant ritual when Bill got home from work, for me to say, "Bill, could you please put the screen door back on its track? Your dog has busted the door again."

I had to resort to closing and locking all doors when the dogs were left alone, whether the dogs were inside or outside, so that I wouldn't come home to dangling screens or doors wide open, swinging in the breeze, bugs and creatures inside, and Walter wherever he wanted to be. If I remembered to lock the doors, the dogs usually were stuck in the place I left them. Thank goodness, Walter had not yet learned to turn a dead bolt.

> Compassion is the keen awareness of the interconnection of things.
> -Albert Einstein

CHAPTER 18

FAMILY DYNAMICS

Bill's children were not kids any longer and the dynamics in the house and our family had changed. Anne, the oldest, had graduated from college and had moved away. Roy was in Santa Fe working and doing his own thing. After living in Maine with her mom for a few years, Jane had returned, bringing her dog Rufus, to live with Bill and me for the end of her junior and senior years in high school. The house was filled with a lot of the dramatic energy that comes with a sixteen year old. Jane kept us on our toes. Rufus was adorable but a handful. The first night he was home, Jane was out with some of her childhood friends, and Bill and I were left in charge of Rufus. Bill dropped a piece of chocolate on the floor.

"Quick, Bill," I said. "Grab that before Rufus gets it. Chocolate isn't good for dogs."

Bill went to grab the chocolate before Rufus could, and Rufus turned on Bill with bared teeth and a snarl, and then bit him on the arm. Blood gushed everywhere. I calmly piled Bill in the car and drove him to the emergency room for stitches. My dogs would let me take anything I wanted out of their mouths, so this was new territory for me.

Upon hearing what happened, Jane said, "Oh yeah, sorry Dad, I forgot to tell you. Don't take anything out of his mouth. He doesn't like it."

"Don't you think you should have mentioned that before?" I asked trying to hide my distress at having a biting dog in the house. Jane understood Rufus, but she was a busy high-schooler and rarely home, so I got the brunt of the work with Rufus. But I didn't mind too much because Jane had explained how important Rufus was to her well-being.

ooooo

I was in the kitchen cleaning up after breakfast one glorious spring Saturday morning talking to the ants who had violated our agreement and wandered in through a crack by the open screen window. Jane was outside on the trampoline.

"Come on, little ant. Climb up here. No, no, not that way. This way. I'm not gonna hurt you," I said, putting my finger real close to the particularly active one. "Just get on my finger and I'll take you outside. And don't forget about our deal. Please stay outside and tell your friends too. I don't want to have to give the big Black Flag warning, thirty minutes to vacate or else." The deal was the ants could have the outside, with no chemicals, if they stayed out of the house. Based on the actions of a few rogue ants, I didn't want to hurt them, and I didn't want to interfere with our negotiation, which had been working.

I never told anyone that I negotiated with the ants to keep them out of my house. If I had, my colleagues would have tried to have me committed, and my friends would have laughed and concluded that I was actually a bit nuttier than they'd thought. But it worked. It really worked. Everyone else had ant problems in their kitchens, not me. Mostly they just stayed outside; I would see them all over the deck rails and along the edge of the house, but they didn't come in.

"Hey, who are you talking to?" Jane asked as she came bursting through the door and startled me from my reflections and my task at hand.

"No one," I said.

"I heard you," Jane said.

"OK, I was just talking to …"

"Yeah, who?" Jane interrupted.

"I was just talking to the ants and reminding them about our deal," I said before I thought about it too much and filtered what I said.

"What deal?" Jane said.

"I negotiated with the ants a while back that they get the outside, with no chemicals, and I get the inside."

"Oh, cool," Jane said.

"To tell you the truth, I don't know if I ever really believed it myself, that they heard me, let alone agreed to the deal. I've just been thankful that they've stayed out of the house. So I keep renewing our negotiation."

"So you don't believe it, but you do it anyway?"

"Yes, I guess it's something like that."

"Why don't you believe the ants can hear you?" she asked.

I stopped to think about the question. On some very deep level, I knew it was true. I knew my negotiation had worked. I just didn't know how or why.

"That's not an easy one to answer," I replied. "I guess I never wanted to believe it because believing ants and other creatures are capable of communication carries with it a lot of responsibility."

"What do you mean?"

"If you believe animals can hear you, or you can hear them," I said, "then it's pretty hard to do anything which might hurt them. Take ants, for example. People spray stuff all over and kill them by the thousands. But they're incredible little creatures who can carry 100 times their weight, who are totally cooperative with each other, and never let up on doing their jobs of cleaning up. So if you see them as individuals, or even as a cohesive group, you have to treat them like that." I was a little reluctant to talk about this with Jane because I didn't want her to think I was the nutty stepmom, but something propelled me along. I looked down and saw Gracie right by my side, watching me intently.

"If I do find them crawling around in the kitchen or I pick up something outside covered with ants, then I think I have a responsibility," I continued with more conviction. "I do my best to move each one individually, to take it outside or back to the spot it came from. Well, you can imagine, some days this can take hours just dealing with the ants. I must admit, sometimes I think I have better things to do with my time than herd ants." I laughed and so did Jane.

"But I keep doing it. And if I do kill one by mistake, then I feel bad, and I say I'm sorry and ask that it be taken to ant heaven or wherever ants go. And I try harder the next time to be more careful. And the whole time I'm usually talking to them. So that's what I was doing," I said.

"Oh, that's cool."

"I'm trying to be more compassionate in my life. If we're all connected, then we need to be kind to one another and feel compassion for all beings, humans, animals, plants, the earth. Ants, too. If we expect to survive and move forward as people, I think we've got to show love and kindness to all."

"It's probably a good idea to be kind," Jane said. "Not so easy when people are being jerks though. Anyway, you're not hurting anybody by talking to ants. Good luck with trying not to kill them. That's a tough one. But chemicals aren't good for the environment, so that's awesome. Is it OK if Alisa comes over and we go out on the pond in the boats? We'll take the dogs with us."

"Great, do we need to pick her up?" I said relieved to change the topic but amazed at how accepting Jane was.

"No, her mom will drop her off," Jane said as she ran upstairs to phone her friend.

> A bird doesn't sing because it has an answer,
> it sings because it has a song.
> -Maya Angelou

CHAPTER 19

JEFFREY

One day Gracie and I were sitting together on the couch. Notebook in hand, I told her I was willing to take her dictation again, even though internally I still wasn't sure about being able to communicate in this fashion. Gracie locked her eyes on mine and stared deeply. I was interested in how things really worked in nature. I shut my eyes, took a breath, and said, "Here we go, Gracie. Would you tell me about gnomes and elementals?"

There are lots and lots of different forms on this planet. You just cannot see them yet because you have closed off your vision and your heart. But they are out there working in the fields, working in nature. They help tend to everything, and they try to restore balance to the natural world that man has interfered with. Nature spirits are abundant, but buildings are pushing them off of the land, and then they have to move. They can't deal with solid cement and concrete—they don't know what to do with it. That is why there are so many where we live. It is like a refuge for them. But sometimes there are too many, and they get a little lost, and they wander around instead of knowing exactly what task they are supposed to accomplish. They like to know what to do, and they like to be asked.

There is a large gnome who lives in our garden. His name is Jeffrey, and he is the boss, the one in charge of all of the elementals and fairies and other light workers who are out there tending to nature. He wants to talk to you. He has things to say, important things about how things run and how he wants to bring in additional helpers to make it easier for you.

He is real—don't think differently. He is really out there every day, working, rain or shine. He is a hard worker even though he has to boss everyone else around. Jeffrey tries to coordinate everyone calmly and peacefully and tries to make sure everyone has something to do, but sometimes there are stragglers, and he gets a little upset that he can't do it all and then the energy gets scattered and there are little beings all over the place.

You know sometimes when I bark at the door and you look out and tell me to calm down, that there is nothing there? Well, you may not see what's happening out there, but trust me; I have reason to bark with all of the goings-on. There are lots of fairies and elves and angels all around, doing their jobs in the garden and taking care of the earth. Sometimes it is so crowded I can only see the big ones like Jeffrey, trying to keep everyone in line. Sometimes they get so happy and excited that they just start going all over the place, and it gets a little confusing outside. Jeffrey does a good job of rounding them up, though. Then they start to laugh at themselves and each other; sometimes they start laughing so hard that they are doubled over, thinking everything is just so much fun. I like it when they laugh; it makes me smile too.

Bill is a big help and the nature spirits and elementals all like to help him when he is in the garden working. They love it when humans are happy and positive. You sometimes see a hundred little ones out there with him laughing, helping him pull weeds, jumping on his back. They think he's fun. Sometimes Bill's back is sore after he is done working outside because the elementals have been jumping on him all day and they get pretty frisky and they hurt him, without meaning to, of course. I've been talking to Jeffrey about that, and he's been trying to get them to stop jumping on his back.

Do you know that is one reason why that phrase 'get off my back' started a long, long time ago when people could still see the elementals and worked with them? The elementals always had that playful side to them and wanted to be jumping up on the people they were working with. Sometimes it would bother the people when the people were doing something which they thought was far more important than playing with the elementals, so the people would tell the elementals to get off their backs, to leave them alone. And so the elementals started to leave humans alone and as things progressed, humans became less and less able to see them. Now it is time for people to begin to see them again.

Sometimes I see Jeffrey, side by side with Bill, helping him. Bill doesn't know where some of his ideas come from. The elementals and nature spirits love him, and Jeffrey does too, so they help him and give him ideas. Bill just needs to tune in more to his spiritual side, although that is up to him. I don't really have too much more to say right now except that the elementals and nature spirits are all different sizes and shapes. They are cute in a sort of weird way; not cute the way I am, though. That's all for now. I need to rest. (Dictated 5/11/06)

I thanked Gracie as she drifted off to sleep.

Since I couldn't see giant gnomes, let alone hear them talk, I just wrote down what I heard from Gracie and tried not to think about it or judge it in any way. I remembered what Crystal had said: "Just take the first idea or thought that is transmitted at the intuitive and heart level. Try not to edit the communication or question or doubt. That shuts the door to the transmission."

When Bill came in that night he sank down next to me on the couch and said, "I got this really great idea this morning when I was out working in the garden. I think I can change the whole way I teach this one class I've been teaching for years. I'm still working out the details, but it's gonna breathe new life into that class."

"That sounds wonderful," I responded. "It always feels good when some new idea about an old problem just pops in your head, doesn't it?" I said vaguely remembering that Gracie had said something about Bill getting inspiration from nature.

"Oh, here's the mail," he said. "You got something from Crystal."

I looked at the large envelope from Crystal in Santa Fe postmarked a few days before. I opened it and found my solar chart, which I'd completely forgotten that I'd ordered. In the quiet of the darkened house, after Bill had gone to bed, I read the spiritual guidance contained in the chart. The words in one section gave me goose bumps:

> There is a gnome that you are working with who would like greater communication with you. There are certain things he would like to make known to you that would strengthen the energy field of your center. His name will be given to you shortly when you contact him. He wants to bring in a larger body of invisible workers to increase the power of the place.

As soon as I read Crystal's words, I knew that I had heard something like that from Gracie earlier that day, and I went back to Gracie's dictation to make sure I was remembering correctly. Gracie had said:

> *There is a large gnome who lives in our garden. His name is Jeffrey, and he is the boss, the one in charge of all of the elementals and fairies and other light workers who are out there tending to nature. He wants to talk to you. He has things to say, important things about how things run and how he wants to bring in additional helpers to make it easier for you. (Dictated 5/11/06).*

This random confirmation from Crystal of the words Gracie had spoken earlier spooked me. It was hard for me to fathom that an almost verbatim message about a giant gnome in my garden had arrived from a person a thousand miles away just a few hours after Gracie communicated the same thing to me. Actually, since the chart came by mail, I analyzed that Crystal's information would have been written before Gracie said anything to me, or before Gracie gave me Jeffrey's name, just as Crystal had predicted. Maybe Crystal communicated with Gracie and told her what to say. I didn't know. Maybe it didn't matter, but it made me wonder. Was Gracie really talking to me? I had sort of believed it before, but now, was this confirmation?

I wasn't sure of much any more. I certainly didn't know about gnomes in the garden or what that meant to me. But if my dog wanted to write a book, so be it. I could be the secretary. Good role reversal, I thought to myself, after having had my own secretary for more than 25 years.

Even my best friends gave me that little smirk with the slightly raised eyebrows, which they didn't think I could see, when I told them I was writing a book with Gracie—that Gracie was dictating the book to me and I was the scribe. That Gracie was a source of spiritual advice. The look told it all. I'd quit being a lawyer, and now I'd flipped. But I didn't feel flipped or delusional. It seemed like the most natural thing in the world to sit down with Gracie and listen to what she had to say. The words just flowed.

CHAPTER 20

ANGELS AND SYNCHRONISITY

I was out with my 35mm camera one day and looked toward the garden for an interesting shape to photograph. I was trying to see the spaces between things in nature. No one could believe that I still wanted to shoot film instead of digital. Somehow digital photography seemed liked cheating to me. I saw Puggers and Gracie just lying calmly amongst the plants and the finished corn stalks, staring at me. I felt compelled to look more closely at the scene because it seemed like there was more to it than I could see visually. Upon closer inspection, I couldn't find anything unusual, but I snapped a photograph of the dogs anyway, without thinking too much more about it. When I got the film back from being processed a few weeks later, I saw an image hovering over the dogs. What was that? I wondered. Something must have been wrong with my camera.

The photos taken before and after this did not contain the angel-like image. This photo was not edited.

The next day I sat by Gracie's side with my notebook in hand and asked her if she wanted to work on the book. I really wanted to know what I'd seen in the garden and thought maybe Gracie could explain. Gracie stared really intently in my eyes, and I moved in really close.

I want to tell you about angels and how all of that works. There are all types and sizes of angels. Some are how you think and others are not. Some are big and some are small. There is one hovering over you at this very moment. She is your protector and helps to keep you safe. She is always around. You got a glimpse of her in the garden, but you just don't want to believe it. You think you need a new camera.

Some creatures on this earth are just part angel. Like me. I am part angel, part dog, so that I can be more visible to you. Everyone can see or feel angels if they want to, if they really look at what is out there. But most people do not actually want to see things that are outside of their comfort zone. That is why some of us come to earth as part angel. We have certain angel powers to help and assist, but we are limited by the bodies our spirits have chosen for this lifetime. Don't get me wrong. It's not bad; it's just that we could do a lot more if we were full angels with angelic powers.

There are also full angels everywhere, but they generally will not interfere unless they are asked to help. That is why you must remember to ask for the angels' help, and for the help of the elementals and other nature spirits, which exist and are at human disposal if you will only ask. But people don't ask so much anymore, or they forget to ask and just get caught up in their busy daily lives. Sorry, I am getting off track. Anyway, I am part angel, and one of my missions is to write this book with you. I have been on earth several times and have even written some of this before, but we really must do it this time. You must believe. You can call on my angel part to help anytime you want.

Remember when you are dealing with any living thing, that it could be part angel. That's just the way it is. So it might be a good idea to show love and respect and compassion for every living thing, just in case. The earth is alive.

It is an actual being. But that is a different topic, and I think I am done for the day.

I put my pen down. Sometimes, like right then, I really thought I could hear Gracie talking. It wasn't spoken words like normal verbal communication, but it was more like an opening in my heart. Then sometimes a stream of thoughts or words or pictures would come gushing forth, as if Gracie were actually talking to me. It was hard for me to understand or explain it to even myself, but sometimes, just sometimes, I went with it and wrote down what I thought I heard. And then the communication would stop as quickly as it began.

The last thing I ever thought I'd be doing was writing a book with my dog. I certainly didn't think I would have had any high-powered clients left if this had happened earlier in my life. But mostly I just questioned whether I was making it up. Maybe I'd just been spending way too much time alone with the dogs now that the kids were mostly out of the house.

ooooo

I was out walking with my friends Maggie and Lisa and our twelve dogs, including Jasper, Lisa's little miniature Dachshund, who just loved coming for a walk on the ranch with all of the giant labs. Lisa said Jasper would start to get excited as soon as they drove in the ranch gates until he could barely contain himself. Gracie, Lily, and Walter all particularly loved Jasper and would race to see him, giving him kisses as he jumped out of the car. As we started our walk that day, all the dogs ran ahead except for Gracie. She stayed very close and walked next to Maggie, Lisa, and me as we talked about synchronicity in the Universe, and how sometimes things just happen to come together effortlessly.

"Let me look up the definition for synchronicity on my phone," Lisa said. After Googling the word, she read: "'Synchronicity is defined as a series of seemingly unrelated events which are connected via a hidden agenda.'"

She added, "It's like we live on the tenth floor or the ninth floor, but there's a place in between, which isn't so solid, where things can come together to work on our behalf, where the hidden agenda lives. And talk about synchronicity, it's really funny we're discussing this today," Lisa continued. "Just yesterday, I read a story which originally appeared in *Life* magazine back in the '50s. Apparently fifteen members of some church choir in Nebraska were due at choir practice at 7:20 p.m., and they were typically on time or early. On one particular evening, everyone was late. The minister and his wife and daughter were delayed, so his wife could finish ironing the daughter's dress. One girl waited to finish a geometry problem; one couldn't start her car. Two waited to hear the end of an exciting radio program. One mother and daughter were late because the mother had to call the daughter twice to wake her from a nap, and so on. The reasons seemed rather ordinary. But there were ten separate and quite unconnected reasons for the lateness of the fifteen persons. Luckily for them, none of them arrived on time because at 7:25 p.m. the church was destroyed in an explosion. Apparently *Life* reported that the members of the choir wondered if their delay was 'an act of God.'"

"That's interesting. I think the odds are staggering against chance being the culprit for that many random events," Maggie said, the statistician part of her speaking out.

"It certainly sounds like a form of synchronicity to me," Lisa added.

"Wow," I said, "that's a great story. I don't have anything that dramatic, but I feel synchronicity working sometimes in my life. You know, how a plan just seems to come together somehow, without too much effort? Like the way I got this place."

"What made you buy this ranch and move to Ojai anyway?" Maggie asked.

"I've never told you that story?" I asked. Maggie shook her head no.

"One day I was flying home from Washington, D.C., with my friend Ellen who lives here and also studies with Crystal," I said. "I know I've told you about my friend Crystal before. Well, Ellen and I had just completed a four-day seminar with Crystal in Virginia that had been pretty intense with meditation and connecting with the unseen dimensions at work in our lives. As Ellen and I chatted and flew back across country, out of the blue I said, 'If you ever run across 100 acres of property, up against the national forest, with a stream running through it, let me know.' She wasn't a real estate broker or anything, but I just put it out there.

"The following week Ellen called me at my office in Los Angeles. 'Well, it isn't 100 acres, only 45, but it has a stream and a pond and a mountaintop with a giant stone labyrinth on it, like the one at the Cathedral in Chartres. And it's up against the national forest, too. It's not really on the market yet, but I was talking to a broker friend of mine, and she said it was for sale. Do you want to come up and see it?' she asked. 'I can arrange it.'

"And that was it. The house was a ramshackle mess with rats living in it, but I saw potential, and I absolutely fell in love with the land. I'd just made a bundle of money on one of my cases and needed to do something with it. I thought it would be a great weekend place to get away from Los Angeles and being able to walk the labyrinth seemed like a bonus. I put in an offer, it was accepted, and—contrary to my second husband Harry's wishes—I waived all contingencies five minutes before our time expired and went forward with the sale. He was furious. In hindsight, that decision was probably the beginning of the end of our relationship. But anyway, that's how I got this magical place, and I'm so glad I did. I'm so grateful and blessed to live here, to have met Bill and the kids, and to have you guys as friends."

Later that day, Gracie followed me around everywhere until I finally realized she wanted to work on the book. I got out my pen and paper, closed my eyes, took a deep breath, and imagined my heart could hear. I always remembered that Crystal said I should pretend my heart had ears. "OK, Gracie. What do you want to tell me?"

I can tell when you are talking about important things with your friends. I know by intuition. This morning when we were out walking, I don't know if you noticed, but I stayed real close when you and Aunt Margaret and Lisa were talking about the 9½th floor. That is what I am talking about too. It is an unseen place that actually exists where things flow and synchronicity just happens without any effort. Everything in the universe is flowing together on the same thread, just one thread where things happen without stress and effort. The universe brings together the people and places for transformation to take place. The importance is in seeing the place, feeling the place, and staying in that flow for as long as you can. You will probably notice that at first you may only get glimpses of the stream, the flow, the thread, the 9 ½th floor—whatever you want to call it, it's all the same. The universe is constantly working on our behalf. Things are happening all of the time. But usually we just miss the signs because we are not paying attention to the present moment. We are worrying about the past or the future and opportunities just pass us by.

But it's OK. It's a process of baby steps. Even if you remember to pay attention to the present once, that is better than not at all. And things will start to happen for you. Your life will be filled with more and more joy. The stresses will fall away because you have God working on your side, doing the work for you. Let go and let God in. You do recognize, don't you, that GOD is DOG backwards? Maybe everyone is so concerned about using the word God because it sounds religious. Well, maybe those are just words and it is the feeling, the essence, that counts. Let go and let DOG in. Now that's more like it. The life force, the creative force, the divine energy, the Great Spirit, Mother Nature, they are just different words for the same thing. Let go and let spirit take over. Whatever sounds right for you.

I hear the sound of the quad getting closer. It might be Bill driving up from the meadow. I really like to see Bill. By the way, I think your religions have really messed things up for people. On a different plane we are all talking about the same thing. It just doesn't matter what name you put on it. It is Love. It is harmony with the earth. It is peace. Whoops, Bill drove by and left again. Let's play. I love this new ball you got for me. It sounds like a little baby crying. That's why I keep it in my mouth to protect it. (Dictated 9/9/06)

After hearing Gracie, I thought back and realized it was synchronicity at work when I got Gracie and when both Gracie and Crystal said the same thing, on the same day, to me about Jeffrey being the gnome in charge in the garden. Maybe the Universe really wanted me to understand that Jeffrey was out there, working every day, so that I would pay attention. I guess I shouldn't be surprised that an intelligent Universe might realize that I was pretty dense, and that I might need to be hit over the head with the same information, from two different sources, at the same time, before I would begin to see how truly complex, how truly simple and how truly perfect it all was when we connected with the flow of divine energy. When we allowed magic to happen.

CHAPTER 21

THE BEACH

Some of my happiest times with Bill and the dogs were at the beach. Although, it was always an adventure to take four dogs to the beach. They were a pack and protected each other from other dogs, and that aspect did cause me a level of stress.

Ever since she'd had her babies, Gracie had become a fierce protector of her gang. She watched out for her own and kept away intruders. Puggers would sometimes get in the act. Walter would approach other dogs, too, although he usually was just interested in acting tough, but he didn't have any follow-through. Lily was always kind with all other dogs and people.

"You know, sweetie," Bill said to me at the beach one day, "your stress just fuels Gracie's need to protect and gets her all riled up."

"I know you're right, but I can't help it," I said. "I worry when other dogs approach. I just don't want any dogfights, so I try to anticipate problems and prevent them."

"Don't worry. I'll watch out," he said. "I'll put her on the leash if I see any trouble coming. I want you to have a good time and relax."

"Thanks, I appreciate that," I said, but I could sense Bill's disapproval that I was being overly protective. He was attentive and accommodating anyway.

"It does take away some of the fun of the beach if you're stressed," he said.

Keeping the dogs happy and engaged was actually pretty easy at the beach. The trick was to constantly throw the stick, and then all other beings on the beach disappeared from Gracie's mind. Gracie was intensely competitive with Walter to see who could recover the stick from the ocean first. Nothing could stop her, and she would play in the water until she was so exhausted she could barely walk. I could feel her happiness at the beach. Walter loved the beach, too, and would swim great distances to retrieve whatever was thrown for him. Puggers liked to play with balls and Frisbees and to compete with Walter, but he didn't really like to swim. Lily just liked to watch and greet strangers as if they were her long lost friends. She didn't like the water. I was just happy to be at the beach with my gang.

When we got home, I gave everyone a bath on the back deck to keep the sand and salt outside. Then I sat next to Gracie as she dried in the late afternoon sun and asked, "When I get stressed when other dogs come around at the beach, does that have an effect on you?"

I am very in tune with you. I can anticipate your actions, and I certainly pick up on your feelings. It is the same for you if you would tune in to what is around you. We do not have to do the tuning in part because we are there, in the moment. But we definitely are affected by the human emotions around us. We take on and personify what you are thinking and feeling—so if you get scared or anxious, we do too, and then our tendencies of fear and aggression may come out. Usually aggression does arise from fear. Fear is just in your head, but it is very powerful. It can make you not believe in what you are doing. It can create all kinds of anxiety and stress and weird behaviors. The natural world, animals in particular, pick up on that easily and will use it to their advantage or to act out in certain ways.

People say we love unconditionally and that is why dogs are so great, but that is not quite correct. We are unconditional love. We do not act that way, we just are. That is our natural state, but we get out of balance too. We pick up on every bit of energy around us. You are calm, we are calm. You are nervous, we are nervous. You are upset, we are upset. We can't help it; we're all connected. We feel very deeply. We feel it all, just like you can. All that you see outside is a reflection of what is inside.

One more thing, pet me more. I love you. (Dictated 5/10/06)

"Thanks, Gracie. I'll try to be a little less stressed and a little calmer. But it's hard for me. I'm a worrier. I want to prevent bad things from happening." I moved to lie down next to her on her dog bed and started to stroke her neck. "Right now I'm worried whether it's time to start treatment for my Hepatitis C. Somehow you knew that I had Hep C years ago, didn't you? When you told me to sit on that rock? I'm scared. I've been trying to stay away from everyone, including Bill. It's hard to feel untouchable. And I'm just tired. You've been staying real close lately, and I appreciate it. Do you understand what I'm saying?"

Gracie had that look as if she knew what I was talking about: she cocked her head to one side, looked directly at me, and smiled. But I didn't hear anything, so I wasn't sure.

"But I really don't want to go through the treatment right now," I continued. "It's like the drugs used for cancer and supposedly hard on you physically. There are lots of side effects. I don't think I can do it right now. And I don't feel that bad. I just feel like I have a low-grade flu all of the time."

Trust yourself. You know what is right for you.

"Gracie, you're so smart. Do you have anything you want to add to your book right now? Or are you too tired from the beach? I've always wondered: is there anything I don't know about you?"

I am very strong in more ways than you know. There is part of me that is an Everlasting from the animal kingdom. We have certain knowledge and wisdom about the animal kingdom and have lived on this earth many times. Animals take on the pain of mankind and sometimes it hurts. Sometimes we absorb the pain, or the illness or the negativity of our human companions, to help them, to save them or to make it a little easier for them to get through their day-to-day lives and the stress they create for themselves. We come to this earth willing to do that for our human partners. I am very adept at using the deflector shield to protect you and me. It would be useful for you to learn to use a shield to protect yourself and others. Transmute the negative energy into positive and bounce it back. I love you. Love is all there is. Send love.

I see the big picture, or at least a piece of it. Sometimes you get lost in trying to figure it out with your head. Things change constantly. It depends on the energy at any particular point in time, and, as far as I know, the whole picture is beyond human or animal comprehension. Maybe it doesn't even exist yet. It's all divine creative energy at work. Love is joy and happiness and peace and calm and kindness and compassion and exuberance and affection, all wrapped up. It is the unifying force of the Universe. Get connected to that flow and your life will change.

"Thanks," I said, writing as fast as I could to keep up with Gracie "How would you feel about going on a little trip to work on your book?" I asked. "Just you and me. I've been preoccupied with the Hepatitis C, and I'd like to get back to your book. How about if I find a place on the beach that takes dogs and we go? Does that sound good?"

Gracie just stared at me with those piercing eyes and soft smile.

I went to look for Bill in the garden.

"Hey, Bill. Would you mind if Gracie and I went away for a few days to work on her book? I need to get out of here. Something always comes up to distract me, and I'd like to get away to have some time to think."

"No problem. Do what you want," he said as he pulled weeds in the garden. "Go, you'll have fun."

"Will you take care of the rest of the gang while we're gone?"

"Of course," Bill replied. "Maria is here, too. Stop worrying so much."

I never knew whether Bill believed in Gracie's dictations or not. He was always supportive and agreeable, but he never talked about his own feelings or beliefs. And he never asked me any questions about the book or my communications with Gracie. I never pushed for a discussion because, deep down, I thought he was just humoring me and that he didn't really believe that Gracie and I could communicate.

CHAPTER 22

ROAD TRIP

I found a beachfront motel that welcomed dogs in Cambria, a little coast town a few hours north of Ojai, and a few weeks later Gracie and I started out on our road trip. As she sat in the passenger seat next to me, I noticed that Gracie seemed stressed by the travel. She started to pant and look around in distress as we drove along the highway.

"What's wrong, Gracie? We're going to the beach on a little vacation, just you and me."

When we stopped at a rest stop about half way, Gracie hopped out, walked to a calm spot, and sat down under a tree. I sat next to her, notebook in hand.

Even though you told me we were going on a trip and what we were going to do, it's different for me. When I see things out of the window, they are all new. Big trucks rumbling by make disturbing noises. It startles me. I feel the disturbances in the universe in the moment. That's why I pant. Animals get used to a routine. Change can cause stress, but being confronted by new situations provides opportunities to grow and become more curious. Every time I go to a new place, I am overcome by the scents and the stimuli, but I connect with my surroundings, ask permission to step on the land, and then tread lightly.

"Thanks for reminding me, Gracie. My indigenous friends constantly stress the importance of being grateful and asking permission before stepping on the earth. It's just hard to remember all of these things when confronted with day-to-day life. Ask permission, be grateful, connect within, listen to your inner voice, and send love. Sometimes I really try, and then sometimes life gets overwhelming and I forget."

That's the most important time to remember.

When we got to the motel and checked in, Gracie received a welcome basket containing home-baked dog biscuits, a special bed spread with paw prints on it, a beach towel to wipe her paws, poop mitts (obviously for me, not Gracie), a flashlight for nighttime excursions, and a magazine called *Fido Friendly*. A big handsome golden retriever was waiting to check in just behind us, and Gracie kept turning around to look at him. When we got to our room, I got a feeling that Gracie was incredibly nervous. I retrieved Gracie's bed and a few of her favorite toys from the car and placed them on the motel room floor, close to my bed, but she wouldn't stop panting. No matter how much I tried to reassure her that everything was fine, she clearly didn't think so.

"We'll go for a walk, Gracie. I just need to pee first." Gracie followed me into the bathroom and lay on my feet, so that I couldn't move without her.

"I'm not going anywhere, Gracie. Don't worry."

While we walked along the path up above the ocean, I noticed that Gracie was suddenly very much in harmony with all around her. She didn't bother the squirrels or even the other dogs she saw. At that particular moment, she seemed respectful of Mother Earth and all of its creatures. She stopped and seemed to acknowledge the earth before she lifted her paw to step on the ground. Since I'd made this trip to work on Gracie's book, I was really concentrating on listening to Gracie, trying to understand what she was saying, and taking good notes.

It's the beach. I keep thinking Lily or Puggers or Walter will just show up. Sometimes when I see other dogs in the distance, I even get happy because I think maybe it's them. But then it's not. I like being alone with you, but it's unsettling too. I have nothing to relate to except you. The beach is here, it's cool, not hot like at home. We're staying in a funny small room with weird smells. My dog bed is there and a few toys, but it's still all strange. And there are lots of other dogs around. I am interested in that handsome golden retriever we saw. He seems about my age or maybe a little older. I think he liked me too, but on second glance, I think he was too old for me.

I chuckled to myself. I never knew what to expect out of Gracie's heart. Gracie and I returned to our room, but she balked and didn't want to enter. It was small and dark and tucked in a funny corner of the motel. She finally went in, but got nervous again and stayed attached to me. When I took a shower, Gracie blocked the shower door, so I couldn't get out and go anywhere without her knowing.

"What is it, Gracie?" I asked. "What's wrong?"

This room has confused energy. It is not calm or peaceful here. It is scattered. I am sensitive and it affects me. It should affect you too. Just sit back and feel how it makes you feel.

I didn't know if I felt the weird vibe, but I called the front desk and asked to change rooms. The owner said he'd be happy to switch our room in the morning, but that he had nothing else available that night.

I picked up the newspaper lying on the desk in our room and started to read to fill some time before dinner. The news about the unrest in the Middle East, including the missile strikes between Lebanon and Israel, was unsettling. I was unsuccessfully trying to make sense of the turmoil in the world when I noticed how calmly Gracie lay next to me. It dawned on me to ask her what was going on and what to do.

"Gracie, what is the most important thing for our times right now?" I asked.

We must maintain an attitude of calm and peace. The consciousness of all living things must be attuned to the oneness, be in line with peace. The events unfolding in the Middle East are bringing a vast disturbance to the universe. Only if enough people maintain calm and peace in their hearts can the negative forces be overcome. Send love. You can't take sides if you love unconditionally. You just must radiate love and peace. Every movement you make must be filled with love and calmness. The collective consciousness must now dominate in a peaceful way. Every time you have a negative or judgmental thought, regardless how small, it has an affect on the whole; it brings the whole down ever so slightly. So when you have lots of disturbances, it really affects the whole in significant ways, and things seem to get worse and worse. That is why it is so important to maintain a positive and loving attitude towards all right now. (Dictated 7/15/06)

A few minutes after I knew Gracie had stopped her dictation, and not really wanting to think about the Middle East anymore, I said "Gracie, let's go into town and get something to eat. We'll find a restaurant with an outside patio, then we'll come back and work more on your book."

Gracie jumped up from her bed, ready to go.

When we returned, I got my notepad and sat close to Gracie, silent, ready to listen. Immediately my mind started to wander as I thought about words. Wasn't it interesting that the words silent and listen were comprised of the same letters? I shook my head and came back to focus on my heart.

I am starting to calm down a bit, but I am still a little nervous. I feel that there are going to be more and more disturbances in the universe in the months to come. You must remain calm and hold the peace for all. It's a hard task to only think in terms of love and peace, but you must. It is so important to get things back in balance and perhaps tipping toward the love and peace side, rather than war and hate. See the wholeness. Accept the perfection of it all.

"It's pretty hard for me to see the perfection in the mess this world is in," I said, "but I'll try. There are so many conflicts nowadays. Why do people hate each other so much anyway?"

Why do people hate? They hate because they are filled with fear, fear of the unknown, fear of something or someone different, fear of thoughts and feelings that are foreign to the construct they have made for themselves. Only when we get beyond our fears can we feel pure essence love and genuine happiness. No judgment, no fear. But I am still a little afraid in this room, so I guess I talk a better game than I live. Like I said, I am here to help you figure it out, but I don't have it down perfectly yet either. If I did, I could just jump into a new situation, no problem, no fears, no judgment, just enjoy it for what it is. Be in the present moment without feeling the duality. I am in the present moment, but the strange sounds, smells, and negative thought forms in this room have an effect on me, but I'll get over it.

"What are you feeling in here?" I asked. "What's the problem in this room?"

You should try to tune in to feel what you feel. Use your senses. I feel there was a disturbance here that still lingers. Nothing terrible, but I feel the negativity and the anxiety, and it affects all of the energy in here and brings it down. I have learned ways to deal with negative energy. I will explain more when the time is right. Things are happening on levels we don't fully understand. Be grateful for all the lessons you are being given, whether you understand them or not.

I decided to close my eyes, engage all of my other senses, and focus on the energy in the room as Gracie suggested. I smelled a lingering smell of cigarette smoke, even though supposedly this was a no smoking room. I felt a little tingling sensation on the back of my neck. I also received a picture of a dog huddled, scared, in the corner of the room. It had peed on the carpet and a man, a cigarette in his mouth, hit the dog really hard. I was surprised at the image. Is that what Gracie felt? Could that have been what happened in that room?

The next morning, while the housekeepers were cleaning, I took Gracie to see our new accommodations. The new room looked out on the central courtyard and faced the ocean. Gracie walked right in to check it out without hesitation. She greeted the housekeepers with a wag and a smile, and then left. Then we went to play on the dog-friendly beach. Gracie was very good with the other dogs playing on the beach and settled right down. I threw sticks, and Gracie retrieved them with reckless abandon. Gracie would've stayed at the beach all day if I'd let her.

I love the beach and the vastness of the ocean.

"Me, too," I said wistfully.

The ocean is beautiful, my soul place and yours. The sea, the waves, the smells, the sounds renew us both. Feel it. Feel the love flowing from nature; feel the love of the ocean.

I sat on the sand with Gracie at my side for a long while, soaking it all in. We finally returned to the motel and rinsed off in the outdoor shower. Gracie led the way directly to our new room, with no prompting from me. She knew exactly which door was ours and walked right in when I opened it. She didn't get nervous when I went to the car. She climbed on her dog bed, stayed alert to the noises of the day for a short time, and then went to sleep.

Gracie clearly hadn't been comfortable in the first room we shared. I don't know if the brief image I'd seen was accurate, but I thought I should take a lesson from her about being more sensitive to my environment. It certainly seemed to have an impact on Gracie's emotional and mental well-being, and presumably on mine, too. I know the image of that dog cowering in the corner stayed with me for a long time.

As Gracie slept, I wondered why she'd been so upset and nervous during our car trip up to Cambria. Then it dawned on me that Gracie was eight years old and had rarely been off the ranch. When she was a puppy, she'd gone with me everywhere, but after about six months, she basically stayed home. Besides frequent outings to Maggie and Fred's house to play in the pool or for dinner, she'd gone on only a few beach outings a year, trips to the vet's office, occasional car rides to the market, a few restaurants, and off to Ventura College for a photo shoot for a project in one of my photography classes; but mostly she'd been at home, free on her glorious ranch. When Bill and I went anywhere, the dogs stayed home with Maria and Sebastian. Gracie's worldly experience was limited.

When she woke up, I asked her, "Hey, Gracie, how do you know so much when your experience is so limited?"

All knowledge is out there in the ether. It's just a matter of accessing it. Don't forget, I was sent to you for the specific purpose of accessing certain information and providing it to you, so that you could write it in a book and let the world know about the importance of love and how we are all connected. Children understand some of these things at an early age, but the seeds of love for all beings are not cultivated or nurtured in them. We are all unique beings with a role to play, but we are also all connected. Let these seeds grow in the minds and hearts of all. Humans spend a lot of time negating creative or different ideas in order for children to conform to outdated modes of thinking. Most people don't believe in anything anymore. You have stopped believing in the magic of it all. You have forgotten how to enjoy the simple things in your path. You will see that all of nature is amazing. You can learn a lot if you would just listen. Got to go out to pee now.

I took Gracie out for a walk, and we both enjoyed the cool sea air. The mist was settling in for the evening, and Gracie and I did the same.

I placed the dog cover with the paw prints on the bed and patted the mattress. "Come sleep on the bed with me," I said tenderly, as I bent over to assist Gracie since her arthritis prevented her from jumping up on her own nowadays.

When I awoke, I looked over at Gracie and smiled. Her snoring was peaceful and rhythmic. I closed my eyes for a second, thinking about greeting the day before doing anything else. Gracie simultaneously opened one eye, confirming for herself that I was actually awake.

Greet each day with gratitude and wonder in your heart. Life on this earth is fantastic. Enjoy this human experience you are having on this earth. It is a miracle. Try a little more heart and a little less mental activity and you will understand more. The mind and heart must work together, in balance.

"Thanks for the reminder, Gracie. The left side of my brain is always trying to control and tell me what to do. It especially likes to be critical. Hey, I know it's early, but what's important for people to understand about love?" I asked, believing, at that moment, in the magic and the miracle of the communication with Gracie.

When the heart is open, love flows through, in and out, and has a chance to move throughout the body and outward to the entire universe. It opens space and time for joy. The more love that is pumped out, the more that flows in, creating energy movement and assistance in elevating the collective consciousness. Everything matters: the bugs, the snakes, the mice, the rocks, and the trees. Every drop of water. Each being is as important as the other; each is as unimportant as the other. When the heart is open, it must include all in the love circle: the two legged, the four legged, the ones who fly, those who swim, the seen, and the unseen. People must fill their hearts with love, nothing else.

Celebrating the heart is celebrating the present moment. Be in the present moment. Only sacred thoughts, sacred words.

We all get wrapped up in the small stuff and we miss what is really important. See what is right here, right now, and try not to bring your preconceptions to it. They just cloud the moment. Be grateful for each moment as it is.

I always want to be with you. I am always aware of where you are, whether you are near or far. We are connected, just like you are connected to everything else, not just me. All children, all animals, all knowledge, all of nature. Life is good, although it is getting a little hot in here.

"Wow, Gracie, that's a lot. I'll try and remember. Thanks. Now I've got to get up and pack so we can go home." I started taking things to the car, and Gracie stayed calmly in the room.

She doesn't know that this was all planned out for her. How I came into her life and why and when. It's all perfect, and we are working on my project. It's been a journey, but I think she finally gets it. I am at peace and calm with the world. It has taken awhile for me too, but today I can rest. We are about to leave Cambria and go home and I am finally relaxed. Isn't that just the way it is? She can go in and out of the room, and I don't get nervous. I don't worry that she won't come back. I know she will and all is good. So let's move on to the next part of our adventure. She knows what she is supposed to do to be of service and to help animals. So let's go home.

The trip back to Ojai was uneventful. It was broiling hot when we got there, but everyone had survived without us, yet they were happy that we were home.

> Every time you are tempted to react in the same old way, ask if you want to be a prisoner of the past or a pioneer of the future.
> -Deepak Chopra

CHAPTER 23

AROUND THE RANCH

When Jane went off to college, Gracie was eight, Puggers, Lily and Rufus, six, and Walter only two. Carl was about eleven or twelve. None of us really knew his exact age. The house seemed quiet and empty without any of the kids. Sometimes I felt like there was a gigantic hole in my life, but the dogs and other animals kept me busy and tied down to the ranch. I took care of the six dogs, two horses, two goats, the birds, the fish, besides a rabbit, a leopard gecko, named Blue Eyes, and any number of injured, sick, or deformed birds that we had rescued along the way.

Lucky was my favorite. Years before, when the kids were young and still at home, I'd accidentally stumbled over a cockatiel nest camouflaged on the floor of the aviary. I'd felt bad at finding three eggs lying there unattended but still warm. So I brought the eggs in the house and Roy, Jane, and I tried to hatch them in a very low temperature oven. Only Lucky popped out. I got up every two hours for many weeks to hand feed him, but it didn't take long to see that his wings and throat were deformed and he would never fly. Still I persisted feeding him specially prepared food through a syringe and keeping him in the kitchen in a uniquely designed nest with a warming lamp, feeling he was my responsibility since I had interfered with nature, hoping that he would survive. Everyone thought I was bonkers to disturb my sleep every night and told me that I should put Lucky out of his misery, but I couldn't. He looked at me with such hope each time I approached him.

One glorious warm day I just knew I needed to take Lucky outside so he could experience the wind in his face and the joy of being outdoors. I placed Lucky gently in my cupped hand and walked outside with him. As we walked I moved my hand slowly, up and down slightly, riding the currents and rhythms of the air, balancing him gently so he could get the feel of flying. We walked around the ranch as I cradled him in my hand and talked to him about flying. "Fly, Lucky, fly, feel the air," I said to him. He even tried to flap his oddly shaped, featherless wings. He seemed content when I put him back in his nest, under the heat lamp, and fed him awhile later. Lucky passed away that night of his own volition. I always felt he had a great last day flying on this earth in his little deformed body that just couldn't keep up with his spirit.

ooooo

Although Jane wanted to figure out how to have Rufus at school with her, she left him with us when she skipped off to freshman year at college in Santa Cruz. As the sixth dog, Rufus pushed me over the proverbial edge, but I hadn't been able to say no. When she first asked to bring Rufus from Maine, I'd acquiesced because I knew having her dog with her was really important to Jane's peace-of-mind and happiness. I understood feeling that strongly about a dog. But for me, just as in many aspects of my life, I was afraid to speak up for myself and say how I really felt. I wanted everyone to like me, and I wanted everyone else to be happy. I was afraid they wouldn't be if I said no, so I put my needs last. Now that Rufus had been with us for almost two years, there wasn't much I could do when Jane left for school. Rufus was a source of constant irritation, and I hid it the best I could. He was definitely worse when Jane wasn't around. He barked incessantly at the phone or the other dogs and he nipped at the dogs' heels out on walks. Everyone was scared of him when it came to food.

"Rufus, stop barking. STOP IT, I can't stand it," I yelled as I ran over and shook my finger at him when he started barking at the phone. "Shussssh, no barking."

You know, yelling at him doesn't do anything. It just disturbs the tranquility. Your anger gets us all riled up. It doesn't help. He'll calm down. Just ignore him rather than giving him attention for bad behavior. He had a solitary upbringing. He was left alone a lot and he is not used to all of this activity. Try some love.

"I know you're right, Gracie. I'm sorry. I don't like the way I feel when I yell at him either. I am just feeding the negativity. And he can be very sweet when we're alone. He follows me around and lies at my feet when I'm in the bathroom. I'll really try to remember to praise him when he is calm and being good. You and the rest of the gang are quiet, except when there is actually something to bark about, but not him. I guess I just expect him to act like you and then I get mad and resentful when he doesn't. Sometimes his constant yapping just drives me nuts. It's a lot like dealing with different people," I said. "Sometimes I have trouble listening to what I consider meaningless yapping. That's so judgmental, isn't it?"

You're in control of your feelings, no one else's. Pause before you react. You have the option in every moment to choose to radiate love. You do not have to allow the circumstances, the negativity or the drama around you to dictate how you react. Choose love and see what happens.

I thought about what Gracie said, and I thought about the word react. Re-act. Acting over and over again in the same manner in response to the same triggers. I did that a lot. Maybe I did have a choice to act differently, rather than to re-act in the same old way. Maya Angelou once said, "I've learned that you can tell a lot about a person by the way (s)he handles these three things: a rainy day, lost luggage, and tangled Christmas tree lights." I think that's a very perceptive statement, but I'd add barking dogs to the list.

Bill worked long hours being a college professor and was rarely home, so I had the brunt of the responsibility around the ranch and with the animals. When he was home, I could usually find him on the computer or alone in the garden working hard. Bill was always calm, kind, easy-going, and removed. He did what I asked, but mostly he did things by himself. I had to push him and organize events for us to do things together. I had to plan everything. Although he rarely initiated an activity, he was willing to participate in whatever I wanted to do, without complaint. I looked forward to the holidays when the kids would be around or when we could go to visit them. We always had a great time when we traveled and being around the kids always gave me great joy. At those times, things always seemed better between Bill and I, or maybe the activity masked what was really happening at home.

The dogs and ranch chores had become my focus. Bill had slipped into the comfortable companion role. I cooked, paid the bills, and took care of the house, the dogs and planning events with family and friends. He went to work, took out the trash, helped with chores and cared for the garden and the orchard.

At the same time, the Hepatitis C always loomed over me and intimacy had long slipped out of our relationship. Our kisses were perfunctory. I sort of felt like he kissed me how he would kiss his grandmother. I was afraid of getting Bill sick, and he didn't seem interested in being close physically. Our talks about this lack in our relationship never went anywhere. It seemed like one or the other of us always had some physical ailment at opposite times. His back was out, I was well; I had a urinary tract infection, he was well; I had surgery, he was well. Four nights a week, Bill came home around 11:00 p.m. after teaching a full day of classes. We would talk about his day while he ate what I had prepared for him earlier. I would report what had happened that day with the dogs and the ranch, and he'd tell me about school. Either he or I was usually exhausted. I never asked for anything and I kept how I really felt to myself. I thought maybe this was just what happened as you grew old with someone, for better or worse, in sickness and in health. It was comfortable and didn't require that much effort, but I didn't feel that happy or fulfilled, except when I was with the dogs or just outside surrounded by nature.

ooooo

Roy was home visiting and came upon me out walking amongst the orange trees. "What are you doing?" he asked.

"I was just looking at the orange trees to see how they are doing. I am a farmer now, you know," I said affectionately. "What are you up to?"

"But I heard you to talking to someone," Roy said.

"Ohh. So what? So I was talking out loud. No big deal," I said calmly.

"But who were you talking to?" he asked.

"Nobody," I said.

Roy gave me that "oh really" look without saying anything.

"I was talking to Jeffrey," I finally admitted sheepishly. I had told the kids about Jeffrey, so Roy knew exactly who I was talking about and didn't seem phased.

"Did you see him?" Roy asked.

"No, I didn't see him. But I know he's here," I said. "So I was just thanking him for all he does out here to make the oranges grow so beautifully and effortlessly."

We kept walking through the orange orchard.

"I was also talking to my guardian angel," I said a few seconds later.

"What?" Roy said.

"I realized today, being out here in the orchard, just looking at the trees and feeling at peace, that on some very deep level I do believe that I have a guardian angel. Gracie says I do. I guess I've always felt protected, but recently I have started calling on her and it has worked."

"Like how?"

"Like the other day I couldn't find Walter anywhere. I walked up and down the orchard yelling for him, offering him a biscuit. You know that trick always gets him to come, but not that afternoon. I started to worry and a fleeting thought came to ask my guardian angel to lead Walter to me. So I did. No sooner had I formulated that thought in my head than Walter came walking out from behind a nearby tree. A tree, mind you, that I had already walked by many times looking for him. I know it doesn't sound like anything extraordinary, but it was for me. Walter simply appeared out of nowhere."

"Awesome," Roy said as he turned toward the house. "I'm going to get something to eat."

The kids didn't seem to have any trouble believing in Jeffrey, talking to ants, or my writing a book with Gracie. I wondered why it was such a struggle for me, but I did try to thank Jeffrey, as often as I remembered, for all of the work he did to make everything grow so beautifully around the ranch.

CHAPTER 24

GRACIE ON ANIMALS

One day I was sitting alone with Gracie in the living room. Everyone was gone, the other dogs were sound asleep after a long walk, and it was quiet. It had been awhile since we'd worked on the book, and I wanted to try again. I asked Gracie, "Can you tell me about animals?" I really wanted to know if there was something I should be doing to be of assistance, or if I was missing something, or not getting something quite right. I sat quietly and tried to suspend disbelief and let go of thoughts so I could connect with her.

That is a very broad topic. I guess I really want people to know that animals in general are part of the angelic kingdom. We are not total angels, though; sometimes we misbehave, but it's not our fault. It just happens; we get confused. We are much into the present moment. We enjoy what goes on around us, or not. It doesn't matter, it just is. When we are not doing something, we sleep; we rejuvenate. To sleep, to rest, is divine. To ride in the car and feel the wind in my face is also divine. You should try it sometime. It is pure joy, so never pass up the opportunity to go for a joy ride. That has many meanings.

Animals get a sense from people and we can see and feel people who are kind and loving to animals. That is the way it should be. But there is a lot of suffering and abuse that goes on in this world. You wonder how do I know that. Because we can feel it. We can feel it when an animal is hurt; we feel their pain. It's not like it hurts us, but it is a feeling in the air—a strain on the entire thread that holds us all together. The more love and compassion humans show towards animals, the more love and compassion they will show towards each other. It just works that way.

We must tip the balance in all aspects of life towards love and peace. Once we have more than half of the weight on the love and peace side at all times, by simple physics the whole will have to follow. It is a matter of energy. I am not explaining very well, but it is fairly simple. Once the scales tip, the dark side will have to keep coming over to the light, and the light will get stronger and stronger. It's like the story about Tinker Bell. She just keeps getting brighter and brighter and stronger and stronger the more you believe in fairies; the same way with the light. By the way, some of the creatures who work in the garden do look a little like Tinker Bell. Just thought you'd like to know. Not all of them are so pretty, though. You really need to watch out about taking care of animals. You need to protect them, and not just dogs, but wild animals too, and all creatures. Respect all life. (Dictated 7/26/06)

Bill was gone to a conference, and I was alone with the dogs. I woke up in the middle of the night to the sound of Gracie's panting and knew she needed to go outside to pee. I jumped out of bed and opened the sliding door to the side patio off the master bedroom. When we stepped out into the darkness, with just a sliver of a moon to light the way, I stepped on something squishy and soft just outside the patio gate as I was leading Gracie to the front lawn.

"Fudge," I said, since I was trying not to swear like a sailor anymore. Sometimes the other "F" word would come out when I drank too much wine, or when I thought it would surprise someone if I said it, but generally I wasn't happy afterwards. I was coming to realize how powerful words were and I saw that saying angry or harmful ones definitely affected the energy around me and inside me.

"I just stepped in dog poop with my bare foot. Great, just great," I thought as I waited for Gracie to pee and then hobbled back into the house, trying to avoid getting poop on the carpet by keeping that one heel up off of the ground. But when I looked, no poop. So Gracie and I just went back to bed.

I woke up early the next morning and went out to greet the sun. As I stepped out the door, I saw lots of slimy-looking snails at the entrance to my patio, all gathered in what looked like a semicircle. "Look at all these snails this morning. Where'd they all come from?" I said to Gracie who had followed me outside. "I've never seen this many snails in one place before. It looks like there are more than fifty of them."

"Don't eat my plants, please," I said out loud to the snails.

Be kind to all sentient beings, be compassionate, we are all one. There is no hierarchy.

I thought about Gracie's comment and bent over to pick up the snails. "OK, little snails. Let me pick you up," I said out loud, as one fell from my hand. "Oops, sorry I dropped you, little one. Don't worry. You're not hurt." I picked up the one that had fallen and scooped up a whole handful of the other snails from the patio and walked on. They felt weird in my hand. "I wonder if you can get any kind of disease from snail juice," I thought.

"You guys all look like one big family. I'll take you somewhere together where you'll be safe and feel at home." I walked out of the enclosed patio area with the snails in hand. When I looked down just beyond the gate, I saw what I must have smushed the night before in the dark, surrounded by other snails. "Sorry, little snail," I said to the dead carcass. "I didn't mean to hurt you. Actually, death *is* a little worse than just hurting you. Sorry."

Then I had a flash of insight—perhaps all of these snails had gathered in such an unusual fashion to mourn the loss of their family member whom I had inadvertently killed the night before. They were at a funeral. I was sure of it. It was a weird, deep knowing. I shook my head slightly as if to loosen that thought from my mind; that was just too strange. But I knew it was the truth.

"Well, you are the inquisitive one, aren't you?" I said turning my attention to the snail who had extended his neck, stuck his feelers out, and began to explore my hand and arm by crawling around. "It must feel weird to be on a human hand."

"Yes, it does," I heard in a strange non-voice-like way.

"Oh, my gosh. What was that? Now a snail is talking to me?" I thought as I picked up my pace to relocate the snails. No matter how often this kept happening, I was still surprised each time. "Here you go." I placed the snails under a large agave plant out by the horse manure pile. "There's plenty to eat and lots of water out here," I said to the snails. "Be happy here. I'm sorry about your friend. I really didn't mean to step on him," I whispered as I walked away, a warm feeling spreading through my heart as the idea of relocating unwanted creatures took hold. But when I got back in the house, I washed my hands, just in case.

CHAPTER 25

GRACIE ON PROTECTION

I was sitting in my meditation chair, looking at Gracie, who lay nearby. "Gracie, remember when we were in Cambria and you said, when the time was right, you'd tell me about protecting ourselves from negative forces? Well, I was just wondering if the time was right. I'd really like to know how to protect myself when I run into negative people. Sometimes lately, when I hear a lot of complaining or anxiety from someone, even if it's about little stuff, it gets difficult to be around. It's like it almost hurts my heart to listen, even though I'm trying not to be so judgmental."

Shields come in all shapes, sizes and strengths. Some are for big jobs, some smaller. Shields are very useful tools. The shield I am talking about to protect you from negative forces is a small one, but very important. It is clear and you just bring it into form when you are in a negative situation, when people are being negative or when you feel a darkness or heaviness around you. Just close your eyes for a second and imagine that you are pulling up a shield around you; almost like you are putting on a cloak, but it is like a hard shell, not soft. This shell is filled with light particles that dance at amazing speeds. Sometimes we refer to this as your light body because it takes on the shape of your human body or our dog bodies. But it is very powerful. When negative energy forces hit the light body, they are transformed. You are protected from the negative energy getting inside you, but more importantly, the negative is transformed and bounced back into the universe as positive energy. It is a very useful tool to have and to use when needed.

The shield is real, though. Don't be mistaken. You are not just making this up or imagining it exists. You will feel much better if you remember to use it, especially in stressful situations and times. The shield is like having a luminous egg surrounding you. It is beautiful. We have them too. Sometimes you can't see them so much; other times they are radiant. You look confused. I have a good example for you so you can understand what I am talking about.

Hasn't someone ever approached you and you just start to feel weird? It is like a dark cloud is around them, and you just want to walk away, but you don't really know why. Then there are other people who radiate a white light quality about them, and you want to draw close. You want to be around them, closer and closer. You feel happy and safe and secure in their presence. That is someone who is exhibiting his or her light body in all of its glory. They are radiating love no matter what is in front of them. Because they are love. Just as we all are. The person with the dark cloud is someone who still focuses on the negative. They are walking on their journey at their own pace, although it is a little slower than we would like. We are trying to get everyone into his or her light bodies and out of the darkness.

I have to go bark at something outside now.

CHAPTER 26

BRINGING THE PAST FORWARD

The next day I was at the sink washing the breakfast dishes after my morning walk with the dogs. The smell of sage coming through the open window was carrying memories of my past back to me. I was trying to conjure up the wonderful memories, like summers in Orient, Long Island, when my mother would relax and leave me alone to swim and sail all day with my friends. I closed my eyes, and I could smell the salty air, and I could see the sunlight dancing on the water of the bay in those glorious days of summer. My dad stayed in New Jersey to work and only came out to Long Island on the weekends, and Mother became a slightly different person when she was on her own. Sometimes I would pick blackberries, and she would make incredible pies with them. Or I would dig potatoes in the garden and she would make the most scrumptious Lithuanian potato pancakes, fried in bacon fat. When she was in a good mood, she'd allow me to stand by her side and eat the potato pancakes before they even got on the plate. But then I started to go deeper into memories about my parents and their relationship with my brothers and me, and it started to get dark and negative and confused in my head.

My father had escaped from Lithuania when he was nine or ten and made his way on a ship to America by himself. His parents had left him in Lithuania with some distant relatives and came to America before him, but he never found his parents again after he finally arrived here. He grew up quickly on the streets and learned to take care of himself by working around cars or on the farms on Long Island. He wasn't formally educated, but he was smart and clever. He built a successful business making tote bags and boat cushions and reupholstering cars, back in the days when cars outlasted the seat covers. His motto was, "V. Kanser Cover Co. We cover everything."

My father was constantly inventing gadgets associated with cars or boats, like special clips to hoist the sails, but my mother held the purse strings and squelched all of his inventions. She said his inventions were ridiculous and wouldn't allow him to spend any money to promote his ideas. She had no confidence in him and was fearful of any risk; fearful that it might all be taken away and she would be poor again; fearful that he might be wildly successful and she really didn't want that for him or anyone else either. Because then we wouldn't need her, and she would lose control. When I thought about it, I realized she was fearful of everything and always thought bad things might happen unless she was in control of it all. We used to call her the 20 percent majority. The five of us in the family all had one vote, but we always did what she wanted, no matter how the vote was cast.

The dishes were finally done, and I decided to go pull weeds from around the basil in the garden in an attempt to clear my head. What was it about the bad thoughts that allowed them to gain such power and control in their attempt to overwhelm a beautiful day? Gracie came outside with me and lay calmly by my side. I tried to focus on what I was doing as I gently pulled the weeds out of the ground. "Sorry little weed," I said. "But you have to go. My basil needs a little room to grow." Immediately, my mind started to wander from the weeds, and thoughts of my parents and being left to my own devices when I was the most vulnerable came bursting through like a whale breaking the ocean's surface for air and instantaneously consumed me.

My father had worked really hard to save cash from his business to build our family a new ranch-style house in an upper-middle-class neighborhood in New Jersey. Shortly after we moved in, when I was about six, the scarlet fever episode happened. My mother didn't want anyone in the new neighborhood to know I had scarlet fever and didn't want the big red quarantine sign posted on our front door, which was required in the '50s when someone was sick with such a contagious disease.

"What will the neighbors think about us if they know we have an ill, contaminated child?" I overheard my mother say to my dad. So instead of caring for me at home, my parents deposited me at friend's mortuary in the town next to ours. It had a room upstairs where I could be hidden, and no one would ever know. No quarantine signs necessary.

Day after day, I remember watching the air gently come through the window behind my bed and swirl around the room. The white lacey curtain moved with the air silently over my head, and it fascinated me. At some level, I knew the wind was there to keep me company. It was my friend. I remember the doctor coming in periodically, with his scuffed black leather bag in his left hand, to check on me.

I remember my parents visiting just once during the month that I was sequestered there, standing at the door to my room and looking at me, but not coming in. I could still see the dark hallway and the dark, dust-covered wood on the walls and I could smell the musty quality of formaldehyde and death coming up the stairs and entering my room. I remember hearing the doctor tell my parents only time would tell if I would live or not. He said that there was nothing else he could do.

Later, when I could sort of laugh about this with my brothers, Vince and Bob, we talked about the effect our parents had on our lives. When I reminded them about this story, Vince said, "Did they really do that? That's terrible."

"Do you think I could make up a story like that? I always figured they were being quite practical. If I died, they would only have to move me downstairs, ready to go. It was right next to our old Catholic church, too," I joked. "Easy to call a priest."

"Bob and I always wondered where you went," Vince laughed nervously. "I remember you were gone a long time, and no one ever told us anything. Who fed you?"

"I don't know. I vaguely remember little plates of food being left on a side table by my bed. Who knows? But I must have gotten fed because I'm still here," I said, smiling. I remember my brothers laughing, the kind of laugh you can only share with siblings who were raised by the same cold, controlling, narcissistic mother and passive, powerless father.

I know my mother was depressed. She believed that she'd given up on her own dreams for us kids, so she blamed us for everything that was wrong in her life, including her loveless marriage. She always felt that she was better than my dad, and that she had settled for someone beneath her. At the same time, she was jealous of me and my relationship with my dad. So she constantly told me that she was much prettier than I was. I realize now it was to bolster her own insecurity, but at the time, I internalized her criticisms.

My mother also told me that I was the cause of the serious fights she had with my father. It was all my fault that my mother picked up a radio, threw it at my dad, and hit him in the head—because they were fighting about me. And throwing the pressure cooker filled with pea soup against the wall, well, somehow that was my fault, too. As I tried to understand how the past has affected me, I wondered if those scenes were pieces in the puzzle of why I felt responsible for everyone's feelings?

Vince told me once that our mother used to hit him really hard; then she'd look at her hand and say, "Look what you made me do. You made me hurt my hand." He was the oldest, so he took the brunt of the violence from both parents. Although dad was tender and kind to me, his little girl, Vince, as the oldest boy, was often the victim of his frustration and wrath.

Bob, the middle child, went unseen and escaped behind Vince. Bob said he just wanted to run away and go live with an old-fashioned family, on a farm, and get way from the "modern family" we had. But he said he could never figure out the right season to leave.

When I think about our upbringing in hindsight, I can see that our mother also couldn't stand it if her children were not perfect. We were not allowed to have flaws in her world, and illness or being different was a flaw. Somehow that reflected on her and needed to be hidden.

And yet, to the outside world, my mother was kind and nice and engaging, and my friends all loved her. She was most concerned with what everyone would think about her, so the surface had to look just right. Everything appeared perfect to the outside world in our perfect little family of five that lived happily on a perfect little street in a nice upper-middle-class neighborhood, with gas-lit street lamps, where my mother orchestrated perfect parties for our perfect neighbors and friends.

So if you believe that you pick your parents for whatever lessons you need to learn on your soul's journey, what was my lesson from my parents? I didn't think it was how to throw a good party, even though I was really good at doing that. As I looked at my past, though, I was becoming aware of patterns and influences in my life that shaped some of my deep-seeded beliefs.

Then thoughts like those would dive deep, waiting for the perfect time to resurface and once more wreck havoc in the still waters I was trying to create in my life. I was still trying to forgive my parents and understand that they did the best they could, given their situation as immigrants, who at the beginning had to struggle just to survive. When I thought about it, I realized my mother wasn't a bad person. She simply was fearful of everything and everyone, and she had no impulse control.

I surfaced from these memories to see Gracie looking at me expectantly as the smell of basil surrounded us in the garden and a pile of weeds lay at my feet.

What was it about the past always jumping in to haunt me? Why couldn't it stay put? Why couldn't I let go of the stories?

ooooo

The next day I was out walking the dogs, who had taken off into the avocado orchard to look for overly ripe avocados hiding in the leaves to eat. Only Gracie stayed by my side. As I walked on the dirt path through the trees, I was having trouble just enjoying the natural surroundings and feeling at peace, as thoughts and scenes from my past again broke through the surface and flooded my mind. It was a story which my mind replayed often, and I didn't know why. This time it was coming back in full detail, even though it normally only replayed like that when I looked in a mirror and saw my scars.

When I was 16, a drunk driver crossed the centerline on a snowy Vermont rode and hit my brother, Vince, and me head-on as we were driving home from a skiing weekend. I remembered grabbing the history book I'd been studying to catch the blood as it poured from my head (thinking that the teacher was going to be really mad at me for ruining the book). I could remember seeing a man's face pressed against the shattered passenger window, talking calmly to me through the falling snow, as he tried desperately to pry open the car door to get me out before the car caught on fire.

And I could still feel each snowflake, like it was a giant brick, hitting the gaping wound on my forehead, as the man laid me on the ground to wait for the ambulance, and the snow kept falling. I was afraid I was going to die, but I remember thinking that I was too young to die, that I had too much to do.

And then those bricks kept falling on my open wound as I lay on the ground, one or two at a time, for fifty-four minutes before the ambulance arrived. Vince, who had a large gash on the top of his head, and I were put in the front seat next to the ambulance driver. My brother helped me hold a towel to my head as we applied pressure. Vince was in medical school at the time, and he told me later he was so scared because he could see my skull, and he didn't see how they were going to put my forehead back together. A big chunk of my forehead was hanging in front of my eyes and it blocked my ability to see. I remember thinking at that moment, "Thank God, I'm not going to die," but, "I'm going to be blind." That thought terrified me. The girl who was thrown from the truck that hit us was in the back of the ambulance, barely making a sound; she ultimately didn't make it.

Our parents had been too busy to come be with us while we stayed in that little hospital in Vermont undergoing multiple surgeries and getting casts on various broken bones. After nine days, my father and my mother, dressed in white gloves and mink stole, finally came to pick us up. My brother's car was totaled, and he didn't have a way to drive us home, so they had to come get us.

Just as my parents arrived at my hospital room, the doctor came to remove the bandages from my head. The first thing my mother said when she saw me was "Don't look at yourself in the mirror, honey. You don't want to see how bad you look." I watched my mother's face turn ashen as she stared at me in horror when the bandages came off.

"Those scars are worse than I thought they'd be," she said as she regained composure, and the color came back to her face. "It'll be tough finding someone to love that face. But, don't worry, honey, it doesn't bother me. I guess you won't be going to the prom."

"Bring me a mirror," I said. "I want to look."

"No, you don't," she said.

"Yes, I do. It's my head! Bring me a mirror." I looked. The swollen face that stared back at me was reminiscent of Frankenstein's daughter, the skin around my eyes fading from black to purple to green, dried blood still caked in my blond hair, with 108 dark nasty looking stitches zigzagging across my forehead, making a loop back, and then through my eyelid, across the bridge of my nose and up into my other eyebrow.

"OK, you can take the mirror away now," I said, not wanting my mother to see the tear forming in my eye. But I did go to the prom, bandages, casts, and all. I figured out how to wear a wig and swoop the bangs over my forehead and eyelids so the impact of the crash was barely visible, except for the cast on my arm.

Then the other story came back about being left alone and my parents refusing to come see me in the hospital even though I was close to dying. I was in my twenties and living in Aspen, Colorado, managing a very popular local restaurant and bar, when I became very ill and was in a lot of abdominal pain. Typical of the times and Aspen, the local doctors said not to worry and just advised me to take pain pills. But the pain intensified. Vince made me get right on a plane and come to California. He picked me up from the airport, and I was in surgery by that afternoon. Vince scrubbed in to watch the surgery, and he said the tumor was the largest, most ugly black thing he had ever seen in all of his days as a doctor. Even his years in a busy emergency room when he was an intern and a resident had not prepared him for something like that, and he had to walk out of my surgery.

He said that the tumor was the size of a volleyball and was being fed by a blood vessel the size of a quarter. He told me that if I'd waited any longer, I could have been walking down the street and the blood vessel could have burst, and I would have been dead before anyone could even get me to a hospital.

Vince was always there for me, but he was scared that I was going to die no matter what he did, and he felt responsible. I begged and begged to be let out of the hospital, and finally after about ten days, Vince acquiesced and brought me to his house. My fever spiked to over 105 that night and back to the hospital I went.

Insidious infections consumed my body during the next 20 days in the hospital, and I needed multiple blood transfusions and more surgeries. It was touch and go whether I would make it. A grey unearthly face stared back at me when I looked in the mirror attached to the hospital bedside table. It wasn't me anymore. The life force was barely visible in my eyes. I went out of my body and looked at myself lying there. It was very peaceful and detached, but then I came back. I still had things to do.

My parents never bothered to come see me. I don't even remember them calling, although I'm sure they must have. Vince said my mother told him they were praying for me. A visit would have required a trip across the country to California, and they didn't feel they had the time—even though my mother didn't work, and they had plenty of money, due to my father constantly working. My brother Bob's wife said she begged and begged my mom to come see me, but my mother simply said, "No."

What kinds of parents don't come see their kids who are near death in a hospital? And what was the impact on me? Did it make me strong and independent, so that I never needed anyone? Did it merely reinforce my belief that I wasn't loved or lovable? Did it further my need to bury any vulnerability so I didn't get hurt? Did it further harden that mold so that I didn't love myself? If my own mother didn't love me, how could I love myself? Or was the result some complex combination of those issues?

"Breathe, look at it, and let it go," I said to myself as I continued on the dusty agricultural road leading away from my house.

Those thoughts had come washing over me from nowhere, and now they were receding, leaving me alone, as I came back to the present and my walk with the dogs. Maybe all the books and classes and other work I had been doing on myself to let go of the past were actually working. Those thoughts didn't contain as much sting as they used to. I had a somewhat clearer perspective and a growing awareness of the influences on my life. I wondered whether I kept attracting the same experiences, in slightly different forms, over and over because I had something to learn from them. I also wondered why my mind repeatedly replayed these negative stories in such detail.

During this walk, Gracie had stayed quietly beside me, allowing me my thoughts, and now the other dogs had regrouped. I looked at Gracie by my side, walking with a hopeful expression on her face. She was a lot like me, always hopeful. Besides, even though my parents hadn't come to be with me, maybe their prayers actually had worked to help me recover from the surgery. Maybe that was all they could do, and maybe it helped. Who knows?

CHAPTER 27

HEPATITIS C

One night I couldn't sleep, so I got up and wandered around the house. I couldn't stop thinking about all of the things going on in my life, including feeling unhappy and distant from Bill and having Hepatitis C. It didn't make sense to me that the transfusions, which had perhaps saved my life in 1976 when I had the black tumor surgery, had wound up giving me Hepatitis C. It just seemed weird to me that a virus could lie dormant in my body, quietly sapping me of strength, for more than 25 years before it was discovered.

It felt like yesterday that I'd watched each drop of blood go from the hanging bag into the needle in my arm. What should have taken an hour, took seven hours with me because my veins kept collapsing and the blood couldn't enter. I remembered watching every second of those seven hours and calling the nurses to restart the transfusion every time the drips would stop and the veins in my arm would start to bulge when the blood refused to enter. Maybe my body knew way back then that the blood I was receiving was contaminated and was trying to shut down to protect me. No one really knows how things work in the Universe anyway.

But I'd had multiple surgeries over the years and multiple blood tests. Why hadn't anyone discovered this before? And what was I supposed to do now? I felt contaminated and untouchable. Intellectually I believed that the events of the past did not have any hold over me and that they didn't affect who I really was today. But I wondered about that? At some level the events of the past had everything to do with who I was and what was happening in my life right now. I also continued to ponder whether there was a lesson in my consecutive illnesses. Did I subconsciously want illnesses, to get attention, or for some other currently unfathomable reason, and so the Universe kept giving me what it thought I wanted? Was the Universe acting to please me?

> [Grace] is the unconditional kindness of the Universe. The gentle power and serenity that lifts us up no matter what it is we are going through... Grace is a state of pure openness and being available—a space where you can allow a new reality to enter into your very being. Grace fills us up quietly and powerfully.
>
> -Oprah Winfrey

CHAPTER 28

MEDITATION

I sat down to meditate in my comfortable chair in the living room. Gracie came over and planted herself directly on my feet, staring at me with such intensity that I had to pay attention to her.

"What, Gracie? What do you want?" I said in a slightly annoyed tone. Not a good way to start a meditation, I thought, as I snapped myself out of annoyance and turned my full attention to what was in front of me—Gracie.

At first she was quiet, almost seeming to assess whether I was really tuned in, and then she started to struggle to use her voice, to make actual sounds of differing qualities, as if she really wanted to talk. Not just communicate mind to mind, not just send mental pictures, but actually speak to me.

I strained to understand the words. I really tried, but I couldn't decipher what Gracie was saying.

"I'm sorry, Gracie, but I can't do it. I don't get it. I know you want to say something, but I don't know what it is."

My need to take care of you, to look out for you and protect you, is very strong—much deeper than you know. That is why I am always keeping an eye open for you and trying to keep away the negative forces. Negative forces can include stress, fear, anger, sadness, words or thoughts, jealousy, judgment, and many other things. These aspects can act in the body and cause the physical body to go out of balance. Fear, when it turns to anger or resentment, can inhibit the effectiveness of an individual and the entire universe. Don't give the negative so much power, influence, or attention. The negatives weaken, the positives strengthen. When things operate from love and harmony, they are effective and efficient, including the body.

I can be your strength through illness. I need to stay by your side. I take on much of the negativity and transmute it into positive energy just for you. It sounds hard, but it isn't. When negative stuff hits, it hits my heart and feels the love inside, so when it bounces back, it turns into love. So when it reaches you, it is love and light. Many animals do that for their human companions.

It would be great if you could do that too. So you need to look at everyone and everything with love. Even if you hear a little growl from someone, try to turn it into love. Try to really feel it. Push out love, send love, no matter what. Allow that Dog light within to shine forth and help others. I love you. (Dictated 5-13-06)

Gracie licked my face. She knew I got it.

CHAPTER 29

TREATMENT

Months later, after much deliberation, I decided to bite the bullet and go for the Hepatitis C treatment, which consisted of taking two powerful drugs, Interferon and Ribaviron. My doctor convinced me that I should undergo treatment while I was still healthy. I knew Gracie would give me strength and protect me. I also made the conscious decision to look at the doctors and the drugs as also being part of the divine. I sent as much love as I could to the doctors and the drugs and I asked that the drugs enter my body and do what they needed to do for the good of the whole.

On the first day of the treatment, Bill went with me to the doctor's office. The nurse showed Bill how to give shots and, without hesitation, he gave me the first injection right on the spot.

"Hey, you're not supposed to enjoy that so much." I teased. "But you were pretty good at it. It didn't really hurt."

Bill laughed. Then I took the first two pills, and we left the doctor's office.

"The doctor told me to take the pills with fatty food to help with absorption. Do you have time to go to the Mexican restaurant across the street?" I asked Bill.

"Yeah, sure. I cleared out my morning so we could do this."

I ordered huevos rancheros and a side of bacon. The amount of fat seemed disgusting, but I didn't want to do anything half heartedly, and it actually tasted quite good. I hadn't had bacon in years.

"You know, the doctor said a lot of people aren't successful because they can't stand the treatment and give up," I said. "How bad can it be?"

"For your sake, I hope not too bad," Bill said.

"Can you believe that they get away with charging several thousand per month for this medication, which is designed to make you sick?" I asked as we ate.

"Not really, but just think of all those promotional goodies you got," he said. "Traveling case, traveling syringe disposal, cold eye packs, and enough warnings, disclaimers, and instructions to keep you in reading material for at least a week. What else could you want?" he asked with a smile.

"Lucky you have good insurance," I added.

Bill took me home and then drove back to Ventura to teach. As the day progressed, I started to feel a little weird, but not too bad, so I decided to take the dogs for a walk. I started to feel a little weak in the legs and knees, but I plowed forward up to the labyrinth where I gave thanks for everything in my life, including my husband, the kids, my dogs, my family, and my friends. I came back toward the house but continued my walk on the back path. When chills and shakes started radiating through my legs and then traveling to other body parts, I decided I better get home before it got too bad. Just as I turned around, Lily and Walter spotted a coyote and took off after it, with Carl in hot pursuit. Gracie and Puggers were by my side. I was able to get Gracie on a leash because she'd slowed down, but my reaction time wasn't fast enough to catch Puggers before he got a whiff of what was going on and took off like a rocket to help the other dogs.

I was starting to feel worse and worse by the second as my yells for the dogs went unheeded. When I realized the dogs had crossed the orchard and climbed high into the mountains on the opposite ridge, I started to panic. I heard my dogs yelp in the distance, interspersed with a growing chorus of coyote yelps, as more and more coyotes joined the fray. The dogs and coyotes howled back and forth, close to each other, but far from me. I called Maggie who said she would get Fred to come on the four-wheeler right away.

"Come get a biscuit … come get a biscuit!" I yelled as loud as I could. This trick, which usually worked, had no effect that night.

I forgot all of my training about asking for help from the unseen forces and started to cry. I thought I heard Gracie ask the angels for help, but I just stood there, paralyzed. Then, as if by magic, the dogs started straggling in, one by one, their tongues hanging out of their mouths, barely able to walk and panting to catch their breath. Only Puggers was missing. Then I spotted him about a half mile away on a ledge overhanging a steep ridge, barking in distress because he couldn't find his way down. The coyotes were silent, but I knew they weren't far away.

"Please, angels, there is no way for me to get to him way up there. Please bring him down safely," I begged out loud.

"Puggers!" I screamed, frightened that he would fall or wouldn't be able to get down from that inaccessible place. "Puggers!"

And then I could see him traversing his way down the mountain, as if he was being guided on some invisible path, going in and out of view when he was in the underbrush. Several minutes later, he arrived safely by my side, covered in burrs and ticks. Exhausted, we all walked slowly home.

I was grateful that they were all safe, but by the time we got to the house, my shakes were in full swing. I was weak and could barely stand. I pushed on, pulled the ticks off of the dogs from the walk, forced myself to give the dogs a bath in case they had gotten into poison oak, and fed them. Then I stayed in the kitchen until 6:30 p.m. when I was supposed to take the next dose of medicine. After downing some fatty food and two more pills, I crawled into bed to bundle up with my chills and Gracie. I turned on the TV and started to knit, dozing in and out of consciousness, with the TV blaring nonsense in the background and Gracie lying by my side.

"All in all, Gracie, if that's as bad as it gets, I can do it," I said. "There are people who are a lot more sick than I am."

ooooo

One day I was working intently on my paperwork, ignoring Gracie and her book. I really didn't feel well. The drugs were taking a toll on me. I knew I was getting depressed, but I didn't want anyone to know.

Instead I started to get things organized in my life. I thought it might take my mind off of things, things like my failure to work on Gracie's book. Maybe I was using the illness as an excuse because I really was afraid of the book; afraid of what other people might think; afraid that it was not going to be good enough; afraid that people would think that I made it all up; afraid of all the critics in my head.

Besides, I had lots to do to take care of the house and the ranch to make sure things ran smoothly, so I didn't have time for the book anyway, let alone time to feel sorry for myself because I felt like crap. I made my to-do lists and made sure everything got done each day. I made sure that the house was well stocked with all of the things Bill liked to eat. I made food and took care of the dogs. I was on top of it and determined to muscle through this illness without anyone knowing how bad I felt.

Bill gave me my shots on the appointed days.

"Thanks, Bill," I told him one morning. "I appreciate your doing this for me."

"No problem. I've got to go to school now. You OK?" he asked.

"I'll be fine. Thanks," I said in as upbeat a tone as I could muster. "See you tonight."

Bill made sure I was taken care of and then left. He was attentive and kind, but I thought he took solace in his work, which left me with lots of time alone to think. And sometimes it was awfully busy up there, in my head.

I thought perhaps I'd lost confidence in my belief that Gracie was dictating the book. My heart knew the truth, but my intellect had taken over. Through the veil of my illness and the drugs, I looked at Gracie and heard those little critical voices of self-doubt. She's just a dog. Dogs can't talk. Dogs work on instinct. They're not concerned with the past or future, only the present moment. "But that's a good thing," I thought. "I'd like to me more like that."

"I am getting depressed," I thought. I tried to convince myself that that was why I didn't have any energy to work on the book. The doctors had warned me that the drugs could make me depressed, even suicidal, and said to call if I felt like taking my own life. "Excellent advice," I thought sarcastically. I certainly didn't feel suicidal, but I realized there was a gigantic cloud of darkness hovering around me.

I felt very alone and very out of it. It was like I was supposed to be sick, but I wasn't allowed to be sick because everyone else needed me to take care of them. At least that's what I thought. I came last, and there was no one to take care of me.

"I don't want to be the one everyone thinks is strong and can be relied on all of the time," I said to myself. "It would be nice to feel that it was OK to feel weak every once in awhile. To be able to feel what I'm feeling and not always think I have to get over myself." Even as I uttered those thoughts out loud, I knew I really didn't have time to be helpless and fall apart. I had to be strong and upbeat, no matter what, and rarely ask for help. No one was allowed into my experience.

My mother's voice always came back to haunt me, the mother who'd reinforced every day of my childhood that I wasn't good enough. It was her critical voice that I adopted as my own. No matter what I did, it wasn't enough. I wasn't pretty or smart enough, even though I got straight A's and excelled in school. I actually believed that no one would ever love me because I was not a lovable person. So when someone did, I didn't trust it. I assumed they had ulterior motives. I knew I had to be strong and take care of myself because no one else ever would.

And whenever I did show any weakness or emotion when I was growing up, my mother would tell me, "Just get over yourself. What makes you think you're so important? There are people out there a lot worse off than you."

"Gracie takes care of me, though," I thought. "She's the only one. She sits by me day and night and watches out for me. If I go take a nap, she comes right with me and lies down by my side. And I always feel better when she is near. Walter still wants to play, but even he knows something's up and only gently approaches to kiss my face."

But these ramblings had nothing to do with my self-doubt about my ability to communicate with Gracie. I had noticed the eye rolling from Bill and other friends when I talked about the book, but I wasn't going to let that bother me. I tried to convince myself that I didn't really care what other people thought. But maybe I did. Despite my outward appearance of being strong, maybe I really was insecure and I had lost my confidence within.

Maybe this book wasn't as important as I thought. Maybe Gracie didn't have a mission. Maybe my mind just made up all of these crazy thoughts. Was all of this just the product of an overly active imagination? Maybe I did need to get back to behaving normally. But what was normal now anyway?

ooooo

I thought I was only going to have to do three months of treatment, but after that time was up, the doctor told me I would need to do another three. I think he knew all along it would be six months. A classic bait and switch to get me to start the treatment. At that point, I didn't know if I could stand the extra three. I tried to walk most days with Maggie and the dogs, but sometimes I just couldn't summon the energy. Lisa and Rachel brought over food. And Gracie stayed with me constantly, giving me lots of love.

One day when I thought I couldn't go on, Rachel arrived with an incredible painting of Gracie. I knew Rachel was talented, but this was the most breathtaking and lifelike painting I had ever seen. I was honored. Gracie's smile greeted me every time I looked at the painting, and it stirred a little happiness in my heart. I felt that somehow Bill, my friends, Gracie, and the magic in that painting got me through the next portion of the treatment, which instead of getting easier was becoming harder and harder to take every day.

I kept myself busy doing paperwork, paying bills, decluttering, and attempting to get things in order around the house because I couldn't really go anywhere. I was exhausted all the time and felt so crappy that I talked with my doctor about terminating treatment. He convinced me to continue. The drugs had taken a toll on every aspect of my life. They destroyed my white blood cells, which my blood work showed were dangerously low. My doctor prescribed shots of Neupogen to get my white cells back into a barely functioning range, instead of the alternative, which was death. Bill dutifully gave me the additional shots as needed.

With a deteriorating immune system, I needed to stay away from people so I didn't catch anything my body couldn't fight off. The drugs had destroyed my thyroid, and I felt weak and depleted without knowing why. By the time I discovered this side effect, late in the game, and a prescription was ordered, my thyroid function was almost non-existent. I sat in the crowded waiting area of the pharmacy, by myself, surrounded by strangers, waiting for my thyroid prescription to be filled. Every once in awhile I would nod out of consciousness, and my head would hit my chest and cause me to bounce back awake.

I was so weak that I could barely remain sitting. One of those nice strangers caught me before I fell off the chair and passed out on the floor. I finally got my prescription and then had to drive home, summon the strength to talk to Bill when he got home, and then climb in bed. But I persevered and finally the day arrived when I was done with the six months of drugs. They did a blood test, and I waited anxiously for the results. The Hepatitis C was undetectable in my blood; the treatment had worked. I didn't know if it was worth it, but I was done.

Squamous cell skin cancers started appearing with regularity on my face and my hands, and I had surgery after surgery to remove them. One doctor said the skin cancers were probably due to my weakened immune system caused by the Hepatitis C drugs.

I felt stronger now that the drugs had slowly dissipated from my system, but Gracie was showing more and more signs of slowing down, and this made me sad. I felt guilty that I hadn't been working on Gracie's book, but I just was not feeling motivated. I was having trouble believing in the project, and life, chores, and events kept getting in the way. I was not feeling my upbeat self, and I was acutely aware that I'd lost the joy of the present moment during the treatment process. I had stopped humming.

CHAPTER 30

GRACIE AND JEFFREY

I was standing at the kitchen sink, staring idly out of the window, squeezing lemons for lemonade and feeling guilty that I had not been working on Gracie's book. I don't know what had come over me, even though I felt better, I had put her book aside. Gracie was resting on my bare feet, making them nice and toasty warm against the cold stone floor. It was a gorgeous day with just the right touch of sun mingled with those delicious cool breezes that melt over the ground after a rainstorm. The backyard meadow was alive, teeming with sounds. I could hear hundreds of birds twittering at different pitches, talking back and forth to one another from branch to branch. There were thousands of bees buzzing, and when the individual sounds of the various creatures combined, the low-level hum dissolved into perfect harmony with the hum I could sometimes hear from the earth. The sound of the frogs singing was deafening; it was as if hundreds of them had spawned in every little puddle created by the rain and they were all happy to be alive, yelling to each other.

"A perfect day to take you guys out to play," I said aloud to the dogs who were in various stages of repose around the house, silently waiting and hoping for something fun to happen, like a walk or a visitor or even a coyote to chase.

Suddenly I had the sense that something was on the back deck. Gracie cocked her head to listen. But surely the dogs would be barking if there were something out there, I thought. Gracie moved slightly, and I reached over to open the kitchen door to see if some animal had wandered into my vast backyard. I really didn't blame them; I had moved into their territory a long time ago, but I was still getting used to sharing space with every bear and bobcat who wanted to visit. As I opened the door, I didn't see anything, but I had the sense that the door had bumped into something.

"Oh, excuse me. I didn't mean to open the door in your face," I said, as I looked around, a little embarrassed that I was talking to the empty backyard. There wasn't anything there except my lingering certainty that I had just bumped into Jeffrey.

I was lying in my usual position right on her feet. That way I was right there to hold the energy and keep it from getting too scattered when it was necessary. Well, that's the party line anyway. Actually, I take this spot so she can't go anywhere without me knowing, but the energy thing is true too.

When I heard the commotion, I begrudgingly lifted my head, not really wanting to move from my comfy spot. Oh, it's just Jeffrey, I mused sleepily, but when I saw what happened, I smiled. I could sense her imagining the scene.

I didn't see Jeffrey, but I got an image in my mind. I imagined that Jeffrey came whizzing past with an old tattered green blanket flying out behind him in sync with his large flapping ears just as I opened the door and the top of the door smacked him right in the chin. I saw him looking stunned and then he closed his eyes in a slight wince, but the impact barely slowed him down. He seemed to be on a mission about something.

I imagined that he had leaves and twigs as decoration in his straggly hair. I thought Gracie would prefer a bit of personal hygiene and a little more cleanliness even in a nine-foot gnome. In my mind, I saw a multi-colored feathered hat, instead of a red pointed one like every other self-respecting gnome, but I wasn't sure what he really looked like. I've attempted to visualize him, even to the extent of dressing up an actor friend for photographs, but I don't think I got him quite right. The only thing I'm sure about is my sense of him.

She didn't get it quite right, but close. He is more amorphous than that. I've known him a long time, and I love him for who he is, no changes necessary. He is kind and dedicated to making the garden beautiful. And he loves to give me flowers.

"Hi, Jeffrey, what's up?"

"Hi, Gracie. I really would like to talk to her."

"What about?"

"I would like to tell her certain things so she understands on an inner level and can work with us more. She needs to feel the connection. She's a little lost."

"She's ok," Gracie said. "She's going at her own pace."

"She's a prisoner of worry. She replays the past, she worries she is not good enough, that she can't do it right, that she is making it up. She worries about everything and her judgment and skepticism is getting in the way of the connection. I would like to talk to her. Arrange it when you feel the time is right, would you?" Jeffrey asked.

I decided to pass on walking the dogs and just sit outside in the sun with them. It seemed like a perfect time to meditate, but I couldn't focus on my breath with Gracie licking my face insistently. Gracie cuddled real close and pressed her pale velvet-like fur against my leg. I knew she was trying to tell me something by the intense yet serene look on her face, but I felt pretty dense most of the time lately and couldn't pick up on what Gracie was trying to tell me anymore.

CHAPTER 31

DEPLETED

Jane was home from college for a visit, and we were sitting on the back deck talking, enjoying the glorious sun at our backs. We had been talking for a long time about everything that was going on in Jane's life. I realized I really missed her when she was away and the last year had been tough without her around. Gracie was lying between us.

"How's Gracie's book coming?" Jane asked finally. "You haven't talked about it lately."

"Oh, I haven't worked on it much. Hardly at all since the Hep C treatment," I said sadly.

"Why not?"

"Oh, I don't know. It just started to sound silly, and I don't want people to laugh at me or think it's stupid. I guess I just stopped believing, and Gracie stopped talking."

"Why do you care what people think? From what you've told me about your mother, that sounds like her, not you."

"You're right. I don't know. I just don't feel motivated. I guess I wonder whether she's really talking to me or whether I'm just making it up. Or maybe I don't believe I can hear her anymore. I think I've lost the connection."

"That's too bad," Jane said, as she took a sip of her iced tea. "You do realize Gracie's getting older and she's not so active anymore."

"I know. It makes me sad, but I have lots to do, and I just don't get around to her book. Sometimes I make a commitment to Gracie and myself to work on it and then something always gets in the way," I said with a sigh.

"Have you noticed she doesn't hear so well either?" Jane said as she reached out to pet Gracie as she slept. "You can walk right up to her, yell at her, and unless she sees you, she doesn't know you're there. Maybe it's more important than ever to talk to her heart to heart."

"I don't know. I just don't believe it anymore. People will think I'm nuts. Sometimes I think I'm nuts. I just can't do it. Other people can talk to animals, just not me."

"I'm really surprised to hear you say that. I thought it was inspiring. I always believed in you and Gracie. And I really do believe that animals can communicate. It seems to me it's the humans who are the stupid ones," Jane said kindly as she got up to go in the house. "I've got to go, but remember, only you know what's best for you."

I was suddenly overwhelmed with emotion and started to cry.

"Ahhh. I hate to see you sad," Jane said with an empathetic look and a pat on my shoulder. "You'll figure it out. You always do. I've got to go to my dentist appointment, though. You OK if I leave?"

"Yes, I'm fine. Go. See you later," I said trying to hide the tears.

Gracie opened one eye and stared intensely at me. The tears flowed as Jane left, and Gracie let me cry.

"You're such a good girl," I said, rubbing her head. "You never judge me. Do you?"

She just stared at me and wouldn't look away for several minutes until I stopped crying.

"OK, Gracie," I said in a whisper. "I don't know what I'm doing anymore. I believe in you, I just don't believe in me most of the time. What do you think? Should we try again or have you given up on me? I will be still and really try to listen without judgment."

I will always wait for you to be ready. Every moment provides the opportunity to start over, to begin anew. When you appreciate the miracle that is happening around you, magic happens. Be true to who you are. Honor yourself. Love yourself. Believe in yourself. Find that spark of divinity within you and stay there. Act from that place within you which is spirit, God, oneness, whatever you want to call it; the word doesn't matter. Allow that creative energy to flow in you. Be loyal to the God within in every act you take and find that divine nature in everyone and everything outside of you too. God is in all. Don't look outside, look within. Only then can you see it outside of you too. Acknowledge the sacredness of every individual, human or animal, plant or mineral, the water, the earth, and all life forms. When you truly see and acknowledge that everything around you is filled with spirit, you will be filled with peace. Love and respect all life, and the world will change. (Dictated 2/8/09)

"I would like things to change in this world," I said so quietly that I almost didn't hear myself. "I don't see how I can make a difference in this world, though. But thank you for that miracle, Gracie. Thanks for having faith in me."

CHAPTER 32

WAITING

I really believed Jeffrey was out there working. Everything was so perfect in the garden without too much effort on our part. Banana and macadamia nut trees grew next to apples and cherries. The cherries were sporadic, but the apples and nuts were prolific. Those trees should have grown in entirely different climates. I attributed the variety and abundance to help from the unseen forces at work, like Jeffrey and his crew. I'd also never forgotten that both Crystal and Gracie had simultaneously told me years before that Jeffrey had something to tell me. Could I possibly talk to a gigantic gnome in the garden that I couldn't see but could only imagine? I knew some people would think I was nuts, but I didn't care. I was frustrated that I could sense his presence, but I couldn't see him. Other people had such abilities. Maybe I just wasn't trying hard enough.

Gracie frequently came close and seemed to urge me forward, so I made a decision to go sit in the garden every day and to open my mind to the possibility that Jeffrey might want to communicate with me. Day after day, I sat and asked that I be given whatever I needed; I was open to the gifts of the Universe. I brought a book with me so it would look like I was reading. That way, if anyone came by, I wouldn't have to explain what I was doing. I had tried to convince myself that I didn't care what other people thought, but apparently my actions revealed that at least some part of me still did care.

But I continued with my plan to sit in the garden. I never heard anyone speaking. I never got any particular ideas or revelations, but it was a pleasant experience. Beyond pleasant, it was joyous. As I sat very still, I saw lots of wondrous things: tiny universes working together; creatures interacting, doing their dance. I felt the strength of the trees and the power of the mountains around me. The songs of the birds left me in awe. The natural world became magnified and filled me with calm.

Gracie came with me and lay by my side. But still I heard nothing. I continued to ask that the Universe provide what was right for me. Then, after many days of spending hours in the garden each day, sitting, Gracie came real close and sat by my side. Gracie began to communicate, and I heard it.

Why are you trying so hard to get it right? There is no right way to do it. There is no one way fits all. You are where you are, with the tools you have. All the knowledge you need is within. You don't need to see Jeffrey to believe in him or to have faith that unseen forces are at work in your life and the lives of everyone on this planet. You know it's true. You just don't trust in yourself or love yourself enough to believe you are worthy to contact those forces. You have had many lessons along the way. Your childhood was not easy. You developed survival mechanisms and ways to control your surroundings. But you can let those things go now. You are ready. Don't let your thoughts about the past define you. You are not your thoughts. None of us will ever really know why things happen, but have faith. If it shouldn't have happened, it wouldn't have happened. You gained gifts from all of those experiences, even if you don't understand, even if they don't seem like gifts. They shaped who you are. It's very difficult to wrap our minds around the thought that darkness and shadow may be necessary in bringing about change, in allowing the light to shine.

I recognized that I had just received a powerful message from Gracie. I continued to sit on the beach chair in the garden and started to reassess everything in my head. Gracie was right. I didn't need to see Jeffrey to believe he was there. I knew he was. I had known that all along, ever since Gracie first told me about him. Maybe even before then.

Suddenly a very strong feeling arose, almost like a big breath of hot air came whooshing over me and settled in my heart. Then I felt a strong presence close by. I looked around, and I couldn't see anything, but I knew Jeffrey was standing there, looking at me through the leaves of the pomegranate tree in the garden.

"Feel," I heard in my heart.

"What?" I said aloud to no one as my heart started to pound out of control.

"Don't think …"

"Yeah, but there's no one here except me," I said.

"You know it's me … Breathe."

"How?" I whispered.

"See beyond the struggle. Feel all as pure and whole … restore balance."

And then, the communication stopped as quickly as it had begun.

"Jeffrey, Jeffrey are you still there? What does that mean? Just tell me what to do. I'm a lawyer. I need specifics and a logical game plan. Why won't anyone just tell me what to do?"

"Love yourself. You've been trained … You have all you need inside. Trust. Let your light shine. It's a big experiment for a shift in consciousness on this planet. Be part of the transformation."

I just sat there, motionless.

"Have I really been talking to a gigantic gnome who looks over my place?" I wondered out loud. I had always considered myself to be a levelheaded, logical, rational person. Animals were one thing, but gnomes? And what experiment, what light was he talking about? I didn't have any light for the world. That sounded so egotistical.

Thinking about what Jeffrey said, later that night I opened my laptop, went online, and reread a favorite quote that I had forgotten about, one which has been attributed to Nelson Mandela, but which I discovered originated with Marianne Williamson:

> Our deepest fear is not that we are inadequate, our deepest fear is that we are powerful beyond measure. It is our light, not our darkness that most frightens us. We ask ourselves who am I to be brilliant, gorgeous, talented, fabulous? Actually, who are you not to be? You are a child of God. Your playing small does not serve the world. There is nothing enlightened about shrinking so that other people won't feel insecure around you. We were born to make manifest the glory of God that is within us. It is not just in some of us; it is in everyone. And as we let our own light shine, we unconsciously give other people permission to do the same. As we are liberated from our own fear, our presence automatically liberates others.
> Marianne Williamson, *A Return to Love: Reflections on the Principles of "A Course in Miracles"*

As I sat in front of the computer in the darkened room, I thought back to my childhood and wondered what it would have been like if I had been encouraged to follow what was natural for me as a kid, if I'd been allowed to let my light shine. I thought again about lying on the floor in our kitchen when I was a kid with my black Lab, Sheik. Sometimes I'd lie facing him, hold his paw, look into his eyes, and sing, "I want to hold your paw" to the Beatles tune. It felt glorious just to be with the dog. Sometimes I would be real quiet and just listen to what he had to say and report it to my mother. But my mother would say, "Don't be ridiculous. You're just making things up in that overly active imagination of yours." She demanded that I act normal. "Get up off that floor, Julianne, and leave that dumb dog alone," she would say. "I do not have crazy children. Just act normal like everyone else. Only insane people hear dogs talk, so stop it." Sometimes I would just hold onto Sheik when my mother started to rant and I'd feel protected.

At the time it seemed natural to be with my dog and to listen to what he had to say. He certainly didn't seem dumb, but a parent is a powerful influence, and I learned it wasn't valued or honored to relate to animals in that way. If she'd encouraged me to follow what seemed natural back then, or at least remained neutral, it might not be so hard for me to believe in communicating with animals now.

My mother did everything she could to thwart my natural abilities and my love of animals. Not only did she say I was crazy for talking to the dog, but I realized I still hadn't forgiven her for making me eat my pet ducks, Jumpsey and Pooper. It surprised me that after all these years, thoughts about my mother and my ducks, still brought up tears. I saw my ducks following me everywhere and me talking to them quietly as they sat hiding under my petticoat. They would hear my father's car coming down the driveway, peep their heads out from under the safety of my skirt, and run to the compost pile as the car approached so Dad and I could dig worms for them. I could see Jumper jumping five feet in the air to eat a worm off my shovel or out of my hand. And Poopsey, I could see him doing what he did best.

One day I came home and my ducks were gone. Just like that. No discussion, no anything. I remembered my mother saying they were too much trouble and that she'd given them to a good home and had been given two dead ducks in return, which we ate for dinner that night.

"You didn't have the right to give them away. They were my friends," I remember crying to my mother. It wasn't until years later, when I was about 17, that she told me the truth when I asked again about my ducks.

"Well, of course, we ate them, dear. We had fed them so well. What did you expect?" The devious, yet guilty, smile that accompanied that statement still haunts me.

I guess I had expected my ducks to be treated with dignity and respect. They were my friends, no better or worse than any other friends I had. And I realized that my mother's smile that day was the final straw in my relationship with her. I went off to college, and that was it. I put distance between us, and I have never been able to eat duck since.

Thinking about it now, I suddenly realized how much anger I was still holding about an event that had happened more than fifty years before. And how close to the surface it was. I tried to let it go. I went to my heart and tried to infuse the whole situation with love. Then a random thought popped into my head, into my heart actually, based on what Gracie had said earlier. Maybe I needed everything that had happened as preparation for this moment, to allow my heart to crack open.

I never realized how I was holding onto that incident and its effect on me. I needed to let it go. My mother did the best she could with what she had, where she was, and what she came from. Her mother had emigrated here from Lithuania and had about five husbands, and they had to take in "boarders" to live. I sometimes wonder what bad things may have happened to my mother in those circumstances, a beautiful young girl with lots of men around. I think mom's biological father deserted them. They were poor and food was scarce. I guess she just saw the ducks as food and didn't attach any feelings to them. Even though she rarely talked about her past, she told us kids once that she used to have to go pick up coal from the railroad tracks to survive. It must have been hard.

I was beginning to understand how things get passed down from generation to generation, but it had taken me all these years to believe that I deserved more than I got from my parents. That all kids do. I wanted a mother who loved me and encouraged me and accepted me for who I was. I wanted parents who supported my natural talents, not ones who criticized and were so victimized by the depression and the times that money was the only thing that was important to them.

I thought about my mother again. I got a mother who viewed me as a reflection of her, and that reflection had to be perfect according to her picture of how things should be, or else. Since none of us kids could live up to her expectations, we weren't worthy of love or being loved for who we were. I realized it had taken me a lot of delving into the past to understand that she was not the loving mother I wanted, but that I couldn't change who she was. She was limited by her experience and her own reality. She was simply missing the tools to be a better mother. She was asleep. I didn't get what I wanted and that was that.

I realized, though, that I had accepted my mother's critical voice as my own voice. It was not her in my head anymore. It was some part of me that reflected her thoughts back. It was not her fault anymore. Maybe it never had been. It was me. I had believed what she said, and allowed my thoughts, based on her mistaken beliefs, to control the way I acted in this world. No matter what I did, I still felt I could never be good enough or nice enough or generous enough or smart enough. So instead, I was really hard on myself and yet I thought I knew what was right for everyone else, just like she did. Then I would be disappointed or judgmental about myself and others when they didn't live up to my standards. Now, that was crazy thinking.

I came back from my reverie and looked around the darkened room, illuminated only by the computer screen and a single lamp across the way. I started thinking again about what Jeffrey had said, and I wondered what was my gift, my light for the world? Gracie had followed me and was laying about five feet away, looking at me with that intense look she got when she wanted to communicate something to me.

"What did Jeffrey mean today, Gracie?" I asked.

This is a time of change on this planet. Nature is in balance and will survive; the form may be different, but it will survive. The being that is earth will survive. The question is whether humans can be a part of that survival. Can humans transform their consciousness and learn to work with nature; to listen and give love to the earth and to all beings on the earth? Can humans begin to understand their partnership with animals and all beings who reside here? Can humans truly understand their partnership with the earth itself and move towards survival for all? It requires an understanding of the inter-

connection of all the parts. Everyone needs to radiate love and see all as pure and whole. That is the experiment. That is the shift in energy and the shift in consciousness. Don't fight against what is. Work together to bring about change so everyone wins. I never have understood humans saying things like Fight for Peace. Those thoughts don't go together. Be Peace and that is what will be around you.

Think of the earth as a huge being, like a gigantic, gigantic person, or a gigantic organism, with all of its living, breathing, integral parts, composed of different combinations of energy. Just as the human body has trillions of cells and organisms on it and in it, comprised of different forms of energy, so does the earth. When the parts of the body work in balance, the human body functions perfectly. It fights disease; it makes new blood; it makes new cells, and the cells all cooperate. The human body moves and does amazing things without any thought or effort. It's truly a miracle.

When things are out of balance in the body, sometimes the body attacks itself. It is all interconnected, but sometimes parts do not function as they were designed to. They get out of whack and do things that are counter to their true natural state of health and well-being. So too, the earth. Humans are connected to the earth and are an integral part of the well-being of this giant organism. Humans, animals, plants are the organisms on the earth who are supposed to be working in cooperation so that the earth remains in its natural and healthy state. The earth was designed perfectly, just as all beings were. We all have our part to play in the health of our mother earth. But many of the organisms on the earth, the humans, have gotten out of balance. Humans put chemicals, drugs, and toxins into their bodies, which can cause inflammation or disease. These things can change the metabolic functioning of the body, just as putting toxic chemicals into the ground can change the metabolic functioning of the earth. Humans take more than they need and use more than they give back. They fight with each other and attack each other, just like cancer cells in the body fight good cells. There are cancers or inflammation at work in the *earth and on the earth too. Humans have free will and can make a choice to live in balance or not. To live in peace or not. To love and not hate. Those are choices all humans can make.*

I really needed to think about what Gracie had just said and what it meant.

CHAPTER 33

GRACIE ON HAVING FAITH

"Gracie, why is this book so important to you?" I said to her one day as she lay next to me on the living room couch.

I am trying to tell you that I am your partner in writing this book. It is the reason I have come here to be with you, and I really want you to work on it. I want to work on it together, and I need to protect you from everything. I am here to serve and protect, but not in a policeman sort of way.

There are lots of changes taking place on this planet, and we all need to work with them to make this a better place to live. The energy is changing rapidly, and people must learn to live in harmony with nature and animals and everything around them. Many do not understand how we are all connected, on a very cellular level, and we need to write it in an easy to understand fashion. Even if just one person gets it, it will be worth the effort. But I really know it must be done.

The book is already written. I know what to say, but sometimes you are a little thick and you don't get it. Also, there has got to be time for naps. We can't go, go, go all day long. I get tired. So sometimes I just want to lie down by your side and be very still. People don't do that often enough as far as I can tell. Everyone seems to be rushing around at some frenetic pace, and they are missing the beauty of what is right under their noses. That is what is important—what is right in front of you, right under your nose. Enjoy that; be one with that.

I really need you to know that time is running out to make change on this planet. You must use all of your light and love and put it back into the ground. Call on the nature spirits and elementals to help. Ask the angels too. They want to help and they want to be asked. We need to work together to restore harmony, to get things back in balance. If you just ask nature to help, it will figure out what to do.

But you really need to know that I am part angel. I say only part, but that is not entirely accurate. It is very difficult to explain how it works, but it does. Many things you must just take on faith.

> My religion is very simple. My religion is kindness.
> -Dalai Lama

CHAPTER 34

RESPECT FOR ALL LIFE

The cooler fall weather had arrived, and I was picking apples in the front garden with the dogs and Roy, who had returned home. My mind was elsewhere, thinking about things I had to do, including a pending doctor's appointment to remove a particularly persistent squamous cell skin cancer on my hand. Every time it was cut out, it kept growing back, necessitating a special Mohs surgical procedure and a skin graft. I had made an appointment for the surgery the following week. I'd had to make arrangements for the dogs and everyone in my life since the doctor told me I would not be able to use my left hand at all for a few weeks to make sure the skin graft took.

But I really wanted to make applesauce and put some up for the winter before that occurred. Gracie, Walter, and Lily were all sitting calmly under the apple tree, just waiting for apples to drop so they could gobble them up. They had already picked and eaten all of the apples from the lower branches, so now they had to be patient and rely on human error for any treats that day. Everyone was quiet. I haphazardly put my hand out to pick an apple and accidentally squished a bee.

"I'm so sorry," I said tenderly and lovingly to the bee, as I felt the sting radiate through my hand and then quickly subside. I noticed that the more I transmitted sincere feelings of love to the cosmos, the more the pain dissipated.

"What happened?" Roy said.

"I squished a bee by mistake, and it stung me. Now that bee is going to die because I was not paying attention. It was out there, minding its own business, doing a service to the world by pollinating the plants, and my not being in the present moment killed it."

"Oh, too bad," Roy said quietly.

"My normal reaction would be to get mad at the bee for stinging me, but I know it didn't want to sting me. And now that it did, it has to die. I did that. So now I'm trying to send it love and gratitude for all that it did and send it off with a blessing. Not that that's enough, but it's all I know to do."

Roy just looked at me without comment and continued picking apples.

I could tell by Gracie's gentle movements that she was trying not to disturb the peaceful energy, but she wanted to talk to me.

When someone stings you, love them. Nature will do what it will do to them, in its time, but you must feel love, compassion, and respect for all life, including the being who stung you. The more love you send forth, the quicker the sting goes away. Also, accidents do happen; we are not perfect. You have a good heart and are trying. Your intention is good. Besides, I see you rescuing many bees from drowning, so you have built up good bee karma. Just try to be and pay attention to the present moment, and you will do better. I would really like an apple if you would throw me one.

I tossed an apple toward Gracie, and she caught it with a slight hop in the air and a smile on her face.

"You know, I really could do a lot better," I said to Roy and Gracie.

"What do you mean?" Roy replied.

"I talk a good game about saving ants and feeling the connection with the Universe, yada, yada, but I really don't like ticks."

"Yeah. So?"

"So, every time I find one on the dogs, I take it off and squish it. Now, that isn't very nice, is it? I apologize and send it off with blessings and all, but I'm not sure 'I'm sorry, little tick' gives me the right to chop its head off. But I do it anyway. I become the self-appointed executioner because I can't find one single good thing about a tick. And talk about judgmental."

"You're funny," Roy said and started to chuckle. "Most people wouldn't even give it a second thought. Everyone hates ticks. You know, though, they are food for some birds," he added as an afterthought.

"I have been trying a different tack lately. Instead of hating them and being fearful of them for the dogs, I'm trying to send them a love vibe. I think maybe my sense of fear has been drawing them closer. So I'm not giving them so much energy anymore."

"And how has that been working out?" Roy said.

"Pretty good," I said with a smile. "I haven't seen a tick in weeks."

ooooo

I couldn't sleep one night and got up out of bed, trying not to disturb Bill. All of a sudden I realized that Gracie was wandering with me, step by step, through the darkened house.

"Gracie, do you want to work on your book now? Is that why you're following me? I'm so sorry I haven't worked on it for awhile," I said. "I don't know what the problem is with me. I pick up the book and then put it down. I get fantastic information from you, and from Jeffrey, work on your book for a few days, and then I put it down again for months. I let chores get in the way. I say I am going to do it and then I don't. I'm sorry. You're committed and faithful," I told her. "I get distracted and jump from thing to thing. It's like I'm afraid to commit to the book or anything else. If I don't commit, I can't fail."

She looked up at me.

"Is there anything you want people to know, Gracie? I will really try to listen right now. It helps for me to hear things again and again. It takes a long time for things to sink in with me."

Love, laughter, loyalty, and gratitude. That's it in simple terms. Love is all there is. I have said this before, but it's the only thing that's important. Please feel that deep within your heart. Don't let the negativity of those around you affect who you are or change you. Be yourself and let that God part shine through you and out into the world. Be of service to others and act from the heart.

Laugh long and laugh often. It is food for the soul and will keep you young. Laugh at yourself and everything around you. You are so hard on yourself that you don't even see how wonderful you are. Try not to be critical or judgmental of yourself or others.

Loyalty is a misused or misguided principle. Loyalty is what I feel for you, but it goes so deep you cannot imagine. Loyalty goes beyond just being there for a friend or being supportive, and it goes beyond sticking with someone even if they do something you don't like. Actually if you do that, you're just learning to not be so judgmental. It means being committed and loyal to every thing you undertake to do. No matter how menial the task, you must do it with total commitment and joy; you must do the best job you can with everything you undertake, even if it's picking up horse manure. There is no task more or less sacred than another, so be joyful with whatever is in front of you. Be loyal to the present so that you do not miss anything that is going on. It's all wondrous and joyous.

And be thankful for any challenges or circumstances, which on their face may seem negative, because they are opportunities for you to grow and learn. Be loyal to those seemingly negative times too, because they are equally as important as the happy times. They may open the space for other things to happen. Be in the present moment, which is all we really have anyway, with all of your senses working. And remember, things change. That's the only thing you can count on.

Trust, have faith, everything is in divine order.

I probably have more to add on these topics, but I do not feel so well. You promised we would work on the book yesterday and we didn't, and tonight I just can't do too much. (Dictated 2/06/09)

"Wow," I said after waiting a minute in silence. "That's a lot. It sure doesn't feel like there's any kind of order in my life, Gracie, let alone divine order. Is there anything else?"

There is a lot more, but not now, we need to go back to bed and get some rest. Oh yeah, always be grateful for a good meal and all that went into it.

> When Siddhartha listened attentively to this river, to this song of a thousand voices; when he did not listen to the sorrow or laughter, when he did not bind his soul to any one particular voice and absorb it in his Self, but heard them all, the whole, the unity; then the great song of a thousand voices consisted of one word: Om—perfection.
> -Hermann Hesse, *Siddhartha*

CHAPTER 35

GRACIE ON ONENESS

I had been reading about the elements and trying to understand their significance in this journey I found myself on. So I thought I would ask Gracie and see what she had to say. I found her asleep under the dining room table and sat down next to her. I gently placed my hand on her side and she woke up. I was surprised she was so alert and ready to communicate.

The elements are very easy. Earth, wind, fire, and water are within you and outside you. It's all the same. We are all the same; we are all connected. That is the supreme example of oneness. Don't you get it? There is no separation of man and the elements, or man and nature; there never has been. Man has created that separation, and now it's time to come back and really feel how we are all connected. If you don't feel it, then just pretend. That's better than nothing. Please really try to feel this deep in your soul because it's very important. Know that you are the created and the creator; you have extreme powers to heal and make change. Everyone does, they just don't feel it.

See the perfection; feel the perfection; see order in chaos; see the beauty around you and be grateful for it; acknowledge the wonderment on a continual basis. You will be amazed at what can and will happen. Life is awesome; you just must be there in the present moment. Don't miss anything that is going on around you, and just go for it if you feel compelled to. Don't analyze everything so much. Be more spontaneous in your life, more like us. (Dictated 1/29/09)

CHAPTER 36

DON ALVERTO TAXO

One day I got an email from one of my Buddhist friends, Anne, who forwarded an email she had received, discussing the teachings of Don Alverto Taxo, a master Iachak (shaman) from Ecuador. It appeared to be an email from a friend of Anne's who had attended a lecture by Don Alverto, in which Alverto described that this was a time of great transformation on the planet and the effect this would have on all of us.

The email from Anne's friend read:

> To ensure a transformation on this planet, the world needs energy from us, a connection to life, a feeling of a gratitude, not a thought about gratitude or a feeling one should be grateful, but a gratitude that begins with the senses.
>
> Alverto offered two exercises. First, when we shower, he said to take in the sensation of the water all over our bodies and let it penetrate, and let the enjoyment of the water in as well. He suggested that we 'see' or 'imagine' the water going into our pores and washing the inside, the organs, and even our thoughts and feelings.
>
> Second, as often as you can, he said to take a piece of fruit, your favorite, and hold it in your hand. Take it in with your eyes. Think about how the fruit came to be. It started from a seed that was planted in the ground. Then roots took hold, a tree grew, branches grew, etc. Think of the months and the days it took to create this miracle in your hand. Think of the process and all the people it took to have it finally arrive in your

hand. Then smell it. Let the smell fill you. Allow the sense of gratitude for this miracle to grow in you, and then eat the fruit. Savoring it. And then allow the gratitude out into the world.

He went on about the importance of this feeling of gratitude, especially now that we were in a time of great change. He claimed the energy moving through all of us is particularly strong. He spoke very seriously about the danger of negativity, anger or fear especially now.

Now for the really fun part. He said to give to the full moon all of our anger, fears, and concerns—anything that stands in the way of this gratitude, and anything that stands in the way of imagining your dreams coming true. He said the moon feeds on this energy and in doing so transforms it to something positive. And he said that if we were to give all of our negativity to the moon, we would discover something new within us.

"Those are cool ideas," I thought out loud. "What a great idea to give thanks to the water when you're taking a shower and to be grateful for a fruit that way."

I decided to pass the email on to a few friends who I knew would appreciate it. I got an almost immediate response from my friend Karen, who lived in Los Angeles.

"He sounds wonderful," Karen replied. "Why don't you invite him to come here and do a workshop? I think people would like to hear what he has to say. I'll help you put it together, sort of co-sponsor him with you."

"Great. I'll see what I can do."

I emailed Anne and suggested we invite Alverto to Ojai to put on a workshop. I mentioned that my friend Karen was interested in co-sponsoring an event. Anne didn't know Karen but replied, "That sounds great, let's do it."

Bill was out in the garden when I went to look for him. "Hey, Bill," I called up the driveway.

"Yeah, I'm over here. What do you need?"

"What do you think about having a shaman from Ecuador come

here to do a workshop and stay with us for a week or so?"

"Whatever you want," Bill said. "It's OK with me."

"Would you participate in the workshop?"

"Maybe. I'll think about it."

"OK," I said. "I'm going to look into it and see about inviting him then."

I looked at Alverto's website and watched a YouTube video about his teachings, which stressed the importance of gratitude and connecting with nature and all of the elements. It was fascinating, and I recognized the similarity to some of Gracie's teachings. I learned that the Shamanic Council of South America had given him the highest honor and responsibility of Master Iachak in 1989. He was a teacher and healer of the Atis people from the Cotopaxi region of Ecuador. His elders believed that he was the one from their area to share their indigenous wisdom with people in the north, based on a five-hundred-year-old prophecy that said harmony would occur on earth when the condor (the indigenous heart from the south) and the eagle (the industrial mind of the north) flew together in the sky. They felt the time referred to in the prophecy was now.

The prophecy, coupled with the fact that a friend of Anne's knew Alverto, was enough for me to want to learn more and to invite him to come to Ojai. He didn't speak English, and I still only spoke gardener Spanish, so I contacted him through an interpreter to ask if he would come to California to share some of his wisdom. Alverto said yes, that he would like to come to California.

The day was set, tickets were purchased, and we had a growing group of people who were interested in attending his workshop. It all happened very quickly and easily. A few months into the process, when his arrival was imminent, Anne and I discussed final details of the various lectures and workshops we had arranged. That's when I discovered that Anne didn't even know who had authored the initial email. She'd just liked the content, which had been sent to her from a friend of a friend, and so she passed it on to me because she thought I would like it too. She thought Karen knew Alverto and that's why Karen wanted to co-sponsor the event.

When I realized that none of us actually knew don Alverto and our whole journey of putting on a seminar with a shaman from Ecuador was based on a series of misunderstood emails, my rational mind took over.

"What the heck am I doing inviting a shaman from Ecuador, who no one knows, who doesn't speak English, to come stay in my home for a week?" I asked myself.

Like many things in my life, I realized it was supposed to happen, even though it didn't make sense. By then the train had left the station anyway, so to speak, and I just took a leap of faith.

As I thought about it, Alverto had to take a leap of faith himself. Here he got a call out of the blue from some lady in California who wanted him to come to her house and teach the magic of gratitude. And he said "yes" without hesitation or question. At a minimum he had to trust that someone would actually be at the airport to pick him up or he'd be stranded.

ooooo

On her way from Los Angeles, Karen picked up Alverto at LAX and drove him to Ojai. When he arrived, he seemed to fit right in. It was like I had known him for years. He was part of the family without any effort. Gracie and Walter were particularly drawn to him and followed him everywhere. He had an easy-going way about him, speaking from the heart and constantly expressing his gratitude for everything by placing his hands over his heart and then opening them to the divine with a smile that changed the energy wherever he was. Even though we had a translator, it wasn't difficult for me to understand what he was trying to convey. It was obvious he was connected on a very deep level to all of nature, and he wanted to share that ability to feel a connection with everyone.

We had scheduled a long weekend of public and private events to introduce don Alverto to the Ojai community. At the first public event, he explained that he was here because it was time for the Eagle and the Condor to fly together, in harmony, to fulfill a prophecy. He stressed how important it was for us to connect with our indigenous hearts, so that we could find that balance of heart and mind within each individual and then allow it to spread out into the world.

The next day a small group gathered at our house to begin a three-day intensive workshop with Alverto, which involved discussions and exercises designed to open our hearts to connect with the elements and Mother Earth. During one exercise, Alverto suggested that the group wander along a little stream by our house because the water had a message for us, something to teach us. Walter decided to come and followed the group to the stream.

"Look for a connection with water," Alverto said. "When you feel a connection, let your heart feel what it feels. Remember, your body is more than 60 percent water, so it will respond to the love you send to water too." Alverto told us to sit, observe, and make friends with the water. "Introduce yourselves to the water, as if you were greeting a friend, and be open to hear what the water has to say."

Apparently Walter wasn't interested in making a new friend that day. He had only one thing on his mind, and it wasn't learning from the stream. He had his own calling, and he up and disappeared. I didn't worry about him because I knew he could find his way home.

Alverto was trying to get us to understand one important message of water. "When water flows and there's any obstruction, the water doesn't go back. It continues to look for another path … If we have difficult circumstances in our life, we can remember how water won't go back. It will look for the exit. It will rise into a space and look for the exit with harmony, softly. It can be slow or fast, but naturally it will proceed."

We had a delightful time communing with the water. Everyone learned something different. I even thought I saw a few little beings hovering over the stream. Since I still had a hard time believing in such things, my logical mind tried to explain it away.

"They are probably just some type of bugs," I thought. The second I "thought" about it, the beings/bugs disappeared.

When I explained this to Alverto, he laughed and said, "Yes, sometimes thinking gets in the way of seeing. We must learn to balance the heart and the mind to see in a different way."

We'd been sitting by the stream for about 30 or 40 minutes when Walter reappeared by my side. I looked at him with a smile and then noticed that his stomach looked extremely swollen, but I didn't give it too much thought as we started back. Walter was always finding something to eat: apples, avocados, whatever. His appetite was insatiable. When we arrived at the house, the group sat on the back deck to share experiences. Walter lay down, exhausted, his belly bulging.

Alverto explained, "Just as we do not see illness when we heal a human or an animal, we see balance and perfection, we must always see the water as pure. If we see water as a pure, alive being—not the contamination, not the illness—then transformation will occur. Water will heal itself through the love it feels all around."

I thought this idea sounded good. I vaguely remembered something Jeffrey had said about seeing things as pure that I hadn't understood at the time. Maybe this was what he had meant. I was still pondering this, but I did know that sending positive, loving energy is empowering.

A few minutes later the phone rang. It was Maggie. "Is Walter home?" she asked.

"Yes. He was gone for awhile but he wandered back a little bit ago."

"Is he OK?"

"He seems fine," I said. "A little fat, though. What's up?"

"Well, don't be surprised if he gets sick."

"Why? What happened?"

"He came over here, let himself in—without anyone noticing—and ate every baked good I had on the counter, including two of the three loaves of bread I'd just taken out of the oven and had cooling for my company this afternoon," she said laughing. "Oh, also a bag of cookies I bought at the farmers market and several croissants left over from breakfast."

"Oh my God. Did you stop him?"

"No, I was too late. I got the last loaf out of his mouth."

"Oh Maggie, I'm so sorry. I'll go right to the store and get you replacements."

"Oh no, don't worry, no problem. I still have that one loaf left. I'll just cut away Walter's bite out of it. No one will ever know." She laughed mischievously. "I just thought you should know Walter might be sick."

Maggie's family included Walter's brother, Duke, so Walter was part of her extended family. I knew my friend wasn't mad. No matter what Walter did, everyone still loved him. He just had that type of personality and his heart was huge.

"I can't believe he walked three quarters of a mile to your house, let himself in, ate what he wanted, and then walked all the way home. That's unbelievable," was all I could think of to say. "Now at least I know why he looked so fat and was having trouble walking."

Maggie just laughed.

"We're in the middle of that seminar with Alverto I told you about. It's really great. This is the best leap of faith I've taken in a long time. I've learned so much about gratitude and making friends with plants and water. It's really interesting to do some of his exercises to listen to the plants."

"Oh, I forgot the seminar is going on," Maggie said. "Sorry I called."

"No worries, we're on a lunch break. I'm really hoping to learn more about communicating with animals," I said. "Alverto's going to talk about that tomorrow night," I told Maggie. "Want to come?"

"Maybe," Maggie said. "I'll let you get back. Bye."

The following day Alverto led us up the dirt road to the labyrinth, where we gave thanks, released anything we wanted to get rid of to the surrounding mountains, and talked to some of the plants. The dogs came with us to the labyrinth and had their own pow-wow.

Then Alverto had us walk backwards, with our eyes closed, all the way back down the hairpin turns on the rutted dirt road. I had to cheat in a few places and open my eyes to make sure I wasn't going to fall off the edge, but it was a great exercise in feeling the earth beneath our feet and trusting our senses.

The whole weekend was amazing, filled with drumming, ceremonies, and private healings, and exercises designed to help us connect with nature and all of the elements. I particularly liked the exercise in which Alverto instructed us to go up to any flower or plant we were attracted to, introduce ourselves, and enter a dialogue with this new friend. He told us to just observe what information we got from the plant without judgment and to ask questions as if we were talking to a friend. It was amazing to hear what some of the flowers told people when we regrouped and shared our experience. Bill participated some in the weekend; Walter never did get sick.

ooooo

A few weeks later, Bill was taking the dogs for a walk and did a loop past Maggie and Fred's house. Everyone returned home after the walk except Walter.

"Hey, Bill, where's Walter?" I asked as Bill walked down the driveway minus one dog.

"I don't know where he is. They were all with me, and then he just disappeared. I looked everywhere and called and called, but he never came. So I just left him and continued home. I'll take the quad out and go look for him. Silly dog."

"OK, thanks," I said as Bill walked to the garage and got on the quad. "I'm sure he'll turn up somewhere, but you know I worry."

Just then Walter came walking down the driveway. His eyes lit up as he saw everyone looking for him, and he picked up the pace to get close.

"Where were you, you silly goose?" I asked him.

Walter just smiled.

The next morning Maggie and I were out walking the dogs. "Hey, Julie," Maggie said. "Did you know Walter came over for a visit yesterday?"

"Oh, so that's where he was. Bill took him for a walk, and he went missing for awhile."

"I was busy on a conference call so I wasn't paying attention to the dogs. I sort of heard someone come through the doggy door, but I didn't think too much about it. I thought it was just Duke."

"Oh, no," I said. "I hope he didn't eat any more of your bread."

"No, the bread was all accounted for. I started putting it up really high where Walter can't reach it. When I was done with my call, I wandered out of my office and I found Walter up on top of the pool table, all fours, eating the cat food, though," she said. "It was hilarious."

"Real funny," I said, embarrassed at Walter's behavior, but amused by the image of all 145-pounds of Walter standing in the middle of the pool table, eating a tiny portion of salmon and chicken cat food.

"I made him get off the table. He walked nonchalantly over to Duke, said goodbye, and then he just left. I guess he thought the play date was over."

And now here is my secret, a very simple secret: It is only with the heart that one can see rightly; what is essential is invisible to the eye.
-Antoine de Saint-Exupéry, *The Little Prince*

CHAPTER 37

GRACIE AND THE ELVES

I noticed Gracie lying on the grass, facing backwards from how she would normally lie on the lawn, staring intently at something.

"What are you looking at, Gracie?" I asked. She just continued to stare at this one spot on the grass as if she wanted me to see something.

"What is it?"

I decided I would just stare at the spot, too. As I quieted down and simply stared, I noticed the grass was moving, but not in synchronicity as if the wind were blowing it.

As a matter of fact, there was no wind; the air was perfectly still, and yet the grass was moving, being pushed down and then springing back at different angles and places in one little section of the lawn. There was a lot of movement on the lawn in that spot. I was confused. What was making the lawn move like that? What was Gracie staring at?

You can see them. Don't concentrate so much. Let your heart do the seeing.

Then all of a sudden I realized what Gracie was looking at. It was little nature spirits, dancing on the lawn, bouncing around, leaving imprints as they moved from place to place. I couldn't see them, but I knew in my heart that was what it was.

"All I can see are the footprints, the impact. But I know they're here,"

I said happily to Gracie, thinking that this was at least a start and that perhaps one day I too would see the garden workers themselves. "Ah, yes, them elves," I thought.

"Thanks, Gracie," I said as I turned to go into the house, wanting to commit this miraculous viewing to paper.

CHAPTER 38

WORKING AGAIN

I was trying to make time for Gracie's dictations again. I was really trying to listen and write it down before she got too old. We were sitting together on the couch, with her head in my lap, when she started in.

I am really happy that you are working on the book again and that you are finishing it. I have said quite a lot. Just remember about oneness; how everything you do affects everyone else, even those who are far away; even those who you do not know. The same way that any positive or compassionate thing that you do affects the whole; it affects every living thing, every inanimate thing; it affects the earth. As the earth heals, so too will the people on it heal. That is why it's so important for you to protect Mother Earth; be conscious of your actions and how they affect the earth because you are affecting every living thing. The earth is life, the earth is love, the earth is you and everyone else.

This is a time of great change. Be that change. As Gandhi said, "Be the change you want to see in this world." I can hear you wondering how do I know what Gandhi said? I can hear you questioning yourself again about whether I am really communicating with you. Don't go there. Just be with it; don't be afraid of what people will think. Gandhi is part of the universal intelligence, just like Buddha or Christ or Mohammed or the Dalai Lama. These beings and their wisdom are part of me, just as they are part of you; be in touch with that universal wisdom. Access it; use it to change the things that are going on. Carry light and love to all and for all. That's all I have to say for now.
(Dictated 1/30/09)

Gracie, what's it like getting older? I asked

It just is. Humans put such connotations on it. They stress, they fear, they worry. Things are different, slower; things hurt a little more, but there is nothing to fear.

People seem to worry a lot about getting old, but there is nothing you can do to stop it. Life just progresses. It is fluid and constantly changing. Getting old is part of the process. Our physical bodies wear out, but our spirits do not. Change is part of the process. Worrying or complaining doesn't help, and it certainly doesn't change what is going on. Actually worry can just serve to attract the negative things that you say you don't want to happen.

When I look like I am sleeping, sometimes I'm really out having a grand ole time in other ethereal planes. I travel to other places and play since this physical body doesn't allow it anymore in this plane. It's OK. Don't be sad about me. Or be sad if you need to, but remember I'll always be with you.

You also have to be in that moment of getting older. I like to have you around more. It is comforting to me to have you near. But I am not afraid. I have done what I am supposed to do. I have been a good and compassionate being on this earth, and I have tried to explain my wisdom in order to be of service to others. So now I can relax and let you finish this book. I know you can do it.

CHAPTER 39

CRYSTAL CALLS

Crystal called one evening from her new location in Utah. She'd told me a few months before that she'd fallen and cracked some ribs, but I hadn't heard from her for several weeks to find out how recovery was going. I knew she had just moved, but I hadn't received news about how the move went either.

"Did you get moved? How are your ribs feeling?" I said quickly when I answered the phone.

"Well actually, I'm in the hospital. It wasn't cracked ribs like I thought. I don't believe it, but the doctors say I have lung cancer."

"Wait a minute, back up. I thought you fell and cracked your ribs."

"Yes, that's what I thought," she said pensively. "I kept soaking in a hot bath and would feel a little better. I just thought the bones were taking a long time to heal. When we moved here last week, I was in a lot of pain, so I finally went to a doctor. Now they say I have Stage 4 lung cancer."

"What does that mean?" I said calmly, but inwardly stressed about her health and well-being. I did a quick mental analysis of the situation, got into 'what can I do to help' mode, and said, "So, what can I do? What's the treatment plan?"

"I don't know yet. They're still assessing things. I can't live here, in Utah, though. The boxes aren't even unpacked yet, and I don't have the strength."

"Could you live with your kids?"

"No, they don't have room."

"Do you want to come to my house in Ojai to recuperate?" I asked without hesitation or thinking.

"Really, that would be great. I love it at your house. All those beautiful trees and plants … Gracie …" She trailed off and then started again. "I'm sure I'll recover quickly with all of that nature around and then I can figure out what to do."

"Let me ask Bill, but I'm sure it'll be fine."

"Did you ask your inner voice?" Crystal said.

I didn't answer.

"I'll need a hospital bed," she said.

As we ended our conversation I said, "I'll call you tomorrow to find out what the doctors say."

I asked Bill. I told him that I couldn't just let Crystal be alone with no one to care for her, and he agreed. The next day I called her and found out that there was no treatment plan because the cancer was too advanced. Instead, the doctors suggested putting Crystal on hospice and keeping her comfortable with pain medication. The thought of her suffering and dying was overwhelming.

"You do understand what hospice means, don't you?" I asked Crystal, having recently completed a home hospice care program for volunteers. I couldn't bring myself to say that it meant some doctor had said she had less than six months to live.

"Yes, but you know I don't believe in dying," she said calmly. "I've been teaching about that for years. Part of my program has always been overcoming the negative, dense thought forms on this planet that people have created, and a lot of that stems from people's views about physical death. Just get me to your house, and I'll be fine in a few weeks. I'm not giving death any energy."

I had heard her talk about the no-death program before, but those concepts were beyond my understanding. I always thought perhaps it was a metaphorical concept.

I set about remodeling the guestroom to accommodate a hospital bed, got the bed and hospice arranged, and Bill and I modified the van so we could bring Crystal home. A week later we drove to the hospital in St. George, Utah, got Crystal released, piled her in the back of the van onto the make-shift bed we had created, and Bill drove us back to Ojai. Crystal was in tremendous amounts of pain, and it was a stressful, long ride, but we made it, and she moved into our guestroom.

We had some amazing moments over the next four weeks, both physically and spiritually. I learned how to give medication, how to feed and care for someone who is dying, and I learned to see through the pain. I also learned patience. Crystal rarely complained except about wanting to get up and go outside to sit in the sunshine so she could get well. That never happened. We would try to get her outside, but she just couldn't make it. Gracie and the other dogs were wonderful with her. They took turns keeping her company and laying by her bed. Bill was incredible through it all; he never complained about all the commotion and visitors in the house; and he constantly helped me move and reposition Crystal in bed.

Crystal had some amazing visions that she shared with us. One night she said she talked with a gorilla in a business suit about how she could make money selling pounds of pain. Another time she said she was going to see Jane. The following morning Jane called from her archeology sight in Africa where she was working and said Crystal had come to her the night before and had held her and comforted her. She said it was so real that she had to call to tell us. When I asked Crystal if she had actually gone to Africa the night before, she just smiled and said, "Must have."

One night as I administered her pain medicine and turned the lights out so she could sleep, I noticed Crystal's breaths were extremely shallow and weak. I gave her some of her breathing medicine, and that seemed to help. I sat next to her for awhile in the darkness and held her hand. I could feel love pouring from her to me. Between the pauses in her breath, in a kind but barely audible tone, she said, "Remember, you have things to do in this world. It's important. Help the animals. Give them a voice." I really didn't know what she'd meant, and I never got to ask. She passed away quietly in her sleep that night and didn't explain that statement before she made her transition. Maybe she'd meant writing the book with Gracie, but I was never certain. Deep down, I thought it was something else. It took me awhile to integrate the experience and feel the grief.

CHAPTER 40

PET THERAPY

"Come on, Walter, let's go," I said as I grabbed a leash from the hook outside the kitchen door. Walter sat up.

"I'm taking you to visit some sick people in the extended care facility behind the hospital. You have been approved by the Humane Society for their pet therapy program, so today's the day we start."

Walter stared at me with a "huh" expression.

"Don't worry, you'll be good at it. I know you get in trouble at home, but you're a great, loving dog. Besides, I think you need a job," I added.

I piled Walter into the car and drove off. Walter took up the entire back seat, but he kept trying to stick his head between the front seats so he could be closer to me and I could pet his ears. When we got to the hospital, I put on his leash. Being an agreeable soul, he went along with the leash idea even though he wasn't used to it. He bounded up the steps, dragging me along, as if he knew where he was going, even though he had never been there before. I opened the door to four or five astonished faces that just stared at Walter, not sure what he was going to do.

"Oh, my gosh. That's the biggest, most beautiful dog I've ever seen," said one of the nurses.

I had given Walter two baths the day before, and his shiny black coat glistened. The twenty or so avocados he ate every day didn't hurt his coat either. The two baths had been necessary because after the first one, Walter must have decided that he smelled too clean. He'd immediately found the smelliest stuff he could find on the ranch—bear poop, some decaying animal, or some combination of the two—and rolled in it. I imagined it was his protective instinct to disappear into the smells around him, to blend in with his surroundings so no one knew he was there. Although that gigantic black figure was able to blend quite easily into the night, he was very visible in the antiseptic hospital waiting room.

"What's his name?" the nurse asked.

"Walter," I said as I signed us in as 'pet therapy' visitors.

"What a perfect name for him," the nurse replied, studying Walter closely.

As I was writing our names in the visitors' book, Walter tugged at the leash and pulled me over to an obviously paralyzed man in a wheelchair. Walter put his head over the arm of the wheelchair, snuggled his face against the patient's face, and planted a big kiss right on the man's pale, exposed cheek. Walter's kiss was met with sounds of glee, and I knew by the glint in this man's eyes that he loved dogs in general, but at that moment, Walter in particular. But I thought I needed to make sure.

"Hi," I said to the stranger in the wheelchair. "I hope you like dogs. If you don't, we can go away. This is Walter."

The man smiled kindly out of one side of his mouth. "Yesh, I lub dogs," he mumbled quietly. "Hi, Wa ... ter."

"I'm Julie. What's your name?"

"Da—vid," he replied slowly.

"How are you feeling today, David?" I asked.

"Not ... sho ... good," he replied.

"Oh, I'm sorry," I said.

"But ... I sure ... like ... Wa ... ter," David said as he struggled to put his crippled hand out to pet Walter's head. Walter didn't miss a beat. He got as close as he could until David's hand rested on his head, and David could feel the glorious black fur and soft ears. "Ahhh," David sighed. "I ... mish ... my dog."

I chatted with David and painstakingly found out that he had had a stroke and had to leave his two dogs at home, and he was worried about them. His daughter was taking care of them, but he just wasn't sure if it was working out. Walter lay by David's feet, one of which drooped lazily toward the floor and rested against Walter, the other stayed on the metal footrest of the wheelchair.

After awhile, I said, "Well, David, it was nice to meet you. Take care of yourself. Perhaps we'll see you again. Actually, I hope you get to go home and we won't see you again unless it's around town. But we need to go visit some of the other people here before Walter gets too tired. Bye for now."

"Come on, Walter," I said. "Let's go."

Walter jumped up, and we walked into a room just down the hall. A little old lady whose white hair lay tasseled on her pillow awoke as we entered. Her ashen face came to life as she sat up quickly in her hospital bed, in spite of her apparent infirmities, and exclaimed, "Oh my goodness, what a fabulous dog. Come over here, big fella. Get up on my bed," she said as she patted a place next to her.

Walter looked at me for permission, and I shook my head no. He seemed to know better than to climb on the bed, but he trotted right over to her bedside, put his big head on the pillow right next to her old wizened face, and kissed her translucent cheek, missing all of the tubes hanging around her. No judgment, no fear, and no questions about her missing front teeth or her slightly decaying smell: just pure love given and received. And so the morning went.

Walter was incredible at bringing joy to everyone in the hospital, patients, staff, and other visitors alike. He treated them all equally and acted as if each one of them was a long lost friend of his. After a few hours, I knew Walter was tired. He'd been an incredible dog, an incredible being, and an incredible teacher and healer.

As I drove home, I realized Walter had been a great example for me. The books I had been reading by the Dalai Lama explain that the Dalai Lama greets strangers and dear friends all the same because there's not much difference—we're all the same. I never really understood what the Dalai Lama was talking about before, but Walter put that in action. It didn't matter to him if someone had Alzheimer's, a broken leg, or was succumbing to old age. He didn't see any differences. He greeted them all the same, with love and respect. I wished I could be more like him.

Even though I hadn't heard too many complaints from the patients, it had been a tough day seeing all of those people stuck in bed or in a wheelchair.

I'm really thankful I'm not sick, I thought. I'm so lucky and blessed.

> He was just a hired hand
> Workin' on the dreams he planned to try,
> The days go by...
> Take another shot of courage
> Wonder why the right words never come,
> You just feel numb.
> -The Eagles, *Tequila Sunrise*

CHAPTER 41

A DARK CLOUD

I'd sensed that Bill had been depressed for quite some time. He rarely smiled or laughed any more, and when he did, it seemed forced. He hardly ever talked to me about how he was feeling, or for that matter, about anything all. When we did talk, it was about mundane things. He was always polite, but it seemed like he took a contrary view to whatever I said. No matter what I did, I felt it was never right, never enough. It was hard to explain, but I just sensed a dark negative cloud over him most of the time.

One day he told me, "Sometimes I just feel like the handyman around here." And I hadn't answered, but a part of me thought he was right. Didn't a lot of relationships become like that? One cooks and does the dishes, and the other takes out the trash? Shared responsibilities. Was that so bad? He was such a nice, easygoing guy, that it had taken me a long time to see that he wasn't supporting me in feeding my soul. And I wasn't supporting him either. Our relationship was superficial, but I had been seduced and distracted by the day-to-day activities, and I tried not to think about it too much.

I knew sometimes I felt unhappy, too, but I wasn't sure why. Since the kids were gone, only when I was with the dogs did I feel a sense of peace and happiness. The darkness around Bill was palpable and difficult for me to be around. I didn't know what to do. I thought he needed professional help, but he wouldn't go to a doctor. I thought everything would be fine if he just understood his depression.

Many days I wandered around the ranch aimlessly. I walked with the dogs and talked to my friends. Rachel constantly challenged me to look at myself from different perspectives, and I really appreciated our ability to talk about almost anything. It's not always easy to look at your own stuff. And I had a lot of it to look at.

My relationship with Bill was cordial but detached. He was distant and emotionally unavailable to me, and as far as I could tell, with everyone else, too. When the kids came to visit, he didn't join in any family activity or game. He'd walk into the room, see us all having a good time, and walk out. He didn't interact or participate.

"No, that's OK. You guys play," he usually said when we invited him to join us in a game. Then he would disappear by himself into the garden or sit off at a distance, and I would catch him watching us. I'd come to think he'd always been like that, but I had never noticed before.

When I thought about it, I remembered the moment when I'd finally given up trying to push him to make a connection with his children. He was at his computer in his loft/office doing something. I was standing in the living room toward the bottom of the stairs looking up.

"Why don't you call Jane and invite her out to lunch?" I said. "I really think she'd like to talk to you about your relationship with her or what happened with you and her mom or anything. As far as I know, you guys rarely talk about stuff like that."

He came to the edge of the loft and stood there looking down at me. "She's busy. She has her own life to live, and she's out there living it."

"I know that," I said. "But, but don't you get it? She wants you as part of that life. She wants a deeper connection with you. She wants you present in her life."

He looked down at me as if I was from another planet.

Obviously we were seeing this family dynamic differently, but from my perspective, he didn't have a clue about what was going on with his daughter. He was a good person, but he had no idea how to start a dialogue about emotional issues, or why anyone would even want to talk about them. It seemed to me that it was easier for him to just keep things on the surface and not delve into how anyone was feeling. I also realized I had been pushing him to have what I thought would be a more meaningful relationship with his kids, which was not necessarily what he wanted or was capable of. He was working with what he knew and who was I to criticize? From what I knew about his childhood, I don't think he had any good role models. When he was growing up, he said he was told to just go outside and play, so he wouldn't be underfoot. I realized that's what he did. He escaped to the garden instead of dealing with things or interacting with the family. Maybe I should have spent more time with him in the garden.

I realized that no amount of pushing was going to help. He had to see and understand the value in communication himself. Me telling him to do it wasn't going to change things. At that moment, standing there, I made a conscious decision to stop pushing my agenda. Who was I to say what was right for him or his kids or what lessons they needed to learn anyway? I never mentioned that he should call them again. Sometimes I would ask if he had.

I also realized that I'd stopped pushing our relationship, too. There was no closeness, no communication, no discussion of hopes or dreams, no romance, and no intimacy. Even when we talked about our relationship, and made a commitment to change things and incorporate intimacy back in our lives, we never did. Or we would change it for a while and then drift back into our old patterns. Mostly, we had a relatively comfortable day-to-day co-existence taking care of things around the ranch.

I worried about Bill, though, because he seemed so troubled and mad all of the time, as if a dust storm was always brewing around him. Sometimes the dust obscured him; sometimes I could see through the dust, just a little, as if the storm were breaking up.

"You know what, Julie?" Bill said one day. "I know you've always wanted a little meditation room of your own, so I'm going to build one for you. We'll clean out the lathe house and put a roof on it. It'll make a perfect meditation room." And so we did, Bill working almost incessantly on this project, just for me.

But then another gust of wind would arise, and he would be obliterated from view again, enveloped in darkness. I could see and feel the darkness when he entered a room. Some days the blackness followed me around and consumed me, too. I would stop and turn and look at it. I would see it coming and just stare at it. I would let it wash over me. I could feel the darkness enter every pore of mine, and then I would start to cry. The tears seemed to help wash away the darkness. Then I would examine the tears, thank them, and let them flow. When I truly allowed the emotions of the moment to happen, I got some relief. But I never knew how long the reprieve would last.

"How long can I take the blackness? How long can I be in this hole with you, Bill? Stop thinking, brain," I shouted silently. The more I thought about it, the darker it got. What had I done wrong? How had I managed to screw up this relationship, too? How could this happen again? I could see the darkness approaching, filling me and I would start to cry once more. The sadness and the tears were exhausting. I had forgotten everything Gracie had taught me.

ooooo

After walking and talking with Rachel one day, and discussing everything that was going on with me, I realized I had to talk to Bill about how I was feeling. I knew this wouldn't be easy for me, so I suggested that we meet for lunch at an Italian restaurant in Ventura where the dogs or the garden wouldn't distract us. When we sat down in the restaurant, even though it was lunchtime, I ordered wine. Somehow wine made it easier for me to open up. I hoped the right words would come.

We started out with small talk. It was hard to talk about difficult issues with him. Maybe I was just like him and wanted to avoid anything potentially unpleasant. Stay in the calm waters—no waves. Don't say anything that might upset him or anyone else. Eventually, I couldn't stand it, and I said, "Bill, we need to talk about us."

"I agree," he said sadly.

"You seem so distant, so disconnected. I love you, but I can't seem to do anything right. No matter what I do, you seem mad at me. If I say the sky is blue, you get mad. If I ask you what color you think it is, you get mad. I can't get it right no matter what I do. What do you want from me? What can I do?" The questions tumbled from my mouth.

"You can't do anything," he said as he stared at his pizza.

"But I'm not happy with how things are," I said. "It's not good. There's no depth to our relationship. We never talk about anything important."

"I'm not happy either."

"I'm willing to try to change."

"So what do we do?" Bill asked.

"Do you want to go to counseling together?" I asked. "I could call Joel." Joel was a therapist in Los Angeles who I knew and trusted. He had gotten Jane through some tough times created by the divorce and changes in living arrangements. "He knows the whole family dynamic from working with Jane, so it wouldn't take any time for him to get up to speed. Maybe he'd see us together."

"OK," Bill said. "I like Joel. That sounds like a good plan."

"I really want to do what it takes to make it work," I said.

We started counseling. It was a long drive to LA to see Joel, but he was a great therapist, and it provided time for us to talk as we drove. After a few sessions, Joel asked if I would mind if he saw Bill alone since the bulk of our time together was spent talking about Bill and his issues. That was fine with me since I really wanted Bill to get a handle on his depression. I thought that might help our relationship more than couple's therapy right then.

"Who's taking care of you, though?" Rachel asked one day as we walked the dogs. She was right. I needed to take care of myself. Underneath I knew it wasn't just about Bill's depression, although I wanted to believe that was the central problem. I decided I would get my own therapist in Santa Barbara, rather than Los Angeles, and I did. I started seeing a therapist my friend Lisa had recommended, who was a Buddhist, M.D., and both Bill and I continued with individual therapy.

Over the next weeks, thoughts swirled and swirled around in my head until I felt dizzy. I'd thought Bill would be the man I would grow old with. He was easy to be with; he was kind and helpful. He was a good person even if he didn't challenge me. It was comfortable and safe, even if it wasn't perfect. And we'd had a lot of really fun, happy times over the years. I was incredibly confused, incredibly sad.

Bill continued with therapy with Joel, and I felt good about that. When I asked Bill how his sessions were going with Joel, he would say, "Fine. I'm working on stuff from my past." But our relationship didn't improve. He seemed more and more depressed, more and more distant.

I suggested couple's counseling again. I said I would find us someone in Ventura. I was devastated at the thought of another relationship ending, but there was no honest discussion between us. He agreed to couple's counseling, though. I found a different therapist. I set up an appointment, and we didn't go. Somehow it didn't seem that important to him, or I guess to me either. Eventually I gave up.

Bill had been spending more and more time going to conferences now that school was out, and he was often gone a few days at a time. One weekend when he was home, he got it in his head to paint the outside of the house. I thought it was weird, with the tension between us, but I was helping him paint the front porch. As we worked side by side, I was trying to talk about our relationship, but I wasn't getting anywhere. He didn't want to talk about it.

"Do you have a girlfriend," I asked finally.

"No," he said quickly. "I wish."

"That's a weird response," I said. "That makes me feel really great."

"I was just kidding."

He went back to painting for a few minutes silently, then he turned and looked at me. His face looked incredibly sad. "I'm sorry, Julie, I'm leaving. I've packed up a few things. I'm going to Montana for the summer, and when I come back, I'm moving out."

I was shocked and numb. I had never imagined such a drastic step. And it seemed so well planned out. Tears started to well up. "Do you want to talk about it?" I asked.

"I'm just not happy. It's not you. It's me."

"What do you mean? What are you talking about?"

"I can't really talk about it right now. I'm confused. I need some time by myself."

"What about our marriage?" I asked, as I realized I truly had planned to grow old with this man no matter what.

"I don't know, I don't know anything right now," Bill said in a very distant, flat tone.

"Have you talked to Joel about this?" I asked.

"Yes."

"What'd he say?"

"He thinks it's a good idea."

I was startled, dumbfounded, sad, confused, and mad at Bill's therapist. I started to cry.

"It's not about you, it's about me," Bill said, tears welling up in his eyes, too. "We never built anything together, there was no struggle, it was all handed to me, but I never felt needed or special. And I never felt I had enough time to do anything the way I wanted to." His voice trailed off.

He walked up the driveway toward the garage, and I just sat there on the front porch surrounded by fresh paint.

"What are you talking about? We didn't build anything?" I whispered to myself, totally confused. Sure we had had some ups and downs recently, but didn't every long-term relationship go through periods like that? You worked them out. We'd been together thirteen years. We raised the kids together, we got Anne and Jane through college, we put on a beautiful wedding for Anne at the labyrinth, Roy had gotten married and had moved back to Ojai with his family and was going to college, and we were happy about that. We bought and renovated Bill's grandmother's old house in Montana for ourselves, we raised the dogs and rescued lots of animals, and we took care of the ranch. We traveled; we took the dogs to Montana in the summers; we had fun; we had lots of friends. We had done a lot together. Or had I instigated and orchestrated it all, and he'd just gone along for the ride?

It amazed me how quickly I was able to go to that place of insecurity where I was responsible for it all, where I was the exaggerated cause of all that was not right in our relationship. Maybe my mother had been right all of these years. It appeared that no one would ever really love me, at least not long enough to stay with me, for better or worse… Now I just felt that our wedding vows had been meaningless.

I had had three marriages and, when I really looked at them, I was acutely aware that the patterns were similar. I chose or attracted passive men who were emotionally unavailable. Subconsciously, I think I chose men who wanted or allowed someone else to run their lives. But then they didn't really like it. Was I just like my mother even though I had tried so hard not to be like her? Did I choose men who were like my kind but powerless father, over and over, because that's the type of man I felt safe with? Bill and my first husband even had the same birthday. My second husband had the same birthday as my mother. What was up with that? I thought.

Maybe I attracted men whom I thought needed to be rescued and taken care of because I truly believed that was the only reason anyone would want to be with me. Not for me, but for what I could do for them. And then when I took over and rescued them, it made them feel bad and resentful. Maybe I never had made Bill feel special. I realized he never made me feel special either. Maybe that wasn't my job or his job.

There also was a piece of me that felt taken advantage of, like Bill had used me to raise his kids and then when that was done, he didn't need me anymore. I realized that was not a very enlightened thought, but it still passed through my head fleetingly. I did know it took two people to make a relationship work, and it took two to contribute to a breakdown. I knew it wasn't just me, but both of us. I also knew I could only change myself.

I wondered whether the Universe kept handing me the same experiences over and over in order to validate my thoughts and feelings about myself. Perhaps the Universe wanted to give me what I expressed about myself and seemed to want. If that was true, I decided I really needed to take responsibility for what I said and did so I could create a different picture. Or perhaps the Universe kept repeating the same patterns with men until I learned the lesson I needed to learn to move forward. Clearly I was not doing such a great job in that department, but I was trying not to be too hard on myself as I thought about these things.

Maybe I couldn't do anything except be aware of what was happening in the present moment. Maybe I needed to understand that I couldn't fix this situation. But in spite of the realizations, I was still so, so sad. I didn't know what to do. It seemed like I had been doing a lot of crying lately and that wasn't helping anymore.

I turned and went to find Gracie. "What should I do, baby? We haven't talked lately. I've been preoccupied with depression, both mine and Bill's. It certainly does have a way of taking over. I'm afraid that you don't hear me anymore. I'm afraid that I don't hear you anymore. I know you're disoriented and deaf in the physical body, but can you still hear me on a different level? Please, Gracie," I said, "I need you. I'm afraid of being alone again and I'm so, so sad. I can barely stand it."

I haven't gone anywhere. I know how sad you are, I know you have been sad for quite some time, but let him go. You cannot control how everyone else feels. Be with your sadness, grieve, feel it. But if you really love him, you want him to be happy. I love him too. He is a good person, a kind man, but he is lost. He has lost his connection with spirit and nature. He has lost his connection with his heart. Not lost it really, it is just buried deep within the trials and tribulations of everyday life and his own past. He has his own fears. He has things to figure out by himself. If he is not happy here, with you, then he must find out for himself what he needs. It is his journey. He must dig deep. You cannot fix it for him or anyone else. You have never been able to do that, but you won't stop trying, or believing that you can. He simply has changed his mind about you. He has his own work to do.

You have your own journey, too; stay on it. Forgive yourself and him. Be compassionate towards yourself and him. Thank him and the kids for bringing animals back in your life. It is a blessing. You are wonderful and perfect just the way you are. Stay aligned. Connect with the oneness. Tune in to your inner power, your higher self. Be in the present moment with all of your senses alive. Connect with nature and all of the elements. There are other things in store for you. Be grateful for the opportunity this brings to you. Allow love to fill the empty spaces.

"Thank you, Gracie, I'll try. That's not so easy to do though," I said sadly. "By the way, what do you mean by 'other things'?"

Not now, you'll see.

I realized I didn't really know who I was any more. I dabbled around in this or that, pursued one kind of spiritual teaching or another, but never settled on anything. I'd been taking on the likes and dislikes of each of my husbands for so long, that I didn't know who I was. I didn't know what I wanted or what I liked. I guess I never really believed I deserved to have what I wanted.

The one thing both Bill and I had in common—that we both really liked to do—was to go sailing. I thought it was pretty sad that in all the years we were together, we went sailing once. It sort of summed it up for me.

"I guess I could try to believe what Alverto says—'that it's all perfect in the cosmos, even if we don't like it,'" I said to myself.

I knew at that moment that I would really like to see Alverto again. I realized how much he had helped me to see things from a different perspective and to feel gratitude for everything that was going on. I also knew I would really like to learn more about communicating with animals.

CHAPTER 42

WALTER'S LEG

When Bill came home from Montana several weeks later, he quickly found an apartment in Ventura and moved most of his stuff out. He'd been gone for more than a month, but I still woke up most days feeling very, very sad that he was not there. I loved him, but there was nothing I could do. He had his own journey, and I wanted him to find happiness. In spite of the therapy and all of the work I was doing on myself, I still sometimes blamed myself for the end of our marriage.

To get yet another fresh start, I was repainting walls and redecorating my bedroom. Again. This time I wanted my surroundings to really reflect me. As I moved furniture around, I realized that in making space for the kids years before, Bill and I had moved a gigantic 18th-century French antique sideboard into our relationship corner. I had totally forgotten about the Feng Shui analysis of that corner when we put it there. But as I thought about it now, that was exactly what had happened to us. Our relationship had become old, an antique. Although I didn't know whether an antique piece of furniture in a corner could have that much influence on a relationship, I moved it immediately. I didn't want a relationship, even one with myself, to be stuck in or attached to the past.

Most days I forced myself to walk with Maggie and our combined family of dogs. She just allowed me to cry when I needed to, without saying a word or offering any advice.

"Look, Maggie," I said one morning. "Is Walter limping?"

"Yes, his right front."

"I noticed it the other day, and it doesn't seem to be getting better," I said. "He probably hurt himself roughhousing with the other dogs."

"Maybe you should keep him in the house for a few days and not take him on walks so it can heal."

"Good idea," I said, not wanting to be an alarmist and rush to the vet. "I'll keep an eye on it."

A few nights later, I reached out to pet him and barely touched his leg. His cry of pain startled me. It wasn't at all like Walter to complain, and I knew it was more than just over-use.

"Walter, we're going to the vet tomorrow. And don't try to talk me out of it," I said. "You've been limping on that leg too long. It's not healing."

The next morning Walter hobbled to the car and jumped in, being careful to protect his front right leg from touching the floor of the van as he landed. After I explained Walter's symptoms to the vet, Dr. Bailey suggested x-raying him. I waited. When he called me back into the examining room, the look on his face said it was not good news. Walter looked up with happiness to see me, his big tail going thump, thump, thump against the metal examining table, showing some but not all of his usual enthusiasm.

"I'm sorry, Julie, but I'm pretty sure Walter has an osteosarcoma in this leg bone," Dr. Bailey said. "Look at the x-ray," he said, pointing to a lump in the bone.

"What's that?" I asked, guessing cancer but hoping it was something that could be taken care of easily. I was trying to hold it together.

"It's a very aggressive form of bone cancer."

"So, what do we do, Matt?" I said as tears began to choke up my voice.

"The only cure is amputation, but even that's not always successful," he said.

Although it was hard for me to concentrate as thoughts about Walter raced around my brain, I tried to listen as Matt explained what the surgery and the recovery would entail.

"But, Julie, you should know the success rate is not good," Matt told me. "Most dogs live six to eight months with the amputation, four to six weeks with no treatment. But amputation would at least eliminate the pain he's having. On the positive side, you caught it early, and that really helps. Besides, Walter has a big heart. Maybe he can beat the odds. Some people put their dogs through chemotherapy after the amputation."

"Does that help?" I asked.

"Some people say it does give them a little more time, but who really knows? The statistics with or without chemo are not that great and not that different. I can put you in touch with an oncology specialist in Ventura," he said. "There's a very slight chance it could be something else, an infection in the bone. The only way to tell for sure is a biopsy, and that can be worse than the amputation in some respects. And sometimes amputation is the choice for a bone infection, too, if antibiotics don't work."

"What would you do if Walter was your dog?" I said, trying to fend off the emotion that threatened to overwhelm me.

"I would do the amputation and not waste time," Matt said. "Do you want someone else to look at the x-ray to confirm my diagnosis? I've had my partner look at it already, but you can get another opinion."

"How sure are you?" I asked.

"98 percent," he said.

"Let's schedule the surgery."

"I can do it next Friday," Matt said, looking at his schedule.

"That's a week," I said. "You said four to six weeks with no surgery. That's too long to wait. One week is like 25 percent of the time he could have left," I said, starting to come apart while I did the math. "Please, can't you do it earlier? Please, Monday. I want to give this big lug the best chance possible," I begged as the tears spilled, and Matt handed me a Kleenex.

"I'll move things around and fit him in Monday morning. Bring him in at 8:30 a.m. Nothing to eat after midnight. Water's OK."

"I need to call Bill and let him know," I said, "but thanks. I really appreciate it." As Matt lowered the table to let Walter off, I realized that I had been stroking his soft black fur the whole time we talked. "I love you, Walter. Let's go home. I want to give you some extra attention."

I called Maggie, in tears, and explained about Walter. I could hear the quiver in her voice over the phone. I called Bill. I realized that I still relied on him and needed him, especially when things were stressful. Also, this was supposedly his dog. As usual, Bill was calm and supportive. He agreed that the surgery needed to be done as quickly as possible. He said he could come to the ranch if I needed him. As it sunk in that I would be facing this by myself, I got really sad and lonely.

"No, I can take him in by myself," I said. "I might need your help after the surgery, though." I scoured the Internet for anything I could find on osteosarcomas and wasn't encouraged by what I read. I finally wandered off to bed, exhausted and scared for Walter. I continued my reading in bed, hoping to find something, anything of a more positive nature. As I lay there, praying for a cure or a miracle, I reached out to gently touch Walter, who was lying stretched out beside me. He rolled over to look me straight in the eye and offered a kiss. Walter was easy to love and the most adaptable dog I had ever known. He was also the biggest rogue.

Now that Bill was gone, Walter had taken up the position right next to me in my bed. Sometimes his head would be on the pillow next to mine; sometimes his big butt and tail would be facing upwards, right towards my head. It was those times that I hoped he would not take on the full-time role of Walter the Farting Dog, from the kids' books. When he did, sometimes it was so bad I had to get up and get out of bed for a few minutes until the air cleared.

But I knew he was there to protect me. If there were a strange noise outside, Walter would awaken from a deep sleep and be instantaneously alert, often sounding the alarm for all of the other dogs. Gracie couldn't hear, so she rarely woke up at sounds in the night anymore. Walter would act brave and rush the darkness with a ferocious bark, but when he was really confronted with something, like a wheelbarrow left in an unfamiliar place, he would immediately back up and let the others do the investigating. Walter really was a big chicken, who just liked to act tough and get everyone else all riled up. But still he charged first into the darkness, barking to scare away whatever was out there.

Walter knew exactly what I needed. If I was sad, he would approach and lick away the tears. When I sat on the couch and he wanted attention, he would turn so that his butt was on the couch sitting next to me, and his front paws on the floor.

"Will he be able to do that with three legs?" I wondered. "Will he be the same lovable rogue after the surgery? Or will he become depressed, stare at his water bowl, and lament, 'Why me'?"

I fussed around the house anxiously all day Sunday, gave Walter lots of attention, and read information online about cancer in dogs. Finally Monday arrived, and it was time to go.

As Walter and I walked up the driveway to get in the car, he kept looking back over his shoulder as if to remind me that I'd forgotten something. I went through my mental checklist and said, "What is it, baby? What did I forget?" Then I realized Walter was reminding me that I'd forgotten to give him his breakfast, and he really wanted it. I hadn't fed any of the dogs that morning out of fairness to Walter, but he knew.

"Sorry, Walter, no food this morning," I said.

I brought him to the vet's office where a kind nurse waited to lead Walter away. After giving me a kiss and absorbing my hug, he hobbled away without even a backwards glance of fear or "Don't leave me." Walter was on to his next thing, whatever that was.

I went home to wait and pray for Walter and a good outcome. A few hours later Matt called to tell me that the operation had gone well; Walter was resting comfortably and had been outside to pee already. Matt said he thought Walter should spend the night, but I could come get him the following day. It felt like the longest night as I waited, not knowing what to expect with a three-legged dog. I'd heard that they did just fine, but Walter was so big—one might even say "fat." How would he be able to carry all of that weight around? Matt told me that Walter needed to lose 20 pounds, but it didn't seem fair to take away his leg and his joy of food at the same time.

ooooo

The next day the phone rang about 9 a.m. When I answered it, Dr. Bailey's nurse said, "Come get him. He's up, he ate, he peed and pooped, and now he wants to go home."

"What?" I said quizzically. "He can come home now? Are you sure it's not too early? You know how it is here, a bit chaotic with all of the dogs. I don't want him to get hurt."

"Actually, we need him to go home," she said. "He's starting to cause some trouble, howling and making a lot of noise and all. He wants out. Just try and keep him as quiet as you can. The stitches come out in two weeks. We'll give you some pain meds for him. It's important to stay ahead of the pain so that he can heal."

"OK, I'll be right down," I said. Leave it to Walter to cause a stir. I immediately called Maggie. "He's ready to come home. Can you come with me to get him? Bill can't come, and I'm afraid I won't be able to lift him into the car by myself."

"Of course," she said. "I'm ready. Come pick me up."

Maggie and I were anxious the whole ride to the vet's office, worrying about how we were going to lift Walter into the car and what it was going to be like with him only having three legs. We both jumped out of the car and almost ran into the vet's office. One of the girls behind the desk noticed our anxious faces and said, "I'll go get him."

All of a sudden Walter appeared on a leash, bouncing along on three legs, a big smile on his face, as happy as a clam, his big tail knocking over everything in its path on both sides. Maggie and I both started to cry as we ran over to him and gave him a big hug, being careful to avoid the dark red 10-inch incision where his right front leg had been removed at the shoulder.

"Can you help us get him in the car?" I asked the nurse. "I'm worried we won't be able to lift him."

"Sure. No problem."

Walter stopped to pee a little unsteadily on the outside wall of the vet's office. As we approached the van, I opened the sliding side door. Before we could even bend over to lift him, Walter jumped right in, his powerful hind legs lifting him with ease, and then he lay down on the cushion as if nothing was different, as if to say, "What's all the fuss about? Let's go home."

"Good boy," was all I could say, amazed at my wonderful Walter.

"No worries," Walter seemed to say.

"What a lesson in acceptance and being in the present moment," I said to Maggie. We both laughed as we watched Walter settle in as if everything was perfect and nothing had changed. We'd worked ourselves into frenzy over just the thought of him losing a leg. Maybe it was all perfect in the present moment regardless of how it appeared. Maybe Walter was my teacher.

Despite Walter's example, I started to worry again as we drove home. "Getting in was all rear muscles, but how will he get out with only one leg in the front to hold him?" But as I should have known, he did just fine. When he jumped out of the car at home, there was a slight falter as his front leg buckled when he hit the ground, but he made a quick recovery and was immediately on his way to the front door.

When I brought Walter in the house, Gracie and the other dogs were initially interested in where he'd been. They sniffed him to find out if he had been anywhere interesting and to see if they'd missed anything. But then they immediately lost interest and didn't seem to even notice his missing leg.

That night I gave all the dogs their regular nighttime biscuits in the kitchen and then we headed off to sleep in my room. I said good night to everyone, and petted them all as they settled in on their various orthopedic beds scattered around my bedroom. I made Walter a comfortable bed on the floor right next to me because he seemed to be struggling, in spite of the pain medication, to find an acceptable position for sleeping. He kept making soft, little "mmm, mmm" sounds in his throat and staring intently at me from his bed. "Go to sleep, Walter," I said gently. I finally climbed into my bed exhausted physically, mentally, and emotionally. I shut off the light and rolled over.

All was quiet, and my body slowly began to relax. Suddenly I heard a shuffling noise and felt a huge thump, thump on my bed in the darkness. I quickly turned on the light, and there was Walter, all smiles, standing on three legs on my bed, no problem. He looked at me happily, did a half turn, assumed his normal sleeping position stretched out next to me and promptly went to sleep, not at all concerned that he'd had his leg amputated the day before.

A few days later Maggie came over to visit. Walter saw her coming down the driveway with Duke. I watched as he mustered all of his strength to rise on his three legs and begin the trek toward her. He started to run and his head bounced drastically up and down as he plowed forward in uneven and sloppy movements. His jowls jostled in the wind as he moved forward, picking up speed, with his huge propeller tail going round and round in giant circles, his tongue hanging from one side of his mouth, and happiness exuding from every fiber of his being at seeing his Aunt

Maggie. He was going a little too fast when he stopped to pick up a towel to bring to her as a present. His front leg stepped on the towel and his body continued forward and he did a gigantic face plant on the lawn. He immediately got up, looked around with a tiny bit of embarrassment to see if anyone had noticed, but proceeded to his goal—to get some love from Maggie and his brother, Duke.

∞∞∞

I sat on the couch one chilly afternoon reading *Connecting with the Elements*, a book by Don Alverto. Walter stood looking directly at me and making his little "mmm, mmm" sounds.

"Come on up, you big lug," I said tenderly, knowing exactly what he wanted.

Walter jumped on the couch and pressed his face against my thigh as he stretched out. I could feel the chill of his nose through my jeans along with the warmth of his fur as I gently stroked his neck and my fingers worked themselves down to his skin. As Walter started to snore gently, I noticed that his hair was growing back where his leg had been amputated. The scar and the shaved spot were barely visible. At first glance, you would hardly even notice that he had only three legs. It was only his peculiar gait that revealed his loss.

"But he doesn't seem to view it as a loss," I thought. "It just is. Now he has three legs and he needs to get around on what he has. No judgment about it and no comparison to his previous physical status. Or at least it didn't seem that way. But who really knows? I continued to pet Walter's silky ears. "Maybe he's really depressed and feeling 'Why me? What did I do to deserve this?'"

Walter's imagined internal monologue continued in my head, "I was a good dog, or at least a gentle and kind soul. Oh sure, I steal food off of the counter, any counter, at any opportunity I can, but there's no real harm in that. I do feel a tiny bit guilty when I get caught and I get yelled at, which is why I try to take the food stealthily, keeping my head down and sneaking away without anyone noticing. By the time they find the empty bags lying around, it's too late to really get mad at me. Besides, I just don't have any will power when it comes to food." Or at least, that's what I thought he could be saying, but probably not. I didn't think Walter put that much thought into his actions and guilt didn't seem like a motivating factor. He always had been an opportunistic, present-moment kind of a guy.

Walter had been talking a lot more lately, trying to communicate. Ever since Gracie had quieted down a bit, Walter had been picking up the slack.

"Maybe I should just ask Walter what he thinks, rather than guessing," I thought.

Then, as Walter continued to lie calmly stretched out on the couch next to me, I realized there was no thought at all at that moment, simply bliss. I felt it, too, even though his cold nose on my leg was adding to the chill in the room and my body. Walter stirred a little and curled into a ball as if responding to my thought.

CHAPTER 43

PUGGERS

One morning I came home from doing errands and found Puggers lying on the kitchen floor, shaking. He'd pressed his face into the cold stone floor, between his paws, and appeared enshrouded with sadness. He barely raised his eyes in a greeting. A similar incident had happened weeks before when Bill happened to be at the house for a birthday party for one of the kids. Ignoring the shaking, Bill had said Puggers was fine and told me to quit worrying so much. Puggers did perk up a few days later.

I knew my dogs, and I knew there was something wrong, but I decided to wait and see if he got better on his own like he had the previous time. He was a healthy dog and maybe he had eaten something bad and had a tummy ache. He seemed worse as the day progressed, though, not better. By the end of the day, he couldn't get up from his position on the front lawn; he couldn't walk; he looked pale and helpless.

I called Maggie, and she rushed over. Together we rolled him from the lawn onto a towel. Roy was home and helped lift Puggers into the car so I could take him to the vet's office. It was late afternoon, and the vet said Puggers seemed to be bleeding internally, and I needed to get him to the emergency hospital right away. I called Bill, who I knew would be teaching at school, and headed to Ventura with Puggers, where he was admitted to the hospital. They did blood tests and took x-rays and, just like that, announced that he had spleen cancer and that it had already spread to his lungs. One of the tumors had burst, causing internal bleeding. I was inconsolable. This was my healthiest, most active dog. He was only eleven; he was arthritis-free, playful, and full of pure love. The others all had their issues.

Bill showed up and together we talked with the doctors about our options. The doctor said the best plan was spleen surgery followed by chemo. He detailed all of the expenses, including $8,000 for the surgery and another $5,000 for the chemo. He said the recovery was long and difficult, without a good long-term prognosis, especially since the cancer had already spread to Puggers' lungs. He only gave Puggers a short time to live even if he had the surgery. The vet said he might recover from this episode with a transfusion and certain medications, but that he was terminally ill. I cried. It wasn't about the money, but in light of the dim prognosis, Bill and I elected for the transfusion and the medicines, but not the surgery. The hospital gave Puggers a transfusion and kept him overnight. I prayed. By the morning he was doing better. The hospital doctor told me to try and keep him quiet so that his tumors didn't tear away and bleed again.

I did several balancing sessions with Puggers, based on techniques I had learned from don Alverto, asking the divine healing spirit in the Universe to balance air, fire, water, and earth in Puggers' body. I held him and touched him and sent him love from my heart. I tried to see him as healed and whole and yet not be attached to the results. I knew energy healing had nothing to do with me. And then it was like a miracle. He was fine. He was chasing rabbits and acting totally normal. I couldn't even believe he'd been sick. I tried to keep him quiet, but it was difficult since he was back to his old playful self.

Over the next month, I thought a lot about alleviating suffering and the decision to put a dog to sleep if he was suffering. I'd been attending meditation classes, reading up on Buddhism and loving kindness meditation, and the concept of ending suffering. I wondered whether we think about ending another being's suffering for us or for them. Is it interfering with the cosmic plan to choose to end a dog's suffering who is terminally ill? And what about the possibility of a miracle? Suppose we choose too early and a miracle was in process and our action thwarted the miracle. Who are we to say? I turned my thoughts over and over in my head and struggled for guidance. Maybe we like to talk about miracles, but we don't really believe in them. If someone is terminally ill, maybe that is their trajectory and no amount of miracles can help.

I didn't want to believe that there was no cure and that it was only a matter of time for Puggers. He didn't seem to be suffering. He seemed totally peaceful. He slept a lot, just as he had before. He seemed as if he was healing himself, getting back in balance and sticking it out. But I couldn't forget that he had an incurable cancer.

I was talking to Maggie one day. "Maybe I don't have the right to interfere with the natural order of things," I said with tears in my eyes. "Maybe it's Puggers journey to die when God decides he is to die, and his journey might include suffering. I don't want to make the decision to put him down. I don't want to interfere."

"But you've already interfered," Maggie said gently. "He would have been dead weeks ago if you'd let him be. You took him to the hospital, gave him a transfusion, and got him on medication. He was in shock from the blood loss. Now he's stable again. I think it's your obligation as his pack leader, his caregiver, his birth mother, to make decisions for him, including a decision to end his suffering if his cancer progresses or he has another episode."

Rachel said, "You're thinking way too much about this, analyzing all of the ramifications. Your heart will tell you when it's time; your dog will tell you when it's time."

I was still in turmoil about this issue and couldn't stop thinking, even obsessing, about it. I had helped give birth to this dog in my bathroom. I'd been with him for more than eleven years. I'd seen him through getting his tooth knocked out by a baseball bat when he was playing softball with Sebastian and being bitten by a rattlesnake when he was rushing to say hello to a friend who stopped over. We had been through a lot together, and I didn't know if I was capable of making a decision to end this beautiful being's life.

I sent an email to Alverto in Ecuador and asked him if it was OK to assist Puggers in his transition if he was suffering. Alverto's response was "Yes, it is good to assist in the transition to end the suffering. The great spirit of life wants the best for all concerned." All three of these comments from friends helped me to find some peace, but I still struggled with thoughts about putting a dog to sleep.

About a week later, Puggers seemed full of energy, gobbled down his breakfast, and went outside on the back deck to rest in the sun. I checked up on him about half an hour later and noticed him shaking and lying with his head in that funny position between his paws again. I called him into the house, and he rose slowly and walked in a little unsteadily.

"Please, Puggers, lie down. Be still."

His shaking got worse and then he collapsed and could barely move. The vet had said if this happened again to check his gums to see if they were pink. I couldn't tell, but I knew he was in a bad way as I cradled his head in my lap.

I called the vet. "Please, Matt. He's suffering; he's shaking all over. What should I do? It's the same symptoms as before."

"I could come up now and put him to sleep if you want," Matt said kindly. "I know it's still a hard decision, but you've been anticipating this, haven't you?"

"Suppose he recovers again like he did last time?" I asked.

"That's possible, I guess," Matt said.

"Let's wait 10 minutes and see if he starts to calm down, and I'll call you back."

I called Maggie and through the sobs said, "I think it's Puggers' time. Can you come over?"

"I'll be right there," she said. And she was.

Puggers' shaking continued to get worse. He couldn't stand; he couldn't even lift his head. The other dogs stayed nearby, but not too close. I called Matt and said through the tears, "He's not getting better. He's bad. I think you better come. I don't want him to suffer any more."

"I'm sorry, Julie. I'll be there within 10 minutes."

Maggie and I stroked Puggers and told him how much we loved him and what a great boy he was. I held him close, as my tears fell on his fur, and he died in my arms, just as Matt and his nurse drove down the driveway. Although his death left a hole in many hearts, I was grateful that he'd had a great last month and that he died quickly in my arms, on his own terms. I was grateful that spirit/God made the final decision, not me.

CHAPTER 44

LEAVING

A few weeks later, Alverto showed up unexpectedly in Ojai from Ecuador and conducted a ceremony to help release some of our sadness over Puggers' passing. Maria and Sebastian, who were really struggling with the loss of Puggers, participated. Alverto gently played the drum and sang to the Great Spirit in his native Kichwa language. We each lit a candle and spoke about Puggers and what he meant to us.

"Puggers was my best friend and my brother," Sebastian said. "I remember when I knocked his tooth out with my bat on a backswing when he was desperately trying to reach the ball at the same time I was swinging. I was so upset that I hurt him. And then another time he tackled me to the ground from behind when we were messing around. I still have a scar on my back from that one. It reminds me of him each time I see it. I love him, and I miss him running to greet me," Sebastian said with tears in his eyes.

Everyone said something, and then we blew some of Puggers' ashes into the air and watched them get taken up with the wind and scatter in all directions. We all felt a little more peace and a little less sadness when we finished the ceremony and the last drumbeat reverberated into the evening sky.

Alverto examined Walter and said his cancer was gone. I was ecstatic to hear this news, and it helped cement my decision not to put Walter through chemotherapy. Alverto did several balancing sessions on Walter. Over the next few days, I frequently walked in the house and found my big black mischievous dog, asleep under the dining room table, covered in brightly colored flowers. The juxtaposition of Walter and flowers always made me smile. Alverto had also brought me Alpaca fiber pillows made by the grandmothers in his village in Ecuador. He explained that these pillows had very powerful healing properties and were blessed. I frequently placed pillows on Walter and Gracie, and I often slept with one or two on my heart for my own healing.

I also gathered some friends, and we participated in a very powerful winter solstice ceremony with Alverto. It was a ceremony designed to give up everything that was no longer useful from the past and to call in new things for the future; it was a time of transformation for all. Alverto made a powerful personal offering for all human and non-human beings on the planet, and he gave each of us a personal cleansing. I heard that everyone felt transformed on some level. I knew I did. Unlike on Alverto's previous visits, Gracie was not able to walk to the labyrinth to participate. She was having trouble walking any significant distance, so she and the other dogs all stayed home and rested.

"Alverto, can I come to visit you in Ecuador?" I asked. "I want to learn more about communicating with animals."

"Sí, es beuno para usted."

Alverto and I made plans for my to visit Ecuador in a few months. I decided on three weeks, which was a long time for me to be away, but I knew I needed to get on with my life and find myself now that Bill was gone. I arranged to stay with Alverto for some of the time. The plan was that I would study with him for ten days about communicating with animals and then travel around for the rest of the time. Although I was still sad and grieving about Bill and Puggers, time was helping a little, and I thought it would be good for me to leave, even though I worried about the dogs being left at home.

Carl was seventeen and showing signs of age. He couldn't hear at all and had a bad case of doggy Alzheimer's. Sometimes he would go to the door, plant his feet, and just stand there looking out. When I would finally let him out, he would stand in one spot outside, plant his feet again, and look around as if to ask, "What am I doing out here? How did I get here?" Then he would turn around and want to come back in. He could do this several times in a row, and I was patient with him and merely continued my job as doorman.

He could still run like the wind and was like a little homing pigeon when we turned around on our walks and started home. But he was having seizures frequently and was moving sideways and falling down more and more frequently. Before leaving for Ecuador, I had a long talk with Carl and told him how wonderful he was and said good-bye to him. I didn't tell anyone, but I had a feeling he might not make it through the three weeks I was going to be gone.

As it turned out, Bill had moved on, or maybe backwards, quite easily. He had gotten back together with his high school sweetheart, but that hadn't worked out for him either. He came back to me, bursting into my bedroom in the middle of the night, the night he broke up with her. He was a total mess, shaking, frantic. My heart started to race as I observed the wild look in his eye. I didn't know what he was going to do. Then he said he only felt safe with me and didn't know where else to go. After getting over the initial shock of him being there, and trying to assess his mental state, I got him into bed, took his shoes off, and lay next to him. I talked to him calmly until he fell asleep. I stayed awake.

A few hours later, as the sun rose, he wanted to talk. Through his tears, he explained about the girlfriend, and how guilty he felt. He said he was sorry, and he felt he had messed up so many lives. He was still shaking and not totally coherent so I made arrangements for him to see a doctor that morning and drove him to the appointment in Santa Barbara. The doctor suggested medication, and he agreed. On the way home, I drove Bill to get some clothes from his apartment, and we both realized he needed to get out of the drab, depressing apartment he had rented.

The medication helped him feel less anxious, and we had a long discussion about what had happened. I wasn't angry. I asked direct questions and got direct answers. And in some respects, finding out the truth about his having a girlfriend, put things in perspective and helped me to understand things that just hadn't made sense when they were happening between us. Still, I didn't want to be a doormat, and I was conflicted about having Bill move back in, even if it was to the guestroom.

I was scheduled to go to a weekend Buddhist retreat and decided to go in spite of Bill's condition. I thought some time in silence might be good for me. My therapist was out of town, but I broke the silence of the retreat and spoke to one of the Buddhist teachers. She suggested I could not go wrong if I acted from my authentic self. She was right, and I knew I would take in a stranger who arrived at my doorstep in such a condition, let alone someone I loved, someone who was still my husband, no matter what he had done.

I was leaving in less than ten days for Ecuador, so the timing was right for Bill to move back in with me at the ranch and stay with the dogs while I was gone.

As I prepared to leave for Ecuador, I said to him, "Are you sure you'll be OK to be alone?"

"I'll be fine."

"Will you be able to handle Gracie and Carl while I'm away? They're a little more trouble now and need constant attention."

"The kids are around to help," he said.

"Yeah, but you haven't been here to see it, the dogs have their quirks. Neither one of them can hear. Carl is very quiet, and he can sneak up to be close and wind up right underfoot. I've stepped on him a few times because I didn't even know he was there, he was so quiet," I reported.

"I'll watch out for him."

"Gracie, on the other hand, has developed a very weird, very annoying yelp. It's like she's confused about what's happening and, unless you're in her direct sight, she yelps. It's a very distressing sound. And she needs to be comforted and paid attention to when she yelps, or she won't stop."

"She certainly knows how to manipulate you," Bill said.

"And you know Gracie is having trouble walking," I said curtly.

"Don't worry. I'll keep them alive while you're gone, I promise."

That sounded so detached, and for a moment I worried whether he was capable of taking care of the animals, but I knew his kids were around to watch out for him and to help with the dogs.

> Your task is not to seek for love, but merely to seek and find all the barriers within yourself that you have built against it.
>
> -Rumi

CHAPTER 45

ECUADOR

I arrived in Quito, Ecuador, late at night and took a taxi from the airport to my hotel. When I got there, the hotel was closed, and no one answered the door or the phone. The nice cab driver took me to a hotel he knew about 10 minutes away. I had no idea how to contact Alverto to explain that I wasn't at the hotel where we'd agreed to meet the following day. The next morning I tried calling various phone numbers I had, but the one person I spoke to said Alverto was already in Quito, and she didn't know how to find him. As I sat having breakfast in the hotel, wondering how I was going to find Alverto, you can imagine my surprise when he appeared. I had no idea how he found me, but I was learning not to question things when Alverto was around.

We took a taxi back to the airport and rented a car. Although I'd listened to Spanish tapes for three months getting ready for the trip, my command of Spanish was still in its infancy. I could say hello and be polite, order food, and get to the bathroom, but that was about it. Somehow, however, I understood Alverto most of the time. As we drove around to a few sacred spots close to Quito, he started my lessons.

"What animals do you like? What animals speak to you?" he asked in Spanish as we drove along looking at the beautiful mountains in the distance.

"Dogs, whales, elephants, horses, dolphins, bears, maybe alpacas, and birds, hawks," I added. "I like all animals really."

"But which one calls to you the most right now?"

"I think dogs."

"The first step is to feel the animal, be the dog. *Soy el perro.*"

"How do you do that?" I wondered out loud in English.

"You and I have walked together before. I was a horse and you were a dog," Alverto said. "We were great friends roaming the plains together. Your connection has remained strong to animals. You are ready."

"Really?"

"My connection, my communication, is more with the elements: the plants and the rivers and the mountains—the cosmos," he said. "Animals are part of the whole. They're part of you. They're part of me. We're all connected."

Alverto explained that he wanted us to visit the ancient site at Rumicucho, so that I could absorb the energy of this pre-Incan place. Once there, I wandered alone and meditated. I saw Alverto standing on a mountaintop in the distance, bowing in prayer, and then extending his arms to the sky, clearly offering himself to the elements. I made an offering to a plant, as instructed, out of some candy Alverto had given me from his pocket.

Later that night at the hotel, I started to feel like I was getting the flu, but we went out anyway and had a delightful Italian dinner in Quito. When I awoke the next morning, I didn't feel well, but I garnered my strength because I was at the beginning of my adventure in Ecuador. Alverto took me to bathe in some volcanic waters of Ecuador. It was delightful. Then we drove about four hours to Alverto's home in the Andes. By the time we got there, I was not well at all. Alverto told me to go to bed and rest, so I did.

For the next several days I lay in bed, shaking with chills and a fever. I would try to stand and then feel like I was going to pass out. So I stayed put. Food was brought to me, but I wasn't hungry. I rarely saw Alverto, although he was right next door. I learned from his wife that he was sick, too, that they were all sick, with a strange illness. I guessed it was some type of spiritual cleansing, or at least that's what I told myself every time I felt bad and almost keeled over. I wondered why Alverto didn't just heal everyone. I knew he had the power to do so. When I remembered to ask him about that later, he said, "Sometimes you can not interfere. Things happen for a reason."

The only thing I could really do was lie in bed, read, and meditate; so I decided to view this trip to Ecuador as a silent retreat, instead of being bummed that I was sick. I started to read Jack Kornfield's book *A Lamp in the Darkness* that a friend had recommended I bring. It was a series of meditations, just perfect for my bed-ridden state and my desire to forgive and let things go from my past. Although the book was filled with simple stories and advice, I particularly liked the part about forgiveness:

> Forgiveness is not primarily for others, but for ourselves. It is a release of our burdens, a relief to our hearts. A story I like to tell is about two ex-prisoners of war who met again years later. One said to the other, 'Have you forgiven our captors yet?' And the second one answered through gritted teeth, 'No, never.' With this the first one looked at him kindly and said, 'Well then, they still have you in prison, don't they?' Only by learning to forgive, can we let go of what is holding us back and move on with our lives.
>
> Forgiveness means giving up all hope for a better past.
> Jack Kornfield, *A Lamp in the Darkness*

Although I'd been analyzing the effect of the past on my behavior for years, through meditation, therapy, and any number of books, classes and exercises, I realized I was still in prison. I still subconsciously wished or hoped for things to be different than they were. When I truly internalized that my past was never going to get better, that it just was what it was, I understood that it didn't have any power to hold me back. If my heart was full of forgiveness and love, I could just let the past go and move on. I could find my authentic self in the present moment. That one phrase—"…giving up all hope for a better past"—helped me move forward that day in Ecuador.

I decided I was going to do a visualization that was suggested in the book about entering a particularly difficult circumstance in one's life. It was a circumstance I knew I still needed to work on, and I was willing to go there. The book said to remember what it was like being in the midst of this difficulty, to recall as many details as possible, to really place yourself there, and to be aware of your body, your state of mind, and everything that was going on, but not to be afraid because it was just visualization.

I could remember every detail of being molested as a child, as if it were yesterday and not something that had happened more than 50 years before. I could still feel his hand in my underpants, and his thick, gnarled sea captain fingers groping around, as he made me sit next to him on the gold and brown paisley couch in his musty living room with the dirty multi-colored shag carpet. He'd told his son, my best friend and constant playmate at the time, to stay on the other side of the room and not come near or he would whip him. He told me he was just playing a game, looking for my ticklish spot. He said everyone had one, and he could find mine. I remember denying that it tickled, hoping that he would get bored with this game and just stop looking. I still remember not knowing what to do, knowing that this was wrong, but this was my father's best friend, and the father of my best friend, and someone I had known and trusted for years. I just wanted to get out of there. I just wanted it to be over.

The instructions for the visualization exercise said to imagine that, in the midst of this difficulty, there is a knock on the door. Let who is coming be a surprise, but know that it would be a marvelous wisdom figure, a luminous being who represented compassion, understanding, and courage in difficulties. The idea was that this luminous being would enter your body, go back into the situation as you, and show you how to handle and fix the situation.

The Dalai Lama appeared in my visualization and said to me, "You are loved." He went right into my body and back into the living room as me all those years ago, and he told the sea captain very forcefully, "Stop it. It's wrong to touch me like that. Leave me alone." Then the Dalai Lama, as me, stood up to the sea captain with power and compassion, saying, "I'm going to leave. Never touch me or any other child again. And stay away from me. I'm going home to tell my parents." The Dalai Lama then sent the sea captain love and forgiveness and walked out of the room.

The Dalai Lama and I each returned to our own bodies, and the Dalai Lama simply said to me, "Forgive. He did not have the ability to be a better person." He handed me a beautiful, tiny silver sword, saying I should keep this sword for protection. I turned it over and over in my fingers, marveling at how small it was, but how powerful it felt—although I couldn't figure out how in the world this miniscule sword was going to protect me.

When I was molested, I never told my parents or anyone else. I knew I couldn't. I knew that they wouldn't believe me, or they'd say it was my fault, just like everything else that was wrong with my parents' relationship was my fault. I think I blamed myself for it happening, too. I never went back to the sea captain's house. From that day forward I never played with my friend again, and I made sure I never laid eyes on the sea captain again. That was how I handled it. I took control so bad things wouldn't happen. As I grew up, I learned to anticipate all of the bad things that might happen in any given situation and then tried to fix them before they occurred.

When my parents asked me why I wasn't playing with my friend, I just didn't answer or said I was playing with new friends. I found excuses to be gone when the sea captain came to our house for dinner, and I avoided all contact. More than ten years later, my parents wanted me to go to his funeral. I said I was busy, and my parents were furious at me, but I didn't care. My parents and the sea captain all went to their graves without my parents knowing what had happened.

It took more than 45 years before I told Rachel about the event, but I knew it had had a profound effect on my ability to trust or to have an intimate relationship with any man who cared about me. I didn't feel those orgasmic moments everyone talked about, but I pretended I did. I participated out of obligation to please my partner, because that was what was expected, but I didn't really enjoy it. I wanted my partner to be satisfied and happy and for it to be over. Until this meditation, I'd never made the connection in my head or my heart between being molested and my feelings about just wanting sex to be over. I never talked with any of my husbands about the event or my feelings about sex, because I didn't want them to feel bad that I wasn't enjoying sex; that I had shut myself down; that I was numb; that I couldn't feel anything; that I was damaged. Somehow I'd convinced myself that I had the power to control how my partners felt, by withholding information, to make them feel better, even if it was at my expense.

I realized I couldn't change the past, but I could now move forward with awareness. As Kornfield said, I had to relinquish hope for a better past and give relief to my heart. I knew I needed to forgive the sea captain first, not for what he did, but for his state of consciousness at the time. Then I needed to forgive myself for carrying those thoughts, unconsciously, into every marriage I'd had. I could only imagine the effect that must have had on my relationships, and I was truly sorry and hoped my husbands could forgive me. I silently asked for their forgiveness.

I realized that I had never allowed myself to feel vulnerable after that. I didn't want to need anyone or let anyone in. You only got hurt when you did that. At all costs, I had to be tough and in control. Those lessons, coupled with the deeply embedded teachings of my mother—that no one would ever love me, and that men only wanted me for sex and would discard me once I "gave it away"—had made a loving, intimate relationship next to impossible for me. I turned this understanding over and over in my mind as I lay in that little bed in Ecuador. I realized it was time to stop playing my mother's tapes in my head. I realized I had a lot of work to do on myself.

The trip certainly was not turning out as I had expected. I started to feel better physically and emotionally, but Alverto was still sick. I was essentially stuck in the middle of nowhere, with no ability to go anywhere. I took walks and tried to feed and communicate with the two alpacas Alverto had, Chocolate and Crema, and I played with Alverto's daughter's little dog. There was very little formal study about animal communication.

Alverto told me to feed the alpacas and sit with them. He said to try to go inside them and see and feel what they were feeling. Then he said I should go somewhere and summon an animal to me.

I went to the top of the hill behind the house and mentally called Chocolate, the more shy and elusive of the two alpacas. I sat there quietly with my eyes closed, and was surprised when I looked up and saw that Chocolate had climbed all the way up the hill and was standing about ten feet in front of me, acting as if she didn't know why she was there.

As instructed, I said, "Hi, Chocolate. Thank you for coming. What's going on with you?"

Chocolate said that she was fearful of people because she didn't know what would happen next and that she needed water. I looked at her, surprised at the message, and said with love and compassion for the scared little alpaca, "You can stay or go when you want. Thank you for coming."

The little alpaca turned and ran back down the hill as fast as she could. I followed her down the hill a little while later and noticed that the alpacas' water bowl was bone dry. I filled the bowl and thanked Chocolate for letting me know. Alverto later told me Chocolate had come from a difficult situation and had been moved around a lot and was afraid of most people.

One evening Alverto stopped over at the house where I was staying. He was feeling a little better. I asked him if I could have some instruction about animal communication since that was my reason for coming to Ecuador.

"Yes," Alverto said. "Now?"

"Sí, perfecto," I replied, anxious to learn.

"Go lie in your bed, get comfortable, meditate, and empty your mind," Alverto instructed. "I'll come and call the animals in. When they come, pay attention to who comes, thank them for coming, and ask if they have any gifts for you. Accept their gifts, thank them, and when you're ready, tell them they can go."

I took my shoes off, put on comfy pants, and lay down, snuggling under the covers of my bed. It was early evening, the sun had already gone down, and my room was dark. I felt a presence in the room but kept my eyes closed. I assumed it was Alverto who entered the room with representatives of fire, earth, air, and water. A drum beat gently in the background, sounds started to fill the room, and animals started arriving. I heard sounds I'd never heard before. They were animal sounds, not human sounds. The animals were there.

A giant white bird came swooping in gracefully, Gracie, Lily, and Walter arrived together, a whale, a bear, and a large feline, not a lion exactly, but similar, all joined me very vividly in the room, as the room started to fill up. There were lots of other animals that weren't so distinct. Later I realized the lion-like thing was a Jaguar. They all just stood or sat quietly. At one point I thought an actual bear sat on the bed next to me, but I wasn't frightened. It felt wonderful, like someone was at my side to protect me and keep me safe. I felt calm and secure.

When the animals were all gathered, I remembered what Alverto had said. I asked them if they had any gifts for me or any wisdom they wanted to share with me. It was silent for a minute.

Then I heard, as clear as day, "If it's alright with you, we'll rest in your heart. We will not leave."

I was stunned and didn't know what to say, but then realized there was plenty of room in my heart for all the animals of the world.

"Please, yes, stay. There's plenty of room," I invited them silently. I sent love, welcomed them into my heart, and thanked them for coming. Then I fell into a restful sleep. I had no idea when Alverto left, but when I awoke, a candle was burning, and I had Noah's ark in my heart.

The next morning when Alverto came over, I explained what had happened and told him that the animals wanted to stay in my heart rather than leave. I'd participated in other indigenous ceremonies over the years, the effects of which usually subsided over night, so I was quite surprised that the animals were still there in the morning.

Alverto just smiled and looked at me intensely, like he was peering through me and seeing the inside.

"I didn't know what to expect," he said. "I didn't know if the animals would come. Last night confirmed that you have been trained for many lifetimes. You have all the knowledge you need to communicate with animals or to help heal them. You just need to trust your gift and access the information from within."

I realized I had received a very powerful gift indeed.

Days later, the animals were still there. I told Alverto that the bear, in particular, felt very powerful and protective, but I really didn't know what to do with the bear or any of the other animals in my heart.

"You will know what to do," he said. "Trust in the cosmos. Remember, you are a conduit. It has nothing to do with you. You might make an offering to the bears out in your orchard when you get home, though," he added.

"What do you mean?"

Alverto's seven-year-old daughter, a shaman in training, who had joined us around the table, chimed in, "Put out some food for them on a plate, offer it to them, make friends. They like berries and fish."

⁘

I wasn't hearing too much from the home front, and I was beginning to worry. I didn't have a phone and email was spotty, but it wasn't like Bill and the rest of the gang not to report in. All of the kids had moved back in the vicinity of Ojai, and they'd promised to check in on the dogs and Bill. I sent emails asking how everyone was and if everything was OK. Still no response. I finally got access to a phone and called Bill's cell.

"Oh, hi," he answered.

"How's everything going? I haven't heard from you guys in awhile."

"Everything's fine, not to worry," he said. "Have a good time. Oh, by the way, Carl's having a few issues, but we're watching him."

"What do you mean a few issues?" I asked.

"He's been having seizures quite frequently and falling down. He fell down the embankment in the backyard the other day and couldn't get up, and we had to climb down and carry him up. He was not happy about that one bit. Tried to bite. The vet says it might just be his time. Seventeen is pretty old."

"So what are you going to do?" I asked.

"I'm actually not home," Bill said. "I'm in Orange County, visiting my brothers, but the kids are watching the dogs, and they have it under control. I understand they've been talking to the vet."

"OK, let me know what's happening," I said trying to rein in the annoyance I felt that he wasn't home like he agreed he would be. "I feel helpless and powerless so far away. And it's really hard not getting any news. My imagination goes into hyper drive when I don't hear anything. I imagine all sorts of things."

Bill ignored my comment with silence.

"Oh, and Gracie had the grossest, smelliest, bright orange diarrhea the other day," he said as if he were reporting on the weather, not some vital piece of information like that. "It didn't get better, so we took her to the vet. Matt said it's probably some liver or pancreas thing. He has her on medication and did some blood work, but we don't know the results yet."

"What? Wait, I don't understand. How is she? Is she in pain? Is she going on walks? Is she eating?"

"Well, she's having a little trouble walking and getting up. We've made her a comfy bed in the dining room, close to the door, with a plastic sheet under it."

"Please don't let her die while I'm gone." I started to cry.

"That's what I told Matt."

"What?"

"I told him, 'You've got to keep Gracie alive until Julie gets back, or I'll never hear the end of it. Do whatever it takes.'"

I sat there in silence, my mind racing all over the place.

"She'll be fine," Bill said. "Matt will take good care of her. I'll let you know the results of the blood work as soon as we get it. Don't worry."

How could I possibly not worry, I thought. I would never be able to live with myself if Gracie died while I was gone. I needed to be with her; Gracie was my baby. "Should I come home early?" I asked through the tears. "I can see if I can change my plane ticket. It's so hard to assess what's going on from here."

"Let's see about the blood work first," he said. "I promise I'll let you know."

"Please, Bill. I don't know what to say or do."

"Well, everyone is sort of falling apart without you. But don't worry. I'll be in touch soon. Bye," Bill said as he hung up the phone.

"Now what?" I thought. "What does falling apart mean? And why isn't he home like he said he'd be?"

The next morning when I awoke there was an email from Roy, saying they'd been with Carl when he made his transition the night before. The message wasn't clear. I didn't know if Carl had died naturally or if they'd put him to sleep. It was almost as if everyone was trying to protect me by not giving me information. I knew they wanted me to have a nice vacation and not be stressed about the dogs. For me, though, no information was worse than knowing what was actually going on. I'd always been able to deal with situations, including injuries, to the dogs, to the kids, or whatever, calmly and with love. I always took over the situation, figured out what needed to be done, and then went into action to make it happen. But this was something new for me, not being in control of what was happening at home. I started to cry for Carl, for me, for Gracie. When my sobs finally subsided, I got up and went to look for Alverto.

I told Alverto about Gracie being sick, and he suggested we do a remote healing ceremony together, so that I could learn the steps to conduct a ceremony and perhaps stop worrying about Gracie. Alverto and I climbed up the hillside to a little secluded place I had been using for meditation, the same place Chocolate had come to be with me when I called. Along the way, we gathered twigs for a fire. We'd brought a drum from the house and a feather for air, a candle for fire, and water to use as symbols. Alverto showed me how to use all of the elements in the ceremony.

"The power isn't in the symbols, but in the air, the water, the fire, the earth. It's our connection with the power of the elements, with all of the cosmos, but it isn't me or you." He explained that rituals were important, but there was no right or wrong way to do this one.

"Follow your heart," he said. "Let it flow from the heart. Having symbols for all of the elements is a good place to start. Chant, dance, sing from the heart. Only a few words are necessary. No strict rules, just an expression from your heart with love and gratitude."

He started to beat the drum and chant and sing in his native language, and I tried to join in the best I could.

"Call to Gracie and ask her to come," he continued, after we stopped chanting. "See her as well and in good spirits. Explain to her where you are. The greatest healing occurs when you have love and gratitude in your heart, in yourself, and all around you. Do not see illness. See the perfection. See the balance."

I tried to feel that love and gratitude and got the sense that Gracie was there, but my mind was very wrapped up in my own sadness and worry. I tried to quiet my mind and go within, but it was difficult.

Alverto said, "Gracie is here. She likes to go play in the fields and run around. That's what she does sometimes when she looks like she is sleeping. She will be OK while you are gone."

I felt better after the ceremony, and I thought Gracie did, too.

The following morning, I received another email from Roy, saying Gracie had been for a little walk. Later that day, I got an email from Bill saying the blood work was in and that it wasn't good, but it wasn't terrible either; he said it had something to do with red blood cells. He told me Matt wanted to talk to me when I got back. They put Gracie on antibiotics and some kind of liver pills. The next day the email made it sound as if things were getting worse again, as if Gracie were getting sicker and sicker.

I was confused. How could things change so dramatically, so quickly?

"Should I come home early?" I asked in an email. "I checked and I can buy a new plane ticket and make arrangements to get home within two or three days." No one would come right out and tell me to come home, that they needed me, but I got that sense. Alverto said I should stay in Ecuador, that I needed more time for myself to heal and rest.

I emailed Maggie, asking, "What's going on at home? I'm not getting any clear answer from anyone. How's Gracie? Should I come home early? It'll cost me a lot to change my ticket at this late date, but I can do it if I have to."

Her response was quick and clear. "I think you'll be sad if you don't come home now, even if it does cost you a lot extra."

I looked for Alverto to talk about this, but he was nowhere to be found. So contrary to Alverto's advice to stay, I called and bought a new one-way economy ticket to Los Angeles, relinquishing my free business-class return seat for a week later. When Alverto returned, he told me not to go, that Gracie would be fine. I explained as best I could in Spanish that it was too late. I'd already changed my ticket, and I couldn't get my business-seat back. I was conflicted over whether I made the right decision or not. Alverto merely accepted what I said.

He drove me to Quito. It was unusually foggy, and we got lost on the way to the airport.

"Please don't do anything to delay me getting on the plane," I said to him nervously. I thought he probably had the power to do something to cause a delay if he wanted to, and I really wanted to get home now. I'm not sure if he understood what I was trying to say.

He gave me a friendly look. "No, no. No problema."

I got to the airport and a day later I arrived at LAX, exhausted. Rachel picked me up from the airport in Los Angeles and drove me home. As I walked in the house, I saw Gracie lying on the dog bed, which the kids had made for her in the dining room, close to the front door. She was barely able to lift her head, her spirit barely visible through her eyes, although she did smile slightly at the sight of me. As I looked at Gracie with love and bent down to kiss and hug her, I was convinced that I'd made it back with only hours to spare. The kids were there to greet me. Bill was at work.

CHAPTER 46

TRANSITION

Once everyone cleared out of the house, I promptly did a balancing ceremony on Gracie with air, water, fire, and earth, as Alverto had taught me. I thanked the cosmos and asked for spirit to please take over. I took a feather and carefully moved it down Gracie's spine. I took water and thanked it for its healing properties and rubbed it on Gracie's head. I lighted a piece of the sacred palo santo tree bark that I'd brought back from Ecuador and waved the smoke over Gracie. Then I went outside and thanked the earth and all of the plants and flowers with gratitude in my heart. I approached a large flowering geranium plant in my front yard and asked if any of the individual flowers wanted to come in the house to help with Gracie's healing, and one spoke up to volunteer. I approached that flower and thanked it for being willing to sacrifice itself. I gently blew air, the life force of the cosmos, through my funneled right hand into the flower and asked that the whole plant, down through its roots, receive the breath of life. I then again thanked the pink geranium for its willingness to be of service and picked it. I took it in the house and rubbed it on Gracie's spine and hips and then placed it on her side so it could remain on her while she slept. I thanked all of the elements and gave gratitude from my heart. After the ceremony, Gracie seemed to settle in to rest calmly.

I gathered all of the other orthopedic dog beds and laid them next to Gracie, so that I would have a bed on the floor next to her. I wanted to be close to her, so that I could touch her throughout the night and be there to help her get up and go out if needed. Gracie could not stand on her own.

Bill came home from work late and found me lying next to Gracie on the floor. "You're going to sleep there?" he asked.

"Yes. I'm exhausted, but I need to be close to Gracie. I'll be fine here," I replied. "These dog beds are actually comfortable."

"OK. Whatever you want. How was your trip?" he asked automatically, not waiting for an answer, as he headed up the steps to the guest room. "I'm going to bed. Glad you're home safe."

It was a long night for me, lying on the floor, all of the dogs in various places around me, but by morning, Gracie seemed a little better. She wanted to eat, and her eyes were more alive.

Bill came down the steps and wandered into the kitchen. "Hi. How was your night?"

"It was a little difficult to get Gracie outside. I think I pulled my back."

"Sorry. Why didn't you wake me up?"

"I thought you needed your sleep. But I've been wondering something."

"What's up?" he said.

"I know we said you'd look for a new place and move out again when I got back from Ecuador, but I don't think Gracie has long. Do you think you could stay here for a few weeks and help me get her in and out of the house, especially at night? It's really hard for me to lift her. I'd really appreciate it. I don't know if I can do it alone."

"Sure. I'll take her out now," Bill replied. "And then I've got to go to work. See you later."

I called the vet to find out about Gracie's blood work. Matt said she probably had cancer because of the disproportionate number of red blood cells, but an ultrasound would be necessary to confirm what he suspected. Even if they confirmed the diagnosis, though, there was really nothing that could be done. It was just a matter of time. I cried.

I didn't see too much of Bill over the next few days. He left early and came home late. After a few nights passed like that, Bill said, "You know, Julie, I said I would stay and help with Gracie, and I will. But every time I think about driving here, every time I get in the car, I get really depressed, and I start to get a terrible headache. When I leave in the morning, I feel a little better. But I said I would help, and I will."

"Oh," was all I could think of to say as Bill turned and went off to bed. I tossed and turned all night. I really didn't want someone in my house who got sick at the idea of coming home to me.

When Bill came into the kitchen the next morning, I said, "I've been thinking about what you said last night. I think it would be better if you moved out as soon as possible. I'll figure it out with Gracie. Don't worry about us. I really don't want you here if it makes you feel bad to be around me. I'm a good person. I deserve better than that," I said with tears filling my eyes as I turned away.

"OK. I'll go stay with friends for a few nights, and then I'll get a place."

His response seemed so cold and detached, but I really wanted to know something, so I asked, "By the way, why did you ask me to marry you if I'm such a terrible person?"

He had never said I was terrible, but I thought I must have been an awful person, without even knowing it, if it made him feel sick to be around me.

He thought about my question and said, "I thought if I showed you I was committed, you might change."

I didn't say anything. I couldn't say anything. I was numb, but I knew I had lots to talk to my therapist about that week.

For a week I slept on the floor next to Gracie in the dining room until my back couldn't take it any longer. Constantly lifting 100 pounds had strained my back and hips to the point that I could barely walk. It was very difficult to lift Gracie up, but once I got her on her feet, Gracie usually could make it—however unsteadily—out the door to the lawn. I arranged for an acupuncture treatment for her and that seemed to help her mobility a tiny bit. One day, Gracie even walked the 50 feet to the aviaries and back. I thought it was important that she keep moving at least a little and not lie in bed all day.

Her eating was sporadic, but hand-fed hot dogs always worked to get her to eat a little. Her pee and poop were still a very troublesome shade of bright orange. It concerned me that Gracie might go for 48 hours without relieving herself. I could tell that Gracie was embarrassed when her rear legs collapsed while she was peeing, and she fell into her pee and then couldn't get back up. I stayed vigilant and raced to Gracie's aid to catch her when I saw she was about to fall over. I cleaned her off with a warm damp cloth and got her settled into a clean bed each time I wasn't fast enough to be by her side before she fell.

I bought a special harness to help me lift Gracie and assist her to walk. She hated it and refused to wear it. She would totally collapse and not support any weight on her legs until I took it off. It was like she was embarrassed about needing a harness. I would lie on the floor next to Gracie most of the time, pet her gently, and tell her I loved her. In my stress and exhaustion, I'd forgotten about talking to Gracie directly and listening for a response.

"Gracie, what do you want me to do?" I finally remembered to ask. "Please tell me."

Please promise me you will finish the book. You haven't worked on it for a long time. I need to know it will be done this time.

"OK, I promise," I said. "I'm sorry I haven't worked on it with you. I was worried about you getting older. And I've been off feeling sorry for myself. Do you have anything else you want to add to the book?"

No, I have said what I wanted, the amount people can understand at this time. Just get it done. Don't forget to give the profits to help animals.

"OK, I will."

"I worry about the future, Gracie. I worry about things I have no control over. But I can't help myself. What if I get sick again? Who will take care of me if I'm alone? I'm happy Bill's kids are part of my life. I know they'll always be there for me, but sometimes, in spite of it all, I miss having Bill around. But my real fear is no one will ever love me the way I want to be loved. So completely that it takes your breath away, like the kind of love you see in movies or hear about in country western songs, but not the cheating kind," I said, focusing a slight smile on Gracie. "The kind of love I feel from you and for you. I'd like to be able to give that kind of love to someone, too. Maybe that's just not in the cards for me. Maybe I'll never have that. Maybe that's not my path."

You have love all around you. Just feel it. It's not always the exciting romantic love, which can last a lifetime or be fleeting. It's the love in the trees, in the plants, in the animals, in the air and the water and the rocks; and it's in the people around you, your friends, and in Walter and Lily. It's in me. It's in you. Just let it embrace you. You are never alone. Please, try and understand on a deep spiritual level what I have been saying—there is divine energy in everything. That everything includes you. So how can you not feel love? You are love and you are worthy of being loved. How could it be any other way if you have a fragment of God within you?

I sat there quietly, letting those words sink in and fill me. "Thank you, Gracie. What will I do when you're gone?" I said, starting to cry.

I'll always be here for you. I love you. You can do it.

"Is it your time to go?" I asked, tears finally spilling over, as the wet spot on Gracie's neck grew larger and larger. I didn't hear a response.

All of my turmoil about making a decision to end a dog's suffering by assisting their transition, which first arose with Puggers, came flooding back as I continued to sit next to Gracie on the floor and worry about her failing condition. What right did I have to make that decision? It was up to spirit, not me. My friends said I would know when the time was right, but that was baloney. The time would never be right. I didn't know what I would do without Gracie in my life. She was my best friend, the only one who really understood me. I knew Gracie didn't have long for this world, but if she had to leave me, I hoped she would pass away on her own, so that I didn't have to make the decision.

It seemed strange to me that my relationship with Bill started with Gracie and now was finally ending with Gracie's transition. We weren't divorced, but he had moved out again. And this time, I was pretty sure it was over. We were sort of friends, but that was it. Was that coincidence or was there a deeper meaning? I didn't know.

"Gracie, it's OK if you have to leave. I understand. I'll make it. Don't worry about me. I don't want you to be in pain, I don't want you to suffer any more," I whispered as I stroked Gracie's soft, velvety ears and massaged her back.

As the days passed, Gracie's inability to move on her own increased. Stairs were impossible. The two areas in the house with ground level access were the dining room/kitchen area and my bedroom downstairs. I kept Gracie's daytime bed in the dining area, so she could see the action. I moved her nighttime bed next to mine downstairs, so that I could sleep in my own bed but still be close to Gracie when she needed help to go out in the night. It was a little farther for Gracie to walk at night, but I had a ramp built up and over the water drainage ditch that ran in front of the house, so that it was a relatively smooth path to the lawn. This way Gracie didn't have to hop over the ditch. Hopping was not in the cards for her any longer.

Gracie's telltale sign of needing to go out was extreme panting. I also recognized this as a sign of pain or anxiety, and it would wake me up instantaneously. Sometimes I'd struggle to get Gracie up when I heard the panting. Gracie would slowly make it out front and stand outside on the lawn in the moonlight and not move a muscle, as if calling the moon to help her, but not needing to relieve herself. Other times she would try to go, but she'd collapse; and I would race to her side. It was difficult on Gracie and me. I felt very fragile emotionally, and my heart ached with the loss of Puggers, Carl, and Bill. Seeing Gracie failing was almost more than I could bear.

Before I'd left for Ecuador, I'd scheduled a special Mohs surgery procedure to remove a new squamous cell carcinoma that had appeared on my right hand. The surgery was coming up in a few days, and I questioned how I was going to lift Gracie with only one arm since I was already struggling with two. The last time I'd had this type of surgery, I had to have a skin graft and wasn't able to move my left arm or hand at all for two weeks to ensure the graft would take. I knew that Roy, who had returned home and lived nearby, would help during the day, but what was I going to do at night if Gracie needed to go out? I was alone and physically and emotionally depleted.

The next night Gracie was panting and anxious and seemed to be in pain, so I gave her a prescription pain medication to help. She lay on her side, panting all night, but not wanting to move. The following morning, Gracie could not raise her head. I called Roy, and we got Gracie up and carried her to her bed upstairs by the front door. I texted Bill, the kids, Maggie, and Rachel and said they should come say their goodbyes. I told them that Gracie couldn't lift her head, and I thought this was the day.

"Hi, it's Julie," I said through the tears to a familiar voice that answered the phone at the vet's office. "It's Gracie. She's really bad. I don't want her to suffer anymore. Can Matt come up today?"

"I'm so sorry, Julie," the nurse said. "I don't think he can do it today, though. He's really swamped with emergencies. Maybe Friday."

"Oh no, I don't want her to suffer that long. She can't lift her head. The light's gone out of her eyes. I can't bear to see her like this. How about after work?" I asked.

"He can't come after work today either. He has a meeting out of town. I'll talk to him and call you back," she said. "I'm so sorry. I love Gracie."

The nurse called back shortly. "He said he'll come up during his lunch hour, around 12:30."

"Oh no, not that soon. I'm not ready," I cried.

"You'll never be ready. Do you want him to come then or not?" she asked kindly.

"Yes, I suppose." I could hardly breathe.

Bill said he'd be right there and showed up within the hour. Jane had said her goodbyes the day before; she said she couldn't take it and wasn't going to come. Anne lived too far away and texted how sorry she was. Roy was there, just as he always was for me, and he gave Gracie some love. Maggie and Rachel arrived. And then Gracie perked up. She smiled at everyone as they arrived, as if holding court, and started to take small biscuits from my hand as she lay on her side with her head in my lap. I spoke to her softly and lovingly. Everyone told Gracie how wonderful she was. I had second thoughts. The phone rang.

"Hi, Julie. I'm so sorry, but Matt can't come at lunchtime. A dog was hit by a car, and he has to do emergency surgery."

"Oh," I said as I went blank.

"He'll try for after work. I'll let you know."

"I thought he couldn't come then."

"He'll try for you."

"Thanks," I said, not really wanting him to be able to come.

"I'll call you."

Everyone who had gathered to be with Gracie when she made her transition had to leave when I said that Matt wasn't coming at lunchtime. No one could wait five or six hours. They said their goodbyes and made their way out, leaving Gracie and me alone with Walter and Lily. I sat on the floor with Gracie and cried. I totally forgot about asking Gracie what she wanted. I was devastated at the thought of putting this beautiful, magnificent being to sleep. I was incredibly sad for Gracie and for myself. Gracie was my baby. I thought it was the wrong decision. I called Jane. I called Maggie. I called Bill. I called Roy. They all thought it was her time and that she was suffering. I waited with Gracie, her head cradled gently in my lap.

"I love you. You are wonderful. I don't know how I'll make it without you, but I promise to finish the book. Is it your time? Do you want to make your transition?"

The phone rang. It was the vet's office. "Julie, Matt just got done and said he can come right now."

"What time is it?"

"It's about 2:30."

"Oh no. She's lifting her head a little. I don't know what to do."

The nurse was silent, allowing me time to process.

"I guess he should come," I said as I hit the end button on my phone.

I called Maggie. "Maggie, Matt's on his way," I said when I heard her voice on the phone.

"I'll be right there."

Matt and his nurse arrived just after Maggie. Gracie looked up from my lap and smiled at them, and then she took a little piece of biscuit from my hand.

"Matt, do you think it's the right thing to do? Look, she's taking food from me."

"I don't know, Julie," he sighed. "Yes, I do know it's right, but it's such a difficult decision and it's yours. She's old for a lab. She's outlived most of her children. She could probably drag on for a few more days, but she'll never regain mobility. She has cancer, and she'll start to suffer more and more as her organs shut down. This is taking a toll on you, too," he said in his affable but empathetic way.

I looked at Maggie who nodded ever so slightly through her own tears. "You're right," I said. "Go ahead, Matt. I don't want her to suffer any more."

"Gracie, I love you so much," I told her. "Have an easy transition to your next assignment. Whatever it is. You've been my best friend and protector, and I appreciate you being in my life. You'll never know how much. I'll finish the book. I love you," I whispered in Gracie's ear as I held her close and sent her as much love from my heart as I could. "I'll miss you."

Gracie looked at me and smiled. She raised her head slightly as the needle went in, and then she passed away calmly and peacefully in my arms, bathed in love and tears, with the most serene look on her face.

I fell apart.

In the days that followed, I could see Gracie everywhere and feel her in my heart, and my heart ached. I questioned everything and felt incredibly guilty for helping her transition. Why did I do that? Maybe she was getting better. Maybe I messed up her karma. I questioned whether letting her go was the correct decision. Should I have done more to prolong her life? Would one more acupuncture treatment have given her another week or ten days? Had everyone else pressured me? Did I make this decision because of my own physical limitations and pending surgery? Why hadn't I just canceled my surgery and let Gracie live for a few more days? Why hadn't I even thought of that until now? These questions haunted me and woke me up each morning as the tears rose, and I realized that I really, really missed Gracie. Grief is a process and a mystery for sure.

CHAPTER 47

WAKING UP

I was lying in bed, half asleep, half awake, tears filling my eyes along with the first light of day, as thoughts about Gracie once again flooded my mind. I rolled over to sleep for just another half an hour, to try and avoid being confronted with the grief for a little while longer. I fell into that instantaneous deep early morning sleep that sometimes comes when you've had a restless night. I was already dreaming, vivid colorful dreams that didn't make any sense, when Walter put his arm across my shoulder and around my neck. He just rested it there in a half hug, and I ignored it, hoping he would go away and let me sleep. Then Walter gave me a very gentle little shake, as if he were trying to wake me up. Then there was a calm spell as he waited for my response. Next he shook me a little harder and with more intensity. I continued to ignore him. Then another brief waiting period. I could almost hear his thoughts: "Please wake up, please." I continued to ignore the shaking, and then Walter started to talk to me, making low guttural mmmaarg, mmmaarg sounds, which intensified the more I tried to pretend I was asleep even as I was inwardly enjoying Walter's tactics.

Finally I couldn't ignore the shaking or the sounds any longer. I rolled over to face Walter. His big head was stretched forward so it was about one inch from my face, his arm still draped around my neck. As I turned toward him, a slow smile spread on his face and his tongue drooped from one side of his mouth. He took a big swipe with his prickly tongue across my lips and then planted smaller, nibbly kisses all over my face. The pleading sounds didn't stop until I took my hands from under the covers and stroked his silky ears and petted his head.

"Good morning, you big goofball," I said. "Don't worry, I'm still here. I love you."

Then he settled down.

"So human-like in gesture and emotion," I thought lazily as I tried to drift back to the place I'd been. He just wanted some love and attention. Walter quieted right down and fell back to sleep, gently snoring, stretched sideways across the whole bed so I had about six inches on one side.

"Oh well, I'm awake now," I said to Walter quietly so I wouldn't wake him. "I might as well get out of bed, greet the sun, and start the day," I added, even though a part of me wanted to curl up next to Walter and go back to sleep.

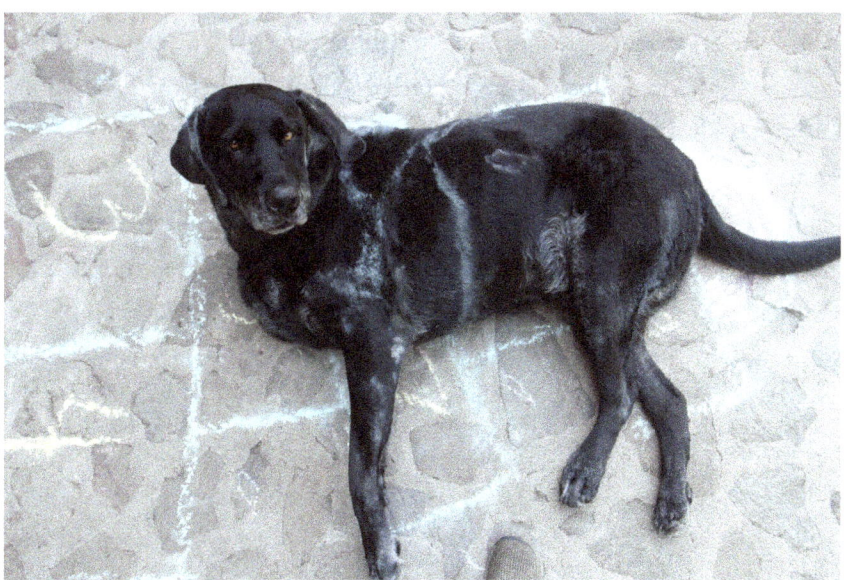

Walter always wanted to be in the middle of any game, even hopscotch.

CHAPTER 48

EPIPHANY

According to Don Alverto, my astrologer, my Buddhist teachings, and everything I was reading about living a more heart-based, intuitive life, this was supposed to be a year of transformation and spiritual growth for me and everyone on the planet. The word in the woo-woo circles was that this was the beginning of a new cycle on earth.

I'd experienced a lot of loss in a short period of time: Puggers, Carl, Gracie, Bill, and Walter's leg, which was a lot worse for Walter than for me. Even Spice, the horse, had made her transition in the last month. It seemed like a lot to take. I know you never get more than you can handle, but some days I felt I was at the breaking point. A quote by Mother Teresa summed up my feelings: "I know God will not give me anything I can't handle. I just wish he didn't trust me so much." A lot of space had been created for something new to come into my life. I could feel that transformation was in process and that I was supposed to be part of it. But how? How was I supposed to get over a heart that had been broken on so many levels?

I meditated. I went to therapy in Santa Barbara. I meditated. I went to Buddhist retreats and group meditations. Just sitting with my breath quietly really helped. I walked and talked to the plants and the trees and the stream. I went to the ocean and sat. I meditated. I just started to be with nature, not thinking about it so much. I felt a deep sense of community, and then I had one of those moments when things come into clarity.

Or at least they become a little clearer.

I realized that I'd lived my entire life believing that if I were myself, I would not be loved. That's what I had heard and that's what I believed deep within myself. That statement had been subconsciously controlling my life and insidiously creeping into everything I did. The solution was simple—be someone different. Make yourself appear just a little better than you are because you are not good enough and never will be no matter what you do.

I suddenly took stock of just how many thoughts had been subconsciously running my life. Don't love yourself because you're not loveable. Don't think about yourself. Don't ever need anything from anyone. Never feel vulnerable. Hide or run from your feelings. Don't feel. Don't ask for help. Give up everything for your partners and become the person you think they want because they certainly wouldn't want you. Say what you think they want to hear. Give up your own likes and take on theirs. Do everything for everyone else—family, friends, strangers—because they deserve it, but you don't. Make it easy on everyone around you by rarely voicing needs or concerns and then get internally annoyed when things don't go as you envisioned. But rarely say anything, because if you stand up for that unlovable you, you won't be loved. But at least then you can prove that your mother was right—you are not loveable. If you stand up for yourself, people will be upset or mad at you, or think you are self-centered, and you can't bear that. You can't stand it if anyone around you is sad or angry or unhappy. It's your fault. It's much easier to feel miserable yourself than have anyone around you feel miserable. Besides you can fix things for everyone else.

"How screwed up is that?" I thought out loud. "Who put me in charge of everyone's feelings anyway?"

But the real epiphany occurred on a much deeper spiritual level, when I truly understood Gracie's final lesson and felt the concept of the divine energy within. How could I not be loved or loveable if there was a fragment of the divine in me too? I truly believed that to be so. I believed that there is spiritual energy in each of us, not just people, but all sentient beings, all of nature, just as Gracie had been hammering in my head for years. Everything is comprised of divine energy. We are divine energy; we are love; and that "we" included me. All I really had to do was be myself, love myself, love and be loved for who I was, and feel the love all around. It was so simple and had taken me so long to integrate into my being. We are spiritual beings having a human experience. Some times the human part of it isn't so easy, but that doesn't change our fundamental nature.

What I had learned from my mother simply wasn't true. Now what the heck did I do about that realization? I wanted to use the "F" word but thought perhaps it was not appropriate with a spiritual epiphany. But what I really wanted was to throw away that tape, which was on a constant loop in my head, and insert one that acknowledged that I was perfect, whole and complete, and loving and worthy of being loved.

> To make the right choices in life, you have to get in touch with your soul. To do this, you need to experience solitude, which most people are afraid of, because in the silence you hear the truth and know the solutions.
>
> -Deepak Chopra

CHAPTER 49

TALKING AGAIN

Someone had told me to write a list between the solar eclipse and the lunar eclipse of 100 things I would like to see happen during the next year. That sounded like a good place to start on a road to transformation and so I sat down to do the list. Things appeared on the list that I'd never thought about before. Travel to Bhutan; I barely knew where Bhutan was. Travel to India; I did know where India was and had always wanted to go there. There were lots of things on the list about strengthening my bond with animals, learning to communicate better with animals, and developing a community. One thing that popped up on my list was to read books about animal communication. I just wrote everything down that came through without questioning it.

The next day I was walking by my bookshelf, and a book I'd purchased five or six years earlier but never read almost jumped off the shelf. It was called *Learning Their Language* by Marta Williams. Normally I would have felt too guilty to read in the middle of the day, thinking that I wasn't being productive, that I should be doing something like volunteering, or taking care of something or somebody. But this was something, something I'd put on my list just days before. So contrary to my normal modus operandi,

I sat down to read this book about animal communication, and I was hooked. The book sparked a fire in me. I wanted to learn everything I could about animal communication. Talking to Gracie was one thing, but branching out to other animals or other species? Why not? Maybe I'd actually been doing that for years, but just hadn't recognized it as communication. Like the ants and the bear. What possibilities existed to communicate with other beings—like Jeffrey. And communication would provide an opportunity to be of service to animals.

As I read the book, I got to one part on the possibility of communicating with a deceased animal. I really wanted to talk to Gracie. I missed her. I had questioned myself at the moment Gracie transitioned, and I questioned myself now, months later. Maybe a miracle was in progress and I had interfered with that miracle. Maybe Gracie had been getting better. No one ever told me I would feel so guilty about choosing to put her to sleep. I kept reading about how to communicate with a deceased animal:

> Sit in a quiet place by yourself, close your eyes and imagine the animal; either see or feel her there right in front of you. Say the animal's name and send love to her. Now say whatever is in your heart and mind. If you felt guilty about something … talk about that … If you are still grieving and can't get beyond the tears, tell her that … Say whatever it is that went unsaid, and ask her to let you know in some way that you have been heard.
>
> Marta Williams, *Learning Their Language*

So I tried it. "Gracie, I love you and I'm incredibly sad that you're gone. My heart feels like it's breaking. I'm so, so sorry I had you put to sleep. I feel incredibly guilty, and I don't know if it was the right decision. Maybe I should have done more to keep you with me. I miss you so much. Please talk to me. Let me know how you are."

I am right here. I only hung on because I knew how hard my passing was going to be on you. I was in a lot of pain and that made it difficult to communicate. I tried to do the best I could for your sake, but it was just too hard in that failing body to keep going. My time on the planet in that form was up. Thank you for helping me make my transition. Didn't you see how peaceful I was as I passed over to the other side in your arms? I can't think of a more comforting place to be than close to you. I hope you can stop feeling bad about it. It is actually easier to be with you now. The communication is clearer now, with fewer distractions. Our connection now truly is heart to heart. The connection is strong, and I am with you always. Please talk to me any time you want. Ask me anything and believe in the answers. I really needed to leave the physical so that you could work on the book. Work on it. I love you.

I started to cry. "Please, Gracie, give me a sign that you really were here with me, and I'm not just making up what I want to hear to make myself feel better."

Candle.

I got the word 'candle,' but I had no idea what that meant. I looked and the four candles I had lit every day were burning side by side in a row while I had been talking with Gracie. I'd been following the Buddhist tradition of lighting a candle each day for 49 days after a passing. Gracie, Carl, Puggers, and Spice each had their own candle on the sideboard where I had created a little altar. I had placed the dogs' ashes, some water, some feathers to symbolize air, flowers for earth, and of course the candles for fire, on the altar, so that all of the elements were represented, as Don Alverto had suggested. It wasn't exactly following the Buddhist tradition since Puggers had died months before, but it felt right to honor everyone under the circumstances, and so I had set up the altar for all of them when Gracie passed away.

After I'd finished talking to Gracie, I stepped into the kitchen to get a drink of water and felt a great weight slowly rising from around my heart.

Gracie's words had really touched me deeply. When I came back a minute later, I noticed that one candle was out. The other three burned exactly as they had for the last several hours. I stared at the candles and pondered why just one had gone out.

"There must have been a breeze," I thought. But the candles were all the same beeswax candles, in the same kind of glass containers, lined up next to each other, so how could the breeze have blown out just one? Why would just the second from the right go out? I wondered. It wasn't logical. It didn't make sense.

"God, am I dense or what?" I said out loud. That was the candle in Gracie's position. It was her sign to me that she'd been there. It was just like me to try to figure it out with my head and explain it away, rather than just believe in the mysteries that occur all the time. I started to cry again. Maybe, just maybe, I really didn't live in a world that operates the way my mind thought it did or should. Maybe there was magic happening all of the time even if I didn't recognize it.

I started thinking about how we spend our time creating so many tidy little boxes to live in, believing things will turn out the way we want them to, thinking we have control over how things go. We make constructs and grids of how things work and why things are the way they are. Then we try to prove it to ourselves. Isn't it just as valid to believe in a different construct? One that acknowledges that we live in an intelligent Universe that knows what we need and when we need it? Albert Einstein knew this in 1929 when he said:

> Everything is determined ... by forces over which we have no control. It is determined for the insect as well as for the star. Human beings, vegetables, or cosmic dust—we all dance to a mysterious tune, intoned in the distance by an invisible piper.

Einstein, who everyone considers to be a really smart guy, said that more than 80 years ago, and it seems some of us are just now figuring it out.

Maybe transformation *is* occurring more rapidly on this planet now, and we just need to get with the program. When we need to talk to someone, we can talk to a tree or a mountain or an animal, and listen to what they have to say.

One day I was out walking with Lily and Walter, and I stopped in front of a tree. Trees are known to be healers, and this one seemed to call out to me.

"What am I supposed to be doing?" I asked the tree.

"Stand strong, stand tall. You must do this alone. Know yourself. Find your true self and then let it blossom in the world," the tree responded.

Then a startling realization filled my whole being. I had never really been alone. I had always had men in my life since I was sixteen years old. Whether they were boyfriends, or random sexual partners, or totally inappropriate men who were emotional placeholders, or husbands, I had never been without some man in my life for any length of time. If I happened to be in between relationships, I was always looking for a relationship to complete me. This was the first time in almost fifty adult years that I was by myself and actually enjoying the solitude and getting to know myself. I didn't have the pressure of a relationship or of wanting a relationship. I was fine just the way I was, and magical things were happening every day in my life. I felt truly happy walking with Lily and Walter and just being out in nature. I felt love all around.

After all of these years, I was finally uncovering my gifts. I was doing what I wanted. Everyone leaving within a short period of time had created a space for my gifts to emerge. I had been emptied out so that I could be filled with something entirely new. I felt gratitude to Bill and the kids for their presence in my life and for the role they had played in bringing animals into my life. Bill had been a gift for me, and yet I felt gratitude for him leaving me, too. The magic was occurring in the space outside the normal belief systems about how things should be in an "until death do us part" world.

What was supposedly normal was so ingrained that it was difficult to break out of that mold. It was particularly difficult to accept that I didn't have to know or understand everything. And yet on some very deep level, I did know. Or at least I knew that I didn't know anything. Each moment was perfect, even if I didn't get what I had planned for or what I thought I wanted. As the Rolling Stones said, "You don't always get what you want … you get what you need." I was having faith in the actual occurrence of things. If it shouldn't have happened, it wouldn't have happened, someone once said.

As humans, difficult and challenging circumstances often occur in our lives. Within each of these moments we are given a special opportunity for growth, a gift. Sometimes it is difficult to accept the gift in the midst of what appears to be a setback or constant drama. I think forward progress occurs when we open our minds and hearts to the blessings that come to us in disguise.

I also realized how important meditation had become in my life. In the stillness of meditation I began to gently release ego thoughts connected with success and failure. Meditation helped me begin to trust the movement of life, knowing that the Universe has much grander plans than I could ever fathom. I finally internalized, as so many teachers had said over the years, that each step along the path of life, regardless of the destination, is a wondrous part of the whole adventure. The moments themselves are the gifts, and the journey, the rich reward.

ooooo

The next day the landline rang. I rarely answered that phone because it was usually a solicitor, and I was getting tired of giving my standard response, "No, sorry, Ms. Bloomer's not here. Could I take a message for her?" The only other people who used that phone and not my cell phone were people from my distant past, and it was fun to hear from them, so for a change I answered the phone.

"Hello."

"Hello, Julie? This is June, Crystal's friend," a voice with a thick British accent said cheerfully over the phone.

"Oh, yes. How are you? It's been a long time," I said, thinking that it had probably been fifteen years since I'd met this woman briefly at a seminar with Crystal in Santa Fe.

"Yes, yes. Well, we spoke a few years back when Crystal was at your house and made her transition. Remember, I called and spoke to her?"

"Oh, yes, sorry. I forgot," I said, the memory flooding me of how wonderful Bill had been to agree to drive with me all the way to Utah, pick Crystal up from the hospital, and drive her home, so I could take care of her until she made her transition. "That was a very stressful time around here. I don't remember too much of those days."

"Yes, well, you did a wonderful thing to keep Crystal with you. It was a blessing for her to be with you, I'm sure."

"Thanks. I don't know about that. I did the best I could, but it was pretty intense … What are you up to?" I asked.

"I'm with a friend in Santa Barbara now, and we were going to come to Ojai tomorrow and would love to pop in and say 'Hi.' Are you going to be around?"

"I think so."

"You'll really like my friend," June said. "She's an anim…," June's voice trailed off so I couldn't hear.

"She's a what?" I asked

"She is an animal … an interspecies communicator," June replied.

"Really?" I said. "I just started reading a book about animal communication."

"Which one?"

"*Learning Their Language*, by a lady in Northern California."

"That's so funny. I'm reading that, too. It's quite good, don't you think?"

"Yes. I want to learn more about animal communication now," I said.

"You've been interested in that for a long time," June replied.

"Have I?"

"Sure. I remember you talking about animal communication twenty years ago."

"I guess that's true," I said, pondering the timing of things in the Universe, how things move at their own pace. Maybe I just wasn't ready before. "I'd really like to study with someone now."

"Hey, Barb," June yelled, laughing to her friend in the background. "She wants to study animal communication."

"That's just the kind of lessons Barb gives," June said to me.

"It's amazing how the Universe provides, isn't it?" I asked.

"It always does. If you are open to it."

CHAPTER 50

LEARNING AND LISTENING

June and Barbara arrived on Sunday afternoon, and the three of us wandered around the ranch. Barbara and I chatted easily about animal communication. Barbara had an infectious laugh that I liked. As we walked along, I could almost sense Barbara's communication with everything; she would walk by an animal or a plant or a bird, stop, and listen. A smile would appear and then her face would erupt into delight, as if someone had just told her a joke. She seemed to absorb humor from nature. Walter stayed by her side everywhere we went, and I could tell he loved her. Of course, Walter loves everyone so I was not surprised.

Finally we wound up back in the living room. Walter sat at Barbara's feet, and Lily parked herself nearby. I asked Barbara about Gracie and showed her Gracie's picture hanging on the wall.

"I feel so bad and so sad that I had Gracie put to sleep. Maybe it was too early. Maybe I interfered with the Universe's plans and screwed things up royally. Maybe I interfered with karma," I said as tears started to well up again. I knew Gracie had said it was fine, but I couldn't stop second-guessing myself. "I can't get over the sadness, even though it's been almost two months that she's been gone. I really miss her, and I keep beating myself up about the decision, even though I know I can't change anything now. Even if I was wrong, she's gone."

"She's right here in this room with you now," Barbara said tenderly.

"Feel her. You know it's true."

"Sometimes I feel it, but I don't trust myself. I think I'm just making stuff up."

"I feel as if she has something to say to you," Barbara said, tuning in. She went quiet for a moment. "Gracie wants you to know that she's here with you, that the communication is stronger and easier for her now. That she has a very clear connection in this form. She meets you in your heart. She is proud of herself and she is proud of you. And you are doing good work together. She also is insistent that you do it now. She says it's a magic time and easy right now. This is me doing the interpretation now. I don't know what it is, but she's showing me that she's almost pestering you about something, being bossy."

"That's my Gracie. She always was bossy. That's almost the same as what she told me last week when I did an exercise from *Learning Their Language*." I told Barbara about Gracie's message and the candle. "I didn't get a chance to tell you, but we're working on a book together. I put it aside for a long time because I stopped believing, but I've taken it up again since she passed. I promised her I would finish it, and it has been therapeutic for me."

Barbara didn't even stop to question the idea or validity of writing a book with my dog. "You know," she said, "Walter has a role in the book, too."

Barbara looked directly at Walter and then chortled with glee. "He has a sense of humor, that one. He's showing me a picture that he's 'throwing up' a wall around you. I believe he's trying to let me know that he's creating a safe space so you can work, not that he's actually throwing up. He and Gracie are partners in this book. He keeps you steady. He holds the energy in his gigantic heart now that Gracie is gone."

I had noticed that Walter had taken up Gracie's place at my feet under the table while I worked on the book, so I wasn't really surprised about that information. If he was outside and saw me working at the computer, he insisted on coming in and getting close.

"But how do you know the connection is real? That it's not just in your head?" I asked.

"How big is Walter? Not his physical size, but how big is he?" Barbara asked.

"He fills the whole room," I said without hesitation.

"How do you know that?"

"I don't know … I just know," I said, my voice trailing off.

Barbara smiled. "Based on my observation and experience, when an animal comes into our lives, it has a very important role. It's a new phase in our lives. It may even sacrifice to bring us gifts. They also create a new phase when they leave. Based on what you've told me, you've had five major leavings in a short period of time. When you examine the old phase, recognize that a new one is beginning. Gracie is here, and she is persistent in this new phase, too."

"I got another confirmation about Gracie last week," I said a little sheepishly. "I went to an intuitive/spiritual counselor. During our medicine card reading, she did a mini-reading about Gracie for me. The card I flipped over for Gracie was a badger. The counselor said, 'Badgers never give up. Gracie is persistent about some project you're working on. I don't know what it is, something about communication, but it feels right for you. It would be good to work on it.'"

Barbara laughed again. "You are blessed. You keep getting confirmation from the Universe, so why don't you believe it?"

"Easier said than done with my logical, need-to-know brain, working non-stop to criticize, sabotage, and distract me," I said, smiling. "What about Lily?"

"Lily is like the antennae," Barbara said. "She gets nervous. She was very interwoven with Gracie and her brother and the other dog, too. She's struggling to get grounded without them. I would recommend that you touch each of Lily's feet, in the morning, in particular, and imagine that roots are growing through her feet to the ground."

"OK," I said.

"She is total love, that one. And talk to her. Tell her where you're going and when you'll be back when you go out. Give her a job while you're away, like keeping the peace or keeping Walter out of trouble."

"That sounds like a good job for her," I said.

"Everything is in communication—consciousness, plants, animals, water, everything. We just must approach them with openness and respect and a willingness to listen. Be kind to all. Think of it like a gigantic computer, that all of nature is out there, online, just waiting for us to connect to access all the information we need."

"Wow, that's an interesting way to look at it. Thanks. I really appreciate everything you've said. I'd really like to take some lessons. Do you ever do that?"

"Call me, and we'll talk about it. Sometimes I do a two-day seminar for groups or private lessons."

"Sounds great. I'll be in touch," I said, as Barbara and June left, laden down with oranges, avocados, and plums that the wonderful, abundant trees had provided—with Jeffrey's help no doubt.

CHAPTER 51

LILY

I really tried to remember to talk to Walter and Lily when I was going anywhere, to give them an explanation and a sense of the time I would return. One of the things that the animal communication book suggested was to pretend that your animals could understand every word, thought, and emotion. It said to suspend disbelief and just do it for two weeks, and then make note of what you observed. So I thought I'd try it. I didn't see how it could hurt anything to just pretend Walter and Lily understood everything I said.

"So, Lily, what's going on with you?" I asked, as I sat on the floor next to her as she lay under the dining room table. "You seem so nervous, and I'm worried about you."

"I was always the unseen dog. I kept it all together for everyone else. I was kind and sweet to all creatures, and I still am, but I was never noticed that much before. Now all this attention from you and this communication is a little much. It makes me nervous. I'm not used to it. Don't worry, I'll get used to it. It may just take a little while. Also, I'm really nervous when you leave that you'll never come back, like all of the others who have left." (Lily, June 21, 2012)

"I'm here, and I'm not going anywhere," I told her. "I have to go out sometimes. I have things to do, but I'll be back. I'll try and let you know how long I'll be gone, OK?" I didn't get a response, but it seemed as if she understood.

And as the weeks progressed, I kept up the chatter with Lily, sending her love and explaining how much I appreciated her in my life. Lily seemed less and less nervous when I went anywhere and was all around happier. Maybe Lily had needed time to grieve and settle in to a new phase, too.

> Within Siddhartha there slowly grew and ripened the knowledge of what wisdom really was and the goal of his long seeking. It was nothing but a preparation of the soul, a capacity, a secret art of thinking, feeling and breathing thoughts of unity at every moment of life.
> —Hermann Hesse, *Siddhartha*

CHAPTER 52

THE LAMAS FROM BHUTAN

One day I received an email from my friend Jill about an empowerment seminar to take place the following week at the Massage School in Meiner's Oaks, the town next to Ojai. I read all of the information on the flyer about a group of monks from Bhutan whose roof had collapsed on their monastery. All of the proceeds from the workshop were to be used to assist with the roof repair. I decided to go because the teachings sounded interesting, and I thought helping a monastery in Bhutan seemed like a good cause in any case.

I was beginning to realize that the things I learned from Crystal, Gracie, Alverto, Barbara, and my Buddhist studies were all basically the same. The words were different, but the concepts were essentially the same; and right now I was trying to find ways to open my heart to the gifts of the Universe. Empowerment just sounded like a good thing to learn to help access my authentic self and figure out what I was supposed to be doing. I was really getting tired of the stories from my past, which just kept replaying themselves endlessly. They no longer seemed helpful. They no longer defined me. So why wouldn't they leave me alone? I thought it was about time to figure it out, and maybe this workshop would help.

I emailed the contact person from the flyer and asked how to reserve a spot since space was limited. I didn't know this person but got an immediate response confirming that I could come, even though I knew nothing about this particular Buddhist practice, and yes, that it was on a donation basis to help the monastery. Almost simultaneously, the phone rang. It was the event organizer, and we talked for a few minutes. He said he was just following up the email and wanted to welcome me to the event.

"You don't know anyone who could host these two monks while they are here, do you?" he asked. "I need someplace for them to stay for a few days."

"They could stay here," I said without hesitation. "I have two empty bedrooms. They'd have to live in the house with me, though. I don't have a separate guesthouse or anything. And they have to like dogs."

"That's fine," he said. "I'm sure it will be perfect. They're really nice. They're brothers, very easygoing. One of them spends some time in the United States, and he speaks some English."

"Do you want to come over and see, to make sure it's OK? Meet me or anything?" I asked, thinking he should want to know where his guests would be staying and make sure I wasn't some weirdo inviting strangers into my house.

"Probably not necessary, but OK, I'll come by tomorrow morning if you're around," he said.

And just like that, after the inspection was approved, five days later, two of the happiest, most wonderful people I had ever met arrived on my doorstep, their saffron robes and smiling faces lighting up the whole property. Lily and Walter were immediately in love with Tsewong Rinpoche and Pema Tenzin and followed them everywhere as they wandered the paths and examined the orchard. Both dogs just wanted to be touched and loved by them. The happiness was infectious while they were around.

Over the next few days, I attended the workshops and experienced some of their Tibetan Buddhist Cho practice. I learned that Rinpoche held the lineage from a great female saint or deity they called MaChig Labdron (sometimes spelled MaChik), who practiced Cho, a profound and extensive system of meditation and ritual that used sacred instruments, music, and mantras. As a practice, Cho is highly famed for its ability to transform beings and awaken them to their true potential. It was not the quiet guided meditation I was used to from other Buddhist practices or retreats. These monks played drums, bells, and flutes all at the same time, and yet despite the noise, it was somehow very soothing and peaceful, and I found that I had too much to do to let my mind wander.

MaChik was a female Buddhist deity, which was unusual in itself, but I was immediately drawn to her because of the similarity of her name to the word magic. The first time I heard Pema talking about the teachings of MaChik, in his soft, simple, slightly Indian accented English, I thought he was saying the word "magic," and learning about magic seemed just right to me. The Cho teachings honored the four directions and the elements, just as did the teachings of don Alverto and other indigenous and shamanistic practices. Cho is also used for healing and correcting the imbalances in the earth and the environment for the benefit of all sentient beings. I talked to Rinpoche, and he agreed that the different practices were basically the same. The words are different, but the feeling of oneness with all beings was the same.

Over the next few days, I learned about Rinpoche and Pema and their monastery high in the Himalayan mountains in Bhutan. I told them that I really wanted to visit Bhutan, and that it was on my list of things to do.

"Come," Pema said. "You will stay at the monastery with us. We'll need to get a car. Our village is a two-and-a-half-day drive from the airport due to mountain roads. We'll drive as far as we can, leave the car at the end of the road and then walk four hours into the mountains to reach our village. We can rest there, and then it's only another short three-hour hike higher up into the mountains to reach our monastery."

I then learned that the monastery was at more than 12,000 feet and had been operating for more than 600 years without running water or electricity, but "lots of wood for fires." The trip seemed like a done deal to them.

"I really want to come," I said, but in my heart I didn't know if I was in good enough shape to make such a trek.

"OK. Next spring would be great," Pema said.

"We'll see," I said.

As Pema continued to tell me about his monastery, he said, "I never saw a car or a pair of shoes until I was fifteen years old."

"But you live in the snow," I said. "How could you not have shoes to protect your feet?"

"I don't know. I never thought about it. I didn't know what they were. We had little sock-like things to put on our feet sometimes."

"What about food? You can't grow much at that altitude."

"The villagers walk up and bring us food," Pema said.

"And water?"

"We have beautiful clear springs in the ground."

"Are there any stores or hotels in your village?" I asked.

Pema and Rinpoche both laughed kindly.

"No stores, just a few houses. People grow their own food," Pema said.

It turned out Pema was an artist and spent about half of his time in the United States, painting and helping at Buddhist centers here. When I asked him about the culture shock of being in the United States in comparison to his village, he admitted calmly, "Sometimes I really miss the simple life I had." He said television was too stressful for him, so he simply didn't watch it. I often thought that if everything ever went to hell in a hand-basket here, I was sure they would be just fine at their monastery in Bhutan. I was also noticing that I rarely watched television anymore myself.

I would frequently see Rinpoche and Pema sitting quietly on the front lawn with Walter and Lily, smiling. I wandered over to them one time. Walter wagged his tail incessantly when I sat down to join the circle.

"When I try to mediate," I said, "sometimes my mind wanders all over the place. I think about all sorts of things. Sometimes I do errands; sometimes I go to the store with my shopping list. How do I get back to the present? How do I stop my mind from wandering?"

Pema translated for Rinpoche. Rinpoche replied, "Don't stop it, it will come back. Probably not a great idea to get up and actually go to the store, though." He laughed. "Just be filled with joy and love. Your mind will come back. Breathe."

One afternoon I was sitting around the dining table with Rinpoche and Pema, talking about their Buddhist practices. I looked down and observed the lovely prayer bead necklace that Rinpoche was wearing. I did a double take when I saw that one of the silver objects hanging from the necklace was identical to the tiny sword the Dalai Lama had given me for protection while I was in meditation in Ecuador. Every detail of the sword was identical: the three-sided blade part and the ornate little silver crown on top, which was the handle. I could vividly remember taking that tiny one-inch sword from the Dalai Lama and holding it between my thumb and index finger, thinking, "How is this little tiny thing going to protect me?"

I told them about the meditation in Ecuador, and Pema translated the story for Rinpoche. Rinpoche smiled at me, that smile that lit up the room, the same look I remembered from a chance encounter, more than forty years earlier, with the actual embodied His Holiness XIV Dalai Lama when he came out of a side door at a lecture at UCLA, and I happened to be standing right there. He almost bumped into me. He stared into my eyes, took my hand, and smiled. He bowed and greeted me like he knew me. Then he laughed, turned, and the throngs surrounded him. I have never forgotten the divine merriment in the Dalai Lama's eyes. It was the same look that Rinpoche shared.

Rinpoche took off his necklace, cradled it in his hands, and breathed into it. He closed his eyes and my heart felt as if he was blessing the little sword, and then he put the necklace around my neck. I was touched beyond words and felt incredibly loved and protected.

> We can't discover new oceans unless we have
> the courage to lose sight of the shore.
> -Anonymous

CHAPTER 53

SUNDAY BRUNCH

I was feeling a little too reclusive. Even though I saw the kids frequently, I spent a good percentage of my time at home with Walter and Lily and was adjusting to that new state of being. It was OK, and I was working on Gracie's book diligently, but I thought it might be healthy to get out. I'd been invited to a charity event at a friend's house, and I decided to go. I thought a Sunday brunch would be easy to attend on my own. I got dressed up, put on jewelry and even a little make-up. I arrived late to avoid a prolonged champagne hour. The backyard was already full of people, some whom I knew quite well and others whom I'd never seen before. I stopped and chatted with a few people, fielding questions about how I was doing.

"I haven't seen you in a long time, Julie," my friend Anna said, as I wandered over toward her with a glass of wine. "How are you?"

"Good question. Do you want the real answer or the standard 'fine' response?"

"The standard 'fine,' please … Don't be silly, you ass, of course the real answer."

"Well, let's see. I've been really, really sad and in recluse mode for a long time. I've had a lot of loss in the last few months. Three dogs, a horse, and a husband. The husband didn't die, though. He just left. Besides that, it's all good. Aren't you glad you asked? How about you?" I replied.

"Wow, that's a lot. I'm surprised you're not more of a mess," Anna said. "Things have been a little chaotic for me, too. Let's sit together for lunch."

I had to repeat that answer a few times in response to inquiries about my well-being. Most people didn't know what to say and just stared at me in shock. I got a plate of food and sat at an empty round table and waved to Anna. The table started to fill up with a few other friends and a few people I didn't know; the combination was nice as far as I was concerned.

"Hi, I'm Julie." I introduced myself to the stranger who sat next to me.

"Hi. My name's Jane, and this is my husband, Bob."

"Nice to meet you. Are you new to Ojai or am I just out of touch with who lives here anymore?" I asked. "I've sort of been out of it for awhile."

"We've only been here a few months."

"Welcome," I said. "It's a great little town."

"What do you do?" Jane asked.

"I'm a … recovering attorney," I said successfully playing for laughs. "Seriously, it's a very challenging twelve-step program," I continued with a straight face. "Actually, I'm a farmer," I said. This made them laugh again, as I knew it would.

I wondered whether I should have the courage to talk about animal communication in this sophisticated crowd that included a few well-heeled strangers and a few good friends. I took a step backwards in my head and worried about what people would think if I said what I was really interested in. I liked getting a laugh, but I didn't want to seem foolish.

"Tell us about Ojai. What's it like here?" Jane asked my friend Lisa, who was sitting across the table.

"Well, there are all sorts of people here—professionals, farmers, and lots of spiritual and woo-woo types. Sometimes those are even wrapped up in the same person," Lisa responded with a smile as she looked directly at me.

"What exactly is woo-woo?" another newcomer across the table asked. "I've heard that term before in connection with Ojai."

"Julie, can you explain woo-woo to our new friends?" Lisa asked.

"I don't know exactly how to define it," I said stalling, as I stared at Lisa with a look of 'Why me?'"

"People on a spiritual path, maybe?" I said. "Actually, that sounds a little egotistical. We're all on a spiritual path, whether we know it or not. Some of us just talk about it more than others." I looked at Lisa to jump in and help me.

When I didn't get any help, I continued, "I think I'm struggling for an answer because what I thought was woo-woo twenty or thirty years ago, like energy healing or animal communication, is not considered so woo-woo now. The term woo-woo also seems a bit derogatory."

"Woo-woo doesn't necessarily have a negative connotation," Lisa interjected. "It's just a different way to look at what we, as humans, think is real or works."

"Maybe being woo-woo means acknowledging the unseen forces, the divine energy, at play in our lives—God, spirit, whatever you want to call it," I added.

"What do you mean?" Jane asked as she turned toward me with a slightly confused look.

"Maybe it's really understanding how we're all connected, that we're all in this together—people, animals, trees, oceans, angels, unseen and seen forces. Somehow we see ourselves as separate, superior, but I don't think we are," I said. "I think we're all part of the oneness, and nature has a lot to teach us. I think we're the dense ones who just don't get it sometimes. That's not really a definition of anything though. That's just truth, well, my truth, at least."

"That's an interesting way to look at life, but I think that would definitely qualify as woo-woo," Anna responded.

"One man's woo-woo is another man's normal, I suppose. Think about it. Lots of things that started as 'far out' years ago are commonplace today. We used to use typewriters and rotary phones, now we can connect all over the world by just pushing a button on our computers," I responded, thinking, oh no, here I go. "I'm writing a book with my dog Gracie and studying animal communication," I continued. "I suppose some people might consider that a little woo-woo, but I don't."

"That's a good idea, pretending your dog is helping you write," someone said.

"I'm not pretending anything," I said with more conviction than I knew I had. "My dog actually dictated portions of the book, and I just wrote them down. Now I'm trying to put it together in a book. Her job is done."

"Ahh, that's woo-woo, alright," Anna interjected.

"But good woo-woo," Lisa added.

"I disagree. I think animal communication is getting to be the norm," I said.

"What is woo-woo to you then?" Lisa asked.

"I think being able to levitate or transport yourself from place to place, like 'Beam me up, Scottie' is woo-woo. Not that I don't think it's possible. I just can't do it … yet," I added with a grin. "But animal communication—not so much out of the norm anymore."

"I sort of agree with you, Julie," my friend Jill said. "I had an interesting experience with my dog recently. She always chewed up this little red stuffed bear of hers and ripped it apart. She loved that bear, so I would constantly find the pieces and sew it back together. A few months ago, she chewed it up again and I said to her, 'I will sew this back together one more time, but if you rip it again, that's it. No more bear for you. You're not supposed to chew up your toys. They were gifts from a very good friend.' The funny thing, she hasn't chewed it since. It was as if I just needed to explain how she was supposed to treat her toys. She never knew. She plays with it now, but with a little uncertainty about what she's supposed to do.

I doubt it was coincidence. I think she really heard me and understood."

"That's fascinating," I said. "I never thought about it that way. They just might not know what's expected of them with respect to their toys. I might have to try talking to Walter about his toys. He'll chew anything, especially to get those little squeakers out of a stuffed animal. It sounds like you had a real moment with your dog, though, Jill. I think that's great."

"Well, I don't really believe in animal communication," Judy, a friend from my book club, interjected. "And I do think it's a little woo-woo. But I talk to my horse, Cash, and sometimes I know exactly what she's thinking."

"What do you mean?" I said.

"Before we came to Ojai, you know we lived in Mammoth. Well, we moved there from Catalina. After we were in Mammoth a few months, a friend asked if I wanted to take our horses in her trailer and do a special ride. Cash has always been curious and willing to walk right into trailers to see if there was any food. We tried for over half an hour to get Cash in that trailer and were about to give up. Her eyes were rolling back so you could see the whites, and she kept rearing up. It was weird and upsetting. Finally I walked Cash away from the trailer. In the past when she was running around the arena, I would think 'Come over here' to her, and usually she would. So I thought at her 'What's the matter?' I heard her say, in my head, as plain as day, 'I'm afraid.' I couldn't understand that because she has always been sassy and fearless. I talked to her, in my head, about what we were doing and where we were going, and she calmed right down. She seemed to understand, walked back quietly, and got in the trailer without a fuss."

"Wow. That's a great animal communication story," I said. "Did you ever figure out what was going on with her?"

"Yeah. Later I realized that the last time she'd been in a trailer was when we moved from Catalina. During that trip, she was stuck on a barge for six hours, and horses can't throw up if they feel sick. And then she was driven eight hours without a break to get to Mammoth. No wonder she was frightened to get in the trailer. But I really think she understood when I explained that this was only a short trip, and there was nothing to fear."

"So you think it's weird to communicate with animals, but you had an experience where you talked to an animal, you knew the animal was listening to you, it communicated back, and you understood what it was saying, but you don't believe it?" I asked.

"Horses are different," Judy said.

I just laughed.

"I occasionally call the pet psychic to find out what's going on with my dog," my friend Deb spoke up. "It's one of those things. I don't believe it, but I do it anyway."

I laughed even harder thinking about the wonderful journey in consciousness. I'd felt the same way just a few years prior.

"I think people communicate with their animals all the time, even if they don't admit it or recognize it as communication," I continued. "Gracie taught me that learning to listen is the key. If some invisible force connects all of us at the soul level, and wants to communicate, then I really want the courage to let go of anything which is holding me back from hearing what's being said."

CHAPTER 54

WALTER TAKES OVER

Walter has taken up where Gracie left off. I know he's Gracie's partner in this book. I also know he wants a more important job than just lying around being a dog, and finishing the book might be it. He talks, but he does it differently. Walter makes sounds of differing tones. Sometimes he trumpets a cross between a walrus and an asthmatic opera singer. Sometimes he makes a squeaky half-bark that starts small and then gets more and more insistent. And all the while—if I don't pay attention or understand him—the look in his eyes gets more and more intense, his tail hits the floor harder and harder, and the sounds get louder and louder, until finally I can't ignore him. He hobbles over on his three legs and puts his face up real close, his tongue darting out to give me a kiss, his eyes sparkling.

"What do you want, big boy?" I know he's talking to me. I know exactly what he wants. He wants attention; he wants love; he wants to get on the couch and sit next to me; he wants to be touched. His messages are always clear and to the point. "Take care of me. Be with me. Love me. I am here." The frantic sounds merge into sounds of contentment as I pet him and send him love.

"Walter, what do you want me to say in the book?"

"Tell everyone how wonderful and funny I am," he says. I realize that he still views himself as a puppy and wants to be active and play. He doesn't want me to treat him like an old dog, even though he tires out easily and has trouble putting weight on his remaining front leg.

So instead of just indulging him with his nighttime biscuits, I decide to make him do a little work for them like he used to when he had all of his legs.

"Sit, Walter."

His giant rear promptly goes down as he looks at me lovingly and sees the biscuit in my hand.

"Walter, give me your paw. Walter, paw," I say, putting my hand out toward him, not knowing what to expect. I don't know whether he will raise up his one remaining front leg and fall over, or what. But I'm ready to catch him.

As I look at him, I see that he keeps lifting his stump for me to take in my hand. The stump goes round and round like he is pawing the air until I understand that he is giving me his paw. It is just invisible. Tears well up as I acknowledge his big, gigantic heart, and gently take hold of and shake his stump.

"Good boy. I love you." Since this was a handshake deal, I complete the transaction and deliver the biscuit to his eagerly awaiting mouth.

Gracie is gone in the physical sense, but she is here, too. I know intellectually there is no death, there is no end, and there is only transformation of the relationship. Gracie exists in a new time, a new place, and a new reality; and so do I. The relationship has transformed from the physical to the spiritual. It hasn't ended; it has just changed. That understanding helps a little, but I miss having Gracie sitting on my feet as I work at the computer. I miss her smiling face, her physical presence. I miss the love I always felt from her, and the love I was able to give her. But Walter and Lily are doing a great job of filling the empty space in my heart. They also have taken up Gracie's spot at my feet as I work on the computer. Still, the tears sometimes fall for Gracie.

I don't know how to explain it, except that my communication with Gracie was different from the communication I've had with any other animal. I received large chunks of information from her. I had to struggle to keep up with her dictations. It's now clear to me that she did have a mission to write this book. She had things to say. Things she told me years ago, now keep getting repeated or surfacing from a variety of sources. And I am just beginning to understand. Finally I have surrendered to the belief that the natural world works in mysterious ways. Ways that are beyond our limited comprehension. I am not a lunatic, just a human being whose awareness is expanding a tiny bit at a time, allowing me to feel the connection between all beings.

I don't know where any of this is taking me, but I'm trying to be open to the ride. I do know that I have started singing in the shower, humming, and laughing again. And that feels great.

I often still question everything, think, doubt, and wonder, but I am learning to forgive myself and others along the way. And I spend a lot of time sending as much love, compassion and gratitude into the Universe as I know how. If we all just chose to exercise our free will and act from our hearts, instead of from the negative and fearful mental patterns of the past, perhaps we could create a significant shift on this planet. Maybe all of the world's issues, environmental or otherwise, could be resolved if we just collaborated with nature, and with each other. Feel the oneness. See the perfection in every being and every moment. Feel how we are all connected by divine energy and choose to co-create a better world—a world based on compassion, kindness, abundance and gratitude for all. Connect to the divine within and radiate love no matter what. I think that's what Gracie would say. I have kept my promise to Gracie to finish this book.

I knew she would.

POSTSCRIPT

Walter made his transition two days before I left for India and Bhutan. He beat the odds by eighteen months, but that is another story, one that makes me sad to even think about. But I know it was right for him. He had given up on that body. I think it became too painful and too small for his spirit. Besides, he told Barbara he really wanted to come to India with me and that was the only way he could see how he could make the trip.

Walter did see me through finishing this book though. After my editor reviewed what I thought was the final draft, she suggested I think about rewriting the entire book in first person since it was sort of a hybrid between a memoir and autobiographical fiction.

I knew she was correct about using the first person, and I began the arduous task of owning my life and Gracie's role in it. Parts of the story were painful to put in first person. Walter saw me through the first 100 pages of the process. I'd actually hoped to have the entire rewrite done before my trip, but the last three weeks of Walter's life were devoted to Walter, not writing. When Walter was sure I could do it without him being here physically, he left his body and came with me on my trip.

I could feel both Gracie and Walter with me in India and Bhutan: Gracie with a running commentary and insights, and Walter as protector and joyous observer. People frequently say, "You can go to psychotherapy for a year or you can go to India." The trip did help put things in perspective for me. Gracie and Walter also helped.

Both Gracie and Walter were with me when I said Namaste to an elephant, acknowledged that she was a magnificent spiritual being, and thanked her for her service to us silly tourists. As I was talking to the elephant, I was surprised when she lifted her trunk to my hands in what seemed like an acknowledgment of what I was saying. My friend Cindy, the professional photographer, of course was right there and captured the moment.

Photo credit Cindy Pitou Burton

Lily was the last dog standing to help me along, and she was home when I returned from my trip. But I didn't know for how long, and just the anticipation of her leaving created another hole in my heart. You would think I would have learned the lesson of living in the present moment by then, rather than focusing on the bad things that might happen. I am getting better, but I'm clearly not there yet. At least I see it when I do it now. Life is a journey, but the journey felt strange with only one old dog around.

I am grateful to Gracie, Walter, and Lily for their patience, diligence, love, laughter, and support in getting this book finished. This book is mostly fact, with a little fiction thrown in for good measure. But everything Gracie said is what she said. Gracie has approved every significant change. She left the commas and punctuation to me.

I know Walter still watches over me in his Bob Marley disguise, saying, "Don't worry 'bout a thing, 'cause every little thing's gonna be alright."

POST-POSTSCRIPT

While I continued to rewrite this book for the third, fourth, and fifth times, Lily too passed away. Each dog's passing set me back with grief and, at the same time, compelled me to push forward. In some respects Lily's passing was the most difficult because, for the first time in more than fifteen years, I came home to an entirely empty house. No people, no animals, no unconditional love to run over and greet me. At first, I couldn't take it, and I never wanted to be home. I even ran away to Hawaii for a healing retreat with Howard Wills to find a way to face the loneliness and the grief.

Howard teaches some simple, but very powerful truths for living a happier and healthier life. Love—Feel—Simplify, and make peace with everyone in your life and your lineage. With Howard's guidance I more fully understand how our thoughts, words and deeds aid in the creation of our reality and affect us physically.

I realized a few important things about myself during my retreat in Hawaii. I realized that throughout my life, I continually ran away or hid from my feelings in the moment. That's what I'd been taught and that's what I had learned so well, not to feel anything in my body and just keep going.

I needed to learn how to surrender and let each moment unfold. To really step back, observe what I was experiencing, and feel it. As soon as I leaned into a moment completely, and faced the thing I was resisting, the resistance seemed to have the space to dissolve. In that space of quiet and forgiveness and compassion for myself, I was able to discover the gift, the gift of releasing the past and allowing the present moment to complete itself and make room for more miracles and more magic to occur. The kind of magic where good, unexpected things just start to happen. The prayers Howard offers to all have helped that magic unfold in my life. He recommends saying at least the first seven lines from the Prayer For the World several times daily to help transform your life:

God, For Me, My Family, Our Entire Lineage And All Humanity
Throughout All Time, Past, Present And Future
Please Help Us All Forgive Each Other
Forgive Ourselves, Forgive All People
And All People Forgive Us
Completely and Totally, Now And Forever
Please God, Thank You God, Amen

After my return from Hawaii, a black cat wandered over to my house and adopted me. She meditates with me and lies on my chest at night and stares into me with her expressive and piercing gold eyes. She purrs and kneads at my stomach. I can feel her transferring healing animal energy to me. Perhaps I'm entering my Julie, the good witch, phase.

NAMASTE
(The divine in me acknowledges the divine in you.)

ACKNOWLEDGEMENTS

I am grateful for so many people in my life who have supported and encouraged me through this writing process. This includes, in particular, my family, friends and animals. You know who you are. Thank you. I love you.

I would also like to give a special thanks to those who helped me finish this book in a variety of specific ways. My heartfelt gratitude, with love, to Rachel Ticotin for her honesty in so many aspects of my life and for her early notes which prompted me to re-write, to Margaret Menninger for always being there as my friend, to Laura Gianni, for listening to me and providing a different perspective, to Manuela Aparicio for her encouragement, to Lisa Cervantes who challenged my thinking, and to my new friend Paula Hanahan who helped me decide so many last minute details. I am also grateful to my friends Cindy Pitou Burton, Scott Council, William Hendricks, Dianne Moon (author photo) and Peter Strauss for their assistance in helping me bring the photographs in this book alive. A big thanks to Chris Nottoli, for dressing up like Jeffrey and cheerfully being my model for hours of shooting, to Deb Norton for being my writing coach for years, to Amy Schneider and David Reeser at Ojai Digital, my book designers, to Stephanie Westphal, my editor, and to Kimberly Gooden, the ultimate proofreader. This book could not have come to fruition without any of you. So thank you.

RESOURCES

I would also like to share a list of resources in case anyone is interested in any of the topics raised in this book. I would highly recommend any of these individuals for their knowledge, skill, patience, creativity, abilities, kindness, and many other attributes, which make them invaluable in my life and perhaps, yours. In other words, I think these people are really good at what they do and I want to thank them for their help and guidance:

Frank Martin Don, LLC, Professional Astrologer, North Palm Beach, FL
frankdon@mac.com, www.frankdon.com

Roger Ford and Kim Vincent, Co-founders, Healing in America
107 W Aliso Street, Ojai, CA 93023, 805.640.0211
office@healinginamerica.com, www.healinginamerica.com

Nancy Furst, Spiritual Counselor and Intuitive, Malibu, California,
www.nancyfursthealer.com

William Hendricks, Professor of Photography, Ventura College
Ventura, California

Barbara Janelle, Interspecies Communicator, Santa Barbara, California
bjanelle@cox.net, www.barbarajanelle.com

Don Alverto Taxo, Master Iachak-Shaman, Ecuador
www.ushai.com

Radule Weininger, M.D., Ph.D, Santa Barbara, California
Therapist and Buddhist Meditation teacher

Howard Wills, Kauai, Hawaii
www.howardwills.com, lifelightandlove@aol.com

www.ingramcontent.com/pod-product-compliance
Lightning Source LLC
Chambersburg PA
CBHW051935290426
4110CB00015B/1987